THE LONSDALE LIBRARY

THE LONSDALE LIBRARY
founded by
THE RIGHT HON. THE 6TH EARL OF LONSDALE
KG, GCVO, DL

MODERN GAME SHOOTING

A pheasant well killed over the tree tops.

THE LONSDALE LIBRARY

MODERN
GAME SHOOTING

RODERICK WILLETT

LONDON
SEELEY, SERVICE & CO
1975

First published in Great Britain 1975
by Seeley, Service and Co
196 Shaftesbury Avenue, London WC2H 8JL
© 1975 by Roderick Willett
ISBN 0 85422 065 8

Printed in Great Britain by
Clarke, Doble & Brendon Ltd
Plymouth

INTRODUCTION

by

THE 7TH EARL OF LONSDALE

I AM indeed honoured to have been asked by the publishers of the Lonsdale Library, to which my great-uncle originally lent his name, to write an introduction for the new volumes in a series which, in its time, was the classic work of reference for sportsmen throughout the world.

I think it is worthwhile quoting a paragraph from his foreword to the old series; words which are as true today as they were then.

'It is now a long time since a Library of volumes on Sport and Games was first put before the public. During these many years great changes have taken place, in men and in methods; how numerous and how great those changes have been, it needs no more than a glance at the text and illustrations of the older existing volumes to discover. The traditions, the customs, the guiding principles of the great sports and games doubtless remain; but as the years go on new discoveries are made, new developments follow, new methods are found to be successful. In the process of time these demand notice and explanation.

I am certain that the new volumes in the Lonsdale Library which incorporates so much of the developments and discoveries in relation to sport and recreation of the last few decades will achieve great popularity, especially as more and more people come to enjoy the increasing facilities which are being provided so extensively nowadays and which are accessible to the public at large in a way they never have been before.

7

FOREWORD

BY RODERICK WILLETT

THE first shooting book I owned was written by Eric Parker, who also compiled the earlier volume on game shooting in the Lonsdale Library. So it is to him that I owe much of my early interest and instruction in the sport. It has therefore been a special pleasure and privilege to produce this new edition.

It is over 35 years since I first took the field with a ·410 and, much to my own and my father's astonishment, killed a wood-pigeon stone dead with my first shot, which, as they say, is how it all began. There have been many superficial changes in the shooting scene over the intervening years. But it is still just as necessary to be a safe shot, rather than a crack shot, and possess a sound basic knowledge of game, its behaviour and needs in order to qualify as a true shooting man.

To write a book of this kind calls for the assembling and check-ing of a great deal of information. I am most grateful for all the help I have received from the Gun Trade, the Game Conser-vancy, W.A.G.B.I., other organizations, and individuals, in par-ticular Harry Lawrence of Purdeys for all he has taught me about guns and gunmaking, the late Norman Clarke (chief instructor at Messrs Holland & Holland's Shooting Ground) for his patience, skill and good humour in teaching me how to shoot, and Joe Huskins, formerly of Eley, and Hugh Clark of the Hull Cartridge Company for their invaluable advice on cartridges and ballistics. My unstinted appreciation is extended to all those who have con-tributed photographs or diagrams, and especially Toby Buchan who prepared the line drawings for me. My warmest thanks go to Terence Blank for his admirable chapter on gamebird diseases, a forbidding subject, which he has tackled with a light but deft touch. Just as diamonds are a girl's best friend, so indigestion is a man's worst enemy, and I would like to think every reader will join me in paying generous tribute to Caroline Verney for her expert assistance in the 'kitchen'.

Finally, I believe there is a need for a book on every sport which deals with its subject comprehensively, even at risk of not covering certain aspects exhaustively because of their complexity. This is the book I have tried to write. I hope it will meet the need of young sportsmen in this respect, and help them to a better understanding and fuller enjoyment of their sport.

CONTENTS

LIST OF PLATES

TEXT ILLUSTRATIONS

INTRODUCTION

THE pursuit of game is a recreation we have enjoyed in Britain for hundreds of years. Means and methods have changed extensively down the ages, but, despite all the alterations that evolution has compelled, the British sportsman today is no less an enthusiast than his Norman forebears. The fact that he shoots with gun and cartridge instead of bow and arrow has made remarkably little difference in essence. We still preserve our land, and conserve our game. We still have to deal with those who seek to order things differently, even if it is only the local poacher. We still have our shooting accidents, often no less inexplicable than that which killed William II in AD 1100. In fact each generation has proved itself sufficiently adaptable and inventive to enjoy good sport in circumstances as they have found them. This seems to me just as true now, when more people are participating in game shooting than ever before, the greater number of whom are syndicate or club members rather than landowners. There is no reason why this state of affairs should basically alter in the foreseeable future, so long as the majority of people in these islands remain determined to enjoy their sporting heritage. Given this, a way will always be found to adapt resources to the needs of the time.

The spacious days when conservation was largely a matter of the squire telling his tenant farmers where he wished certain crops to be grown are a thing of the past. Modern commercial farming prohibits such autocracy and the amount of land which is primarily devoted to the interests of game is small, consisting increasingly of odd strips and corners, the cultivation of which is uneconomic for purely agricultural purposes. Turning such comparatively slender resources to the best possible account calls for ever greater expertise and ingenuity on the part of shoot managers and gamekeepers.

The position regarding forestry and game is slightly different. So-called commercial forestry has never been able to achieve the spectacular and sustained rise in productivity which has enabled farming to retain the status of 'big business'. It is, of course, a much longer-term operation and the marketability of a 'crop' can change dramatically and unforeseeably during the time it takes to reach maturity. With shooting rights in growing demand, there are signs of a greater awareness among foresters of the importance of the income which can be earned by giving more weight to such amenity considerations in the planning and planting of woodlands. This is a welcome change of heart and, it is hoped, may mean an end of the planting of vast, soulless blocks of conifers such as the Forestry Commission has spewed across the British Isles in the past fifty years. For game flourishes best in mixed woodland, where 5% of the acreage can be devoted exclusively to its interests. As this includes space for main rides—20 yards in width—required just as much by forestry as by game interests, the actual encroachment on timber necessary to cater for game is very small indeed. This makes it all the more incredible how fiercely the request for any such concession is usually contested by the dedicated forester.

A sad feature of the country scene since the early '50s has been the decline of the partridge. This has undoubtedly in the main been attributable to changes in farming methods, in particular to the increase in field size and the widespread substitution of barbed-wire fences for hedges. Attempts to make good the partridge population with reared birds have run into certain snags not previously encountered in the rearing of pheasants.

Wild pheasant populations have also suffered from changes in land usage, though the degree to which this has occurred has been to a large extent concealed by the yearly influx of high numbers of reared birds. But, even so, the pheasant has superseded the partridge as the principal lowland gamebird and the mainstay of the rough shoot.

Grouse populations continue to fluctuate much as they have always done but it has become clearly established that the key to well-stocked moors is good heather management, in which the main item should be 'muirburn' properly planned on a rotation appropriate to the rate of heather growth on the various parts of a moor.

After years of persecution by forestry interests, between the two World Wars, blackgame have shown a welcome upsurge in numbers. Capercaillie also seem to be steadily spreading throughout the north of Scotland.

The hare is another member of our fauna which has not taken kindly to changes in farming practice. Hare populations have always been known to have their ups and downs for reasons which yet remain to be discovered, but in some parts of Britain since the 1950s they have vanished altogether.

Apart from the obvious difficulties posed by urban and industrial encroachment on the country-side, there are many problems which confront the game conservationist of today. All shootings in Britain are in private ownership. There is no such thing as 'public shooting', as understood on the Continent or in America. It is, therefore, perhaps natural that there is no state body or department, as in countries such as Holland, Denmark and the USA, to look after the interests of game. This has been left to private enterprise and, thanks to the initiative of the Eley cartridge-making division of Imperial Chemical Industries in the 1930s in starting a Game Advisory Service with proper scientific backing, we have today the Game Conservancy. This is a membership association sustained by private subscription and donation, entirely independent of any government department. It operates a field advisory service and engages in research projects such as investigating the reasons for decline in game populations, the incidence and control of diseases and so on. It is a most necessary and excellent organization, and the work which it has done since 1951, in both the practical and scientific fields, in enabling game management to come to terms with the extensive and rapid changes in methods of land usage has been invaluable. It will undoubtedly play a key part in the years ahead in ensuring the continuance of good shooting in this country.

Another organization to which a great deal is owed for the stimulus it has given to practical wildfowl conservation is the Wildfowlers Association of Great Britain and Ireland (W.A.G.B.I.). It has also done a great deal to improve standards of conduct and behaviour in the shooting field.

In former times most of those who shot were born to it. They became accustomed to the handling and usage of firearms at an early age, as well as to correct procedure and etiquette in the shooting field. But this is no longer true : of the modern generation of shooting men, many only took up shooting in middle age. But for those prepared to learn there is no unfathomable mystery about the sport, the guns and cartridges used in it, or the methods and equipment employed to conserve game. The purpose of this book is to provide the basic information on these subjects which can enable anyone to take a knowledgeable interest, and find genuine enjoyment in his shooting, so that in due course yet another generation will inherit a sporting legacy no less well endowed than that handed down to their forebears.

CHAPTER ONE

THE SHOTGUN

Introduction

THE full-blooded dedication with which our Victorian ancestors pursued their field sports is nowadays more often a source of mild amusement than a compelling example. It is doubtful if any modern sportsman would seriously contemplate on his wedding day packing his bride off on the train for the honeymoon as soon as the ceremony was over, whilst he himself departed to attend a field trial, offering as his only excuse for cutting the reception the fact that he was already late! Yet this is what a well-known sportsman at the turn of the century is alleged to have done. Such behaviour is no longer in keeping with the spirit of the times. But even so, a dash of dedication does not come amiss, and after his wife and dog, a shooting man may quite properly regard his gun as his most treasured possession.

Selection

At prevailing prices (1973), a plain but serviceable boxlock ejector of reputable foreign make may be obtained for under £100, a first-quality British boxlock ejector for around £800, whilst a best London sidelock, easy-opening ejector costs over £3500. Sound secondhand guns are a few pounds cheaper at the lower end of the scale, and at the top end may fetch anything from £2500 to £3000 for a modern gun in 'as new' condition and carrying the name of a leading maker. The days when keen shots could equip themselves with a veritable armoury of first-class guns to meet every contingency at no great cost are gone. The majority are content with one gun for all their shooting; those who enjoy the cream of driven game shooting may have a pair, and the keen wildfowler may add a well-choked magnum or semi-magnum; if there is a young shot in the family a 28-bore or ·410 may also be useful, but individuals who acquire a wider variety of guns of different gauges and types simply for their own interest are nowadays rare. A good gun is not only itself a valuable item, but one which ought to be selected with care if its owner is to get the best value from it in the shooting field. To ensure this it is desirable that the prospective purchaser should have a reasonable working knowledge of shotguns and their performance so that he does not have to rely entirely on the guidance of the vendor, even though the latter may be a thoroughly reputable member of the gun trade.

Mechanism

The various parts of a typical 12-bore hammerless, ejector game gun are shown in Figure 1. Hammer guns are still made in small quantities by some foreign makers and ones of British make can sometimes be obtained secondhand. But for practical purposes they are obsolete and, except for those interested in collecting antique arms, I would advise strongly against buying one for everyday shooting.

The principle on which a gun works is simple. A cartridge containing a shot load—behind which is a driving wad to give obturation, and behind that again a charge of powder, known as the propellant—is placed in the chamber of the barrel. When the breech is closed and the trigger pulled a percussion mechanism is released, the tumbler or hammer of which strikes a detonating cap in the base of the cartridge. This ignites the powder which is converted into gases. The pressure thus generated drives the shot up the barrel and onwards to the target.

Shotgun Gauges

Early firearms shot a lead ball. Hence nowadays cartridges containing a single missile, e.g. a rifle bullet, are referred to generically as 'ball' ammunition, while a single cartridge of any type of ammunition is commonly known as a 'round'. Early cannon were classified according to the weight of the lead ball they fired. Thus one which shot a 2 lb lead sphere was defined as a two-pounder and so on. When, at a later date, hand-guns made their appearance, this system of classification had to be modified because the weight of the ball fired was less than a pound. They were referred to instead by the number of rounds which went to make up the pound. Thus if a 1 oz lead sphere accurately fitted the bore, the

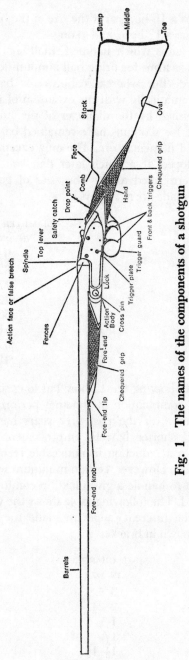

Fig. 1 The names of the components of a shotgun

gun was known as a 16-bore, or if the size of the ball went twelve to the pound, it was a 12-bore, and so on.

Early sporting guns which handled small shot were made in the same calibres as arms for firing ball ammunition, and so were similarly classified. But whereas calibres for ball ammunition have changed dramatically with the evolution of rifled arms and are now distinguished by the diameter of the bore in inches or millimetres, those for shotguns have remained basically the same and retain the old nomenclature. The only exception is the ·410 which was developed at a much later date and so follows the fashion for modern rifled arms. The sizes of gauges in which modern guns are made are as follows :

GAUGE	DIAMETER OF BORE IN INCHES
4	·938
8	·835
10	·775
12	·729
16	·662
20	·615
28	·550
(·410	·410)

For general game shooting the 12-bore has long since been found to offer the best combination of shooting performance and gun weight. The trend over the past fifty years has been towards lighter guns and shorter barrels. Improvements in cartridges, which have led to a reduction in noticeable recoil, have been a major factor in this. However, certain minimum weights to which guns can be built to handle a given load in comfort have become clearly established. The following table shows the weight to which modern guns of the different gauges are made, the chamber length in inches being shown in brackets :

GUN GAUGE	SHOT CHARGE IN OZS	GUN WEIGHT IN LBS
4 (4 in)	3–4	$14\frac{1}{2}$–19
8 ($3\frac{1}{4}$ in)	2–$2\frac{1}{2}$	$10\frac{1}{2}$–13
10 ($2\frac{7}{8}$ in)	$1\frac{7}{16}$	8 – 9
10 ($2\frac{5}{8}$ in)	$1\frac{5}{16}$	$7\frac{1}{2}$– 8
12 (3 in)	$1\frac{1}{2}$–$1\frac{5}{8}$	$8\frac{1}{4}$– 9

GUN GAUGE	SHOT CHARGE IN OZS	GUN WEIGHT IN LBS
12 (2¾ in)	1¼–1½	7 – 8¼
12 (2½ in)	1 –1⅛	6 – 6¾
12 (2 in)	⅞	5¼– 5¾
16 (2¾ in)	1⅛	6½– 6¾
16 (2½ in)	15/16	5¾– 6
20 (2¾ in)	1	5¾– 6¼
20 (2½ in)	13/16	5¼– 5½
28 (2½ in)	9/16	4¾– 5¼
·410 (3 in)	⅝	5 – 5¼
·410 (2¾ in)	7/16	4 – 4¾
·410 (2½ in)	5/16	3¾– 4

N.B. It is quite possible that examples of guns outside these weight limits may be found from time to time, but the figures should prove a sound guide as to what can normally be expected.

Guns are little different from cars in that the shooter will usually be best served by buying the best he can afford, and of course the more he can afford the wider will be the range from which he can choose. But before going shopping for a gun it is important that the shooter should be clear in his mind exactly what sort of shooting he intends in the main to enjoy. There is no such thing as a gun that is ideal for all occasions. But, by attention to appropriate points of detail, a gun primarily intended for driven game shooting will also be able to serve very adequately for rough shooting and the many wildfowling occasions on which success does not depend primarily on heavy charges of large shot.

The Barrel

The barrels of modern shotguns are made of steel. Damascus barrels are made from iron and steel twisted and welded together. They are obsolete, but secondhand guns may still be found with them. They are easily recognized by the distinctive scroll pattern of the metal and were usually 'browned' instead of 'blued' like steel barrels. However, the process of rebrowning Damascus barrels is expensive, and instances may be found where they have been blued. This obscures the distinctive pattern of the metal and makes careful inspection necessary to detect them for what they are.

The barrels of double-barrelled guns are brazed together at the

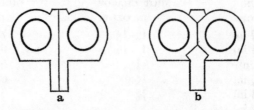

Fig. 2   Two methods of joining the barrels at the breech end

a The Chopper Lump method.
b The Dovetailing method.

breech. This is usually done in one of two ways, either by the chopper lump method shown in Figure 2a above, or by that of dovetailing shown in Figure 2b. The former is the stronger and also the more costly because the tube has to have extra metal at what will become the breech to form the 'chopper'. This has to be tempered differently so that it is harder than the rest. Chopper lump barrels are usually, therefore, a mark of a best gun, though all models in the A.Y.A. range of Spanish guns employ this

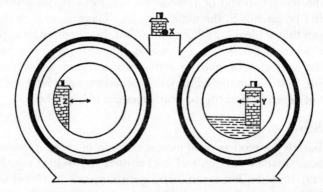

Fig. 3   How the barrels are aligned so that they shoot together

As the axis of the bore of each barrel is to one side of the axis of the gun, each when fired tends to throw the shot charge out to that side. To counteract this, and enable the pattern of each barrel to centre on a given mark, the axes of the bores have to be set so that they converge slightly. Thus when a gun is aligned on a distant object, X, the effect when viewed along the axis of each bore will be as at Y and Z respectively.

method of joining the barrels. But the inferiority of the dovetailing method of joining the barrels has for practical purposes been largely eliminated by the advent of modern fluxes and brazing techniques, and where this method is used by a reputable gun-maker it can be considered entirely satisfactory. (See Figure 3.)

Once the barrels have been joined at the breech, the loop to hold the fore-end in place is positioned. This may be simply soldered under the barrels or have a shaped extension which goes up to mid-way between the barrels or even a little further and be brazed in position. Opinion amongst gunmakers is rather divided as to which is the better, and though some best guns have the loop brazed in place others do not. In less expensive guns it is almost invariably soldered. Two or three distance pieces, which in better quality guns are shaped to the barrels, are spaced between the loop and the muzzles, and the gap is then sealed by the top and bottom ribs being soldered in place. In some foreign guns the ribs are brazed instead of soldered; it is claimed that this gives a stronger join, but as there is no real need for strength in this instance it appears a rather bogus justification. Brazing, unless well executed, can impair the temper of the steel of the barrels, and weight is lent to the belief that this may have happened when the rib itself is distorted, as is sometimes plain to the eye in cheap foreign guns.

The chamber to take the cartridge is bored at the breech end of the barrel. It is connected to the bore by means of a cone. The length of this cone can vary quite considerably, but about $\frac{3}{8}$ in is normal in British guns.

Choke

At the muzzle some form of constriction, known as choke, is incorporated to control the spread of the shot charge. This is contrived in one of three ways, either by boring, which is the traditional method, or by recessing, which is usually an expedient to provide or increase choke in a barrel where none or insufficient existed before, or by swaging, which is a comparatively new method giving excellent results and the use of which is growing.

When choke is bored the effect is as shown in Figure 4a. It will be seen that it consists of a cone and a parallel, and the greater the degree of choke the longer both will be. Again opinions differ quite widely as to the exact combination of lengths of cone and parallel in any specific instance which will give the best results, but dimensions normally vary between the limits shown.

The effect of recessing is shown in Figure 4b. It is a process that has to be used in regulating choke, but when used in its own right to provide choke, it will be appreciated that its application is very limited, and dependent on the thickness of the barrel walls just behind the muzzle. Except for trying to convert true cylinder barrels into improved cylinders, it is little used.

Swaging consists of compressing the muzzle in a special machine, with the result shown in Figure 4c. It can be used to provide choke in barrels which have been cut and shortened. It produces a cone and no parallel and, dependent on the state of the barrels, as much as a quarter choke can be provided. It has been found in practice that swaged chokes shoot outstandingly good and regular patterns. The reasons for this are not fully understood, but it is thought that the hammering the steel receives during the process of compression has a hardening effect on it. The method is so well thought of by some Continental gunmakers

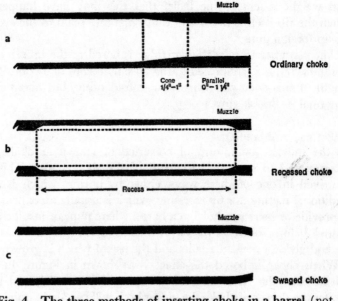

Fig. 4   The three methods of inserting choke in a barrel (not to scale)

that sometimes in new barrels the whole choke complete with cone and parallel is swaged in.

The nominal constrictions used in standard choke borings in different gauges of gun are as follows:

BORE OF GUN	CONSTRICTION IN THOUSANDTHS OF AN INCH				
	IMP CYL	$\frac{1}{4}$ CHOKE	$\frac{1}{2}$ CHOKE	$\frac{3}{4}$ CHOKE	FULL CHOKE
·410	3	6	12	16	24
28	3	7	14	21	30
20	3–5	8	16	24	34
16	3–5	9	18	26	37
12	3–5	10	20	30	40
10	5	11	22	32	43

These figures should only be used as a guide to likely performance. Some full-choke constrictions will shoot half-choke patterns and vice versa. At least one leading gunmaker bores his improved cylinder barrels with nine points of choke. The only way to be certain how a gun is shooting is to pattern it on the plate, but we will come to that in a later chapter.

The Rib

Guns equipped with a top rib of a type other than that known as the standard concave game, or foulard rib, were seldom seen up to fifty years ago, as the purpose of the rib was considered ornamental rather than useful. However, a belief has grown that the top rib may help in correct alignment of the barrels in actual shooting. Although the shooter's eye should be focused on his target and not on the muzzles of his gun when he takes his shot (see Chapter 4), there is no doubt that as the muzzles are swung on to the target, the shooter becomes aware of them as they encroach on his line of sight. If his gun is properly fitted, the centreline of the barrels, i.e. the top rib, should coincide exactly with his line of sight to the target at the moment his eye indicates to his brain that the trigger should be pulled. It therefore seems logical to assume that a prominent rib will assist the eye in this task.

Some wildfowlers have always maintained that a raised, flat, file-cut rib is an aid to shooting in bad light. This sort of rib

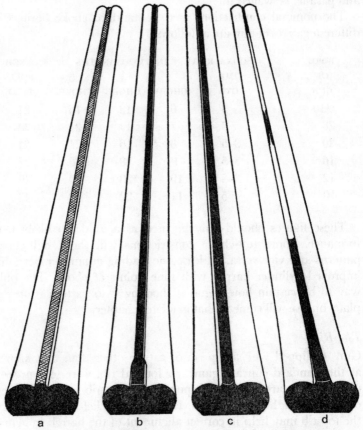

Fig. 5   Three different types of rib and a ribless gun

a The raised, flat, file-cut rib favoured by some wildfowlers, because of its eye-catching attributes.

b The Churchill 'quick sighting' rib developed specially for his 25 in barrelled guns, but now sometimes used in conjunction with 26–28 in barrels.

c The standard 'Foulard' concave rib with which the majority of game guns are normally equipped.

d The Alex Martin ribless gun; it is noteworthy how eye-catching a centre line the absence of the rib provides.

looks all right on a magnum, but gives a lighter, shorter-barrelled game gun a rather 'heavy' appearance. However, this is overcome by having a raised, tapered rib, of which the best known is the 'Churchill' type, specially developed for the 25 in barrelled guns associated with this name. There are others as well, and a rib of this kind has been finding increasing favour amongst game shots in recent years irrespective of the barrel length of the gun.

Examples of various types of rib in use on guns today are shown in Figure 5.

The Breech

There are two ways in which access to the breech can be obtained for the purpose of loading and unloading: either a moving breech-block can be used, as in automatics and repeaters, and Darne-actioned double-barrelled guns, which allows a rigid attachment of the barrels to the action, or the barrels must be moved away from the standing breech, or action face. This necessitates some method of securing them when they are closed on to the

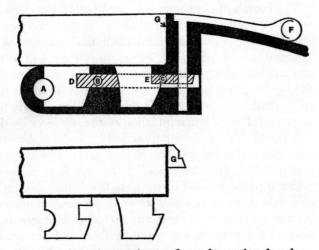

Fig. 6 How the barrels are fastened to the action by the Purdey double-bolt

The Purdey double-bolt is shown at B and C fitting into the bites in the lumps at D and E; where a top extension is employed to provide an additional fastening, it will be situated in the region of G.

B

latter for firing. Because of the advantages it confers in quick loading and unloading, and the ease with which it permits the bores to be checked, the second method has been found the most satisfactory in the shooting field, and, with the exception of the Darne action, has been universally adopted in the design and making of double-barrelled sporting arms.

Figure 6 shows how the barrels pivot about a cross-pin in the knuckle at A. This may be an actual pin, which, if wear causes the barrels to come 'off the face' of the action, can be removed and replaced by one slightly larger, or alternatively it may be cut out of the solid knuckle. The former is always employed in the making of best guns. The barrels are secured to the action by a 'Purdey double-bolt', shown at B and C respectively, which is operated by the top lever F. The bolt at B, fitting into the bite in the forward lump at D, although it should be well fitted, acts more in the nature of a guide. It is the bolt C, fitting into the bite in the rear lump at E, which must be made to bear down as firmly as the easy operation of the top lever F against its return spring allows, so as to give a good closure.

The barrels of some guns are fitted with a top extension in the region of point G, which involves yet another bolt bearing down on a surface. There are valid theoretical reasons for having a fastening at this point but, in practice, if the bolt at G is to be made to bear as efficiently as that at C the return spring actuating the top lever will need to be made twice as strong, as it will have to do double the work. But if this spring has already been made as powerful as easy manipulation of the top lever by the shooter will permit, this will be impracticable, and an efficient fit at G only obtainable by sacrifice of that at C, which is undesirable and pointless. The 'doll's head' is the only form of top extension, which if properly fitted is free from this failing, and on magnums and light game guns really serves its purpose. However, in good guns made of modern steels, and up to weight, there should be no need of a top extension, whilst in those of lesser quality where such a reinforcement might be truly desirable, it will almost certainly be ineffectual because its fitting calls for workmanship of the highest standard which is not found in low quality guns. So, unless the name on a gun, and its other features, are overwhelmingly in its favour, it is best to avoid those with a top extension.

The Action

The action of a gun is the most complex and expensive part of it; it also takes the longest time to make. It is here therefore that many of the distinctions between best, good and inferior guns are to be found.

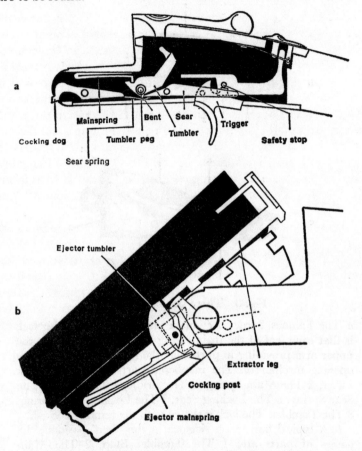

a

Mainspring   **Bent**   **Sear**   **Trigger**
Cocking dog   **Tumbler peg**   **Tumbler**   **Safety stop**
Sear spring

b

Ejector tumbler

Extractor leg
Cocking post
Ejector mainspring

Fig. 7a   The Webley & Scott boxlock action
b   The Southgate ejector system

This boxlock action is probably one of the most robust and reliable used in modern gunmaking. Both materials and workmanship are first class. In conjunction with the Southgate ejector, it has deservedly earned these guns a high reputation among sportsmen all over the world.

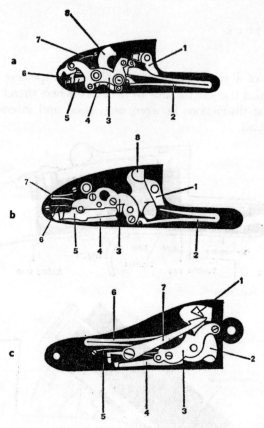

Fig. 8　Three sidelock actions

a The Famous Purdey Action; a unique feature of this lock
is that each leaf of the main spring has a functional role, the
upper arm providing in particular the motivation of the easy
opening mechanism. The numbered parts are, 1 The Lock
Lifter, 2 The Main Spring, 3 The Bridle, 4 The Sear, 5 The
Sear Spring, 6 The Locking Sear, 7 The Locking Sear Spring,
8 The Tumbler. The lock is shown with the tumbler cocked.

b A typical bar action sidelock in the 'fired' position; the
names of parts are: 1 The Tumbler Stop, 2 The Main
Spring (Note how differently shaped the top arm is from that
of the Purdey), 3 The Bridle, 4 The Sear, 5 The Intercepting
Safety, 6 The Intercepting Safety Spring, 7 The Sear Spring,
8 The Tumbler.

c A typical back action sidelock, in which the main spring is
situated behind the tumbler. The names of the parts are : 1 The
Intercepting Safety Sear on the Tumbler, 2 The Tumbler, 3
The Bridle, 4 The Sear, 5 Intercepting Safety Spring, 6 The
Main Spring, 7 The Intercepting Safety.

Boxlock and Sidelock

The two actions with which the shooter is primarily concerned are the boxlock and sidelock. An example of the former is shown in Figure 7 and various examples of the latter in Figure 8a, b and c. In a boxlock the mechanism of both locks is housed in the bar and body of the action; in a sidelock each lock is carried on a separate plate, the main bulk of the mechanism fitting into a space cut in each side of the head of the stock behind the bar of the action. In this room has only to be found for the main spring— not even that in the case of a back action sidelock (see Figure 8c). The small space available in the boxlock design places a premium on simplicity, so that the essential working parts can be positioned to the greatest technical advantage. It is unusual therefore to find intercepting safety devices and easy opening mechanisms incorporated in boxlock guns, though they are standard equipment in good sidelocks.

Because a boxlock is simpler in design it is also cheaper and easier to make and is therefore used in less expensive guns. However, it is worth noting that since Messrs Anson and Deeley introduced their design in 1875 it has remained virtually unchanged and is still the most widely used in modern gunmaking throughout the world. This would not have been so had it not been found to have merit enough to offset the claims to superiority of the sidelock in certain respects.

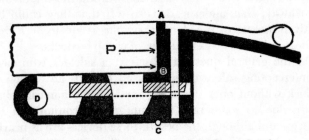

Fig. 9   The effect of pressure against the action face

When a gun is fired the pressure indicated by the arrows in Figure 9 acts against the face of the action. This creates a tendency for the bar to flex about point C, in direct extension of the line of the face, AB; it is not about the crosspin, as might be thought. If the flexing caused by successive discharges sets up metal fatigue, a fracture would ultimately result, just as it might if excessive flexing was caused by firing too heavy a load on any one occasion. It is therefore important to have the section of the action body through the line BC as strong as possible. Here the boxlock is at a disadvantage to the sidelock, and this is aggravated by the hole to take the tumbler peg (see Figure 7) having to be bored almost in the line BC, which does not arise with a sidelock.

But although, everything else being equal, a sidelock is unquestionably the stronger action, a well-made modern boxlock, built from good materials, should comfortably stand up to a life-time of normal hard shooting, and if it is properly looked after will give its owner just as good service as a sidelock. It will not, however, withstand abuse so well.

A sidelock is more mechanically efficient. Although modern cartridges have done a lot to discount the practical advantages of this, it does also allow of finer trigger adjustment. The front trigger is normally adjusted to a pull of $3\frac{1}{2}$–4 lb, and the back trigger to one of 4–$4\frac{1}{2}$ lb on account of the greater leverage obtained. However, well-adjusted triggers on a boxlock should give as 'crisp' a pull as most men require, and there is certainly no reason whatever to tolerate 'drag', within the normal meaning of the term. But this is where the limitations of cheap guns may become apparent, because the tempering of the parts of the locks is often such that any adjustment to the pulls is impossible, and once the hard outer skin of metal on sear nose and bent has worn away, that underneath is so soft that they could become positively unsafe to use. Unhappily this is apt to be a weakness of cheap sidelocks just as much as of cheap boxlocks.

On the general question of safety, a sidelock equipped with an intercepting safety device has an obvious advantage over a boxlock without one. However, anything mechanical is liable to failure due to some rare and unforeseen conjunction of mis-chances, and although the best of these devices are as nearly fool-proof as human ingenuity can make them, a gun equipped with them should be handled no less carefully in the shooting field than one without them. A safety catch only locks the triggers.

Other Actions

There are other actions, three of which deserve mention on account of their special virtues. The *Dickson trigger plate* action,

or 'Round Action' as it is better known, is unique. It is quite
distinct from either boxlock or sidelock, the parts of the locks
being built up on a vertical central plate attached to the trigger
plate, and being held in place by an outer bridle on each side,
as illustrated in Plate 2. The ejectors are housed in the body
of the action, and work on an entirely different principle from
either the Southgate or Deeley ejector systems, or any of their
variants with which boxlocks and sidelocks are normally equipped.
The 'Round Action' is technically excellent; it allows the bar of
the action to be made exceptionally strong, an intercepting safety
device is incorporated, and it compares favourably in all respects
with the best sidelock actions.

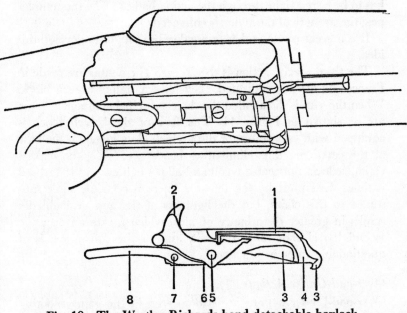

Fig. 10 The Westley Richards hand detachable boxlock

This unique action was only made as 'best', and the quality of
the workmanship and finish throughout is superb. The upper
diagram shows the action with the bottom plate removed and
the locks *in situ*; below is shown one of the locks by itself; the
parts are : 1 The Main Spring, 2 The Tumbler, 3 The Cocking
Lever, 4 The Ejector Activator, 5 The Tumbler Axle (Note
this is mounted on the lock plate, NOT the wall of the action
body), 6 The Sear Nose, 7 The Sear Peg, 8 The Sear Arm.

All sidelocks are hand-detachable in that anyone capable of using a screwdriver efficiently can remove them at will. But there has only ever been one hand-detachable boxlock action, that produced by Messrs Westley Richards until 1970, when it was discontinued. This again was a product of the inventiveness of Messrs Anson and Deeley. As shown in Figure 10, the bottom plate of these boxlocks has a catch at the front which can be operated when the fore-end is removed, allowing the plate to be taken off. The locks can then be simply lifted out, and similarly replaced when need be; they are not held in position by any screws or fastening. The ease of access for cleaning and oiling, especially after shooting in the rain, is admirable. Also, as no hole has to be bored right through the action body to take the tumbler peg, the strength of the action is enhanced.

It is a great pity no other gunmaker has sought to develop this idea.

The third special action is the *Darne*. These guns are made in France. As already indicated, they have a sliding breech block. When the gun is dismantled the three principal component parts are as shown in Figure 11. The face of the breech block is equipped with two obturator discs which close home on the base of the cartridge, thus eliminating headspace. This, the makers claim, reduces noticeable recoil and allows lighter guns to be used without discomfort by the shooter. There is certainly some substance to this claim, but the lightness of the gun undoubtedly results in greater disturbance of aim, which makes an accurate second barrel shot more difficult, and so this advantage is of questionable value in practice.

Over-and-Under Actions

Over-and-Under actions are seldom seen in the game shooting field. They pose two main problems : the first is to keep the depth of the action body as shallow as possible, and the second is to keep the weight down. The first is usually achieved by having bifurcated lumps, i.e. on either side of the bottom barrel, as in the Purdey Over-and-Under action shown in Figure 12. In this design the depth is just about as shallow as it is possible to make it and lends the gun a very pleasing line. But even when this is taken into account, it has to be made about a $\frac{1}{4}$ lb heavier than

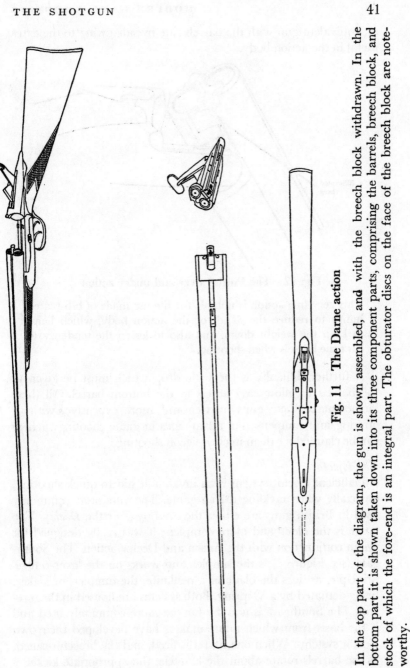

Fig. 11 The Darne action

In the top part of the diagram, the gun is shown assembled, and with the breech block withdrawn. In the bottom part it is shown taken down into its three component parts, comprising the barrels, breech block, and stock of which the fore-end is an integral part. The obturator discs on the face of the breech block are noteworthy.

an equivalent gun with the barrels side by side owing to the extra metal in the action body.

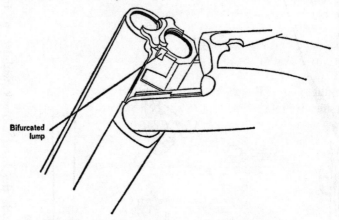

Fig. 12   The Purdey over and under action

This very fine action is notable for the use made of bifurcated lumps to reduce the depth of the action body, which helps to keep the weight down, and also to lessen the tendency to cant the barrels when shooting.

A further difficulty is the wide drop which must be given to the barrels to allow easy access to the bottom barrel. All these factors make these guns heavier and more expensive, without offering any compensating advantages in game shooting such as can be claimed for them in clay pigeon shooting.

The Ejector

An efficient ejector system is an invaluable aid to quick shooting, especially when tackling driven game. The ones most commonly used in British guns are either the *Southgate* or the *Deeley*. The latter is the older and more complex; it was really designed for use in conjunction with the Anson and Deeley action. The Southgate (see Figure 7) is the simpler and works on the 'over-centre' principle, as does the blade of a penknife, the tumbler, or kicker, being actuated by a V-spring. Both systems are housed in the fore-end. The Southgate is now by far the more commonly used and is the basis from which many makers have developed their own ejector systems. When one barrel is fired, and the breech opened, as the barrels rotate about the knuckle, the appropriate kicker is released as it goes over-centre and strikes the base of its extractor leg a smart blow, which causes the fired case to be ejected. As the barrels are raised to close the breech the kicker is re-cocked.

Easy-Opening Mechanisms
An easy-opening mechanism is almost always the adjunct of a best gun. That of Messrs Holland and Holland is unique in its simplicity and efficiency, and in allowing quite exceptionally easy closing. It is shown in Figure 13. Most other designs are operated

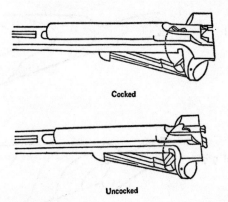

Cocked

Uncocked

Fig. 13 The Holland & Holland self-opening mechanism
This admirable device consists basically of a spring loaded cylinder which is fitted into a specially constructed groove at the rear of the upper face of the fore-end. It has the genius of simplicity and is most effective; as it comprises only three separate parts, including the spring, there is almost nothing that can go wrong with it.

by a V-spring in the action body which exerts a continuing downward pressure when the gun is broken. This invariably makes them noticeably stiff to close. However the benefit in quick reloading conferred by the easy opening more than compensates for the slight extra effort required in closing the gun.

Single Triggers
Single triggers are beneficial for those who like them, or through physical handicap need them, but my experience over many years leads me to doubt whether there is any substance at all in the

claims that they allow quicker or more accurate second-barrel shooting. There are many different mechanisms in existence; all require the trigger to be fully released after the first barrel is fired, before it can be pulled again to fire the second. Some need to be released over a longer distance than others; it is a definite advantage for this distance to be as short as possible to avoid a hang up on the second barrel.

Some mechanisms are selective in that by operating a special lever, which may be embodied in the safety catch, the shooter can

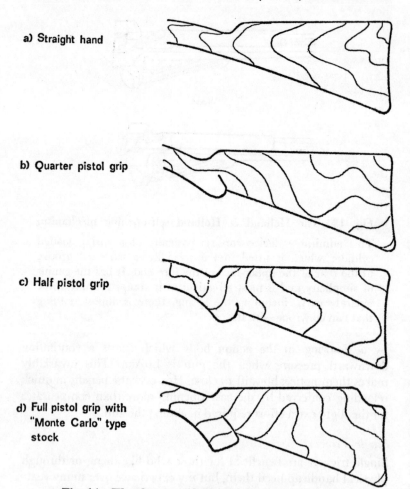

a) Straight hand

b) Quarter pistol grip

c) Half pistol grip

d) Full pistol grip with "Monte Carlo" type stock

Fig. 14 The shapes of different types of gun stocks

fire either barrel first; others are non-selective. Demand is now-adays very much more for the former than the latter. Purdey, Boss, Holland and Westley Richards, to name but some, all make thoroughly reliable selective mechanisms.

The Stock and Fore-End

The stocks of all good-quality guns are made from French walnut, but owing to the high cost of timber in France, other sources are now being investigated, such as Persia. British game guns usually have a straight hand-stock, as depicted in Figure 14a, but quarter pistol-grips, half pistol-grips, and even a full pistol-grip are some-times seen on a stock, as shown in Figure 14b, c and d. The 'Monte Carlo' type stock in Figure 14d is intended to provide a high cheekpiece at the comb for a man with a long neck; it is more often found on the clay shooter's gun than one used by a game shot.

The inadequacy of the traditional shaped and sized fore-end on a game gun in providing a good hand hold, especially when the barrels get warm, is well known. However, the American beavertail fore-end is an ugly and cumbersome substitute. By far the neatest answer to this problem is an ordinary leather-covered handguard fitted with a special clip fastening to the fore-end.

CHAPTER TWO

THE CARTRIDGE

Introduction

AS mentioned in the last chapter the principal components of a cartridge are the shot charge, the main wad and the propellant. A section of a modern British game cartridge detailing these and all the other parts is shown in Figure 15.

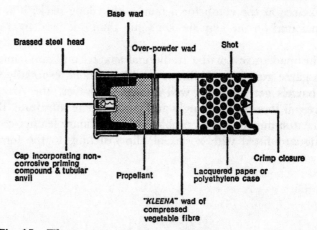

Base wad

Brassed steel head   Over-powder wad   Shot

Cap incorporating non-
corrosive priming
compound & tubular
anvil   Propellant

Lacquered paper or
polyethylene case

Crimp closure

"KLEENA" wad of
compressed
vegetable fibre

Fig. 15   The components of a typical Eley game cartridge

Propellants

All modern powders used as propellants in shotgun cartridges are smokeless. To serve their purpose properly they should possess the following characteristics:

a They should give good, consistent ballistics.

b They should be stable, i.e. they should not be liable to explode when struck inadvertently, and should be relatively immune from deterioration due to changes in humidity and temperature.

c They should combust instantaneously when ignited by a suitable cap.

d They should have a reasonably high density, so that they do not occupy too much space in a cartridge.

e They should leave a minimal residue of fouling in the barrel, which should be non-corrosive.

The *Nobel-Glasgow Series 60* powders used by Eley in their cartridges are particularly notable for their stability. The powders used by other British cartridge makers may be a trifle less so, but in other respects their products are generally no wit inferior to those of Eley, and those of one or two, such as The Hull Cartridge Company, give quite exceptionally good ballistics, which, as I will show in the next chapter, is by far the most important factor in ensuring a clean kill when the quarry is properly centred in the pattern.

Caps

All good modern caps contain a non-corrosive detonating compound, which is proofed against atmospheric changes by being covered with a thin coat of varnish and possibly also one of metal foil. A tubular anvil, as used in all Eley cartridges, is desirable, as this eliminates any possibility of a blowback on to the face of the action, which will cause pitting round the striker holes, such as may sometimes be noticed in old secondhand guns. It is essential that a cap is properly matched to the powder in a cartridge, so that the temperature generated by the detonating compound when the cap is struck is correct for ensuring the complete and instantaneous combustion of the powder. A compound generating too high a temperature and too violent a flame for a powder can be just as dangerous as one which, by generating too low a temperature and small a flame, causes a 'hangfire'.

The Wad

Next we come to the main wad. This has to provide the obturation as the shot charge is propelled down the bore. The material of which it is made must, therefore, be sufficiently elastic to enable it to form a gas-tight fit in the bore when it is squeezed between the pressure exerted by the gases behind it and the weight of the shot column in front of it. It should also be as light as possible to help keep recoil down. The Eley patent 'Kleena' wad is made of compressed vegetable fibre, which, to assist its passage through the bore, is slightly greased. It fulfils the two requisite conditions admirably. Other cartridges, particularly those of Continental origin, still make use of felt wadding. Provided top-quality felt is used, and again is slightly greased, it too gives excellent obturation. The drawback to such wads is that they are expensive, and cheaper, poorer quality felt does not give such satisfactory obturation. Cork is sometimes used, mainly on account of its lightness, but it lacks elasticity and is not a good obturator. Cartridges loaded with cork wadding almost invariably give rather low ballistics. The most recent material is plastic. Wads made from this may be a simple cup shape, or have a thin skirt extending forwards that is slit into quarters, and forms a container to hold the shot charge. This is known as a 'shot protector', and one is shown in Figure 16. The plastic wad, even with the addition of the shot protector, is exceptionally light, and has been found to give such good obturation that it has been possible slightly to reduce powder charges in cartridges loaded with such wads without incurring any loss of performance. This, of course, means that a small reduction in recoil is obtained too.

The Shot Protector

The shot protector saves the pellets from deformation against the barrel wall as the charge goes down the bore. As soon as it

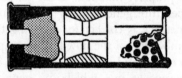

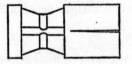

Fig. 16 The Eley plastic 'Monowad'

The shot 'protector', extending from the main driving wad, is a thin walled plastic container which is slit into quarters to allow the shot to spread as soon as the wad clears the muzzle.

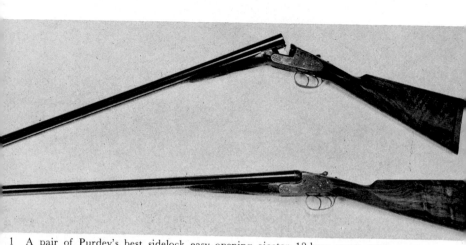

1 A pair of Purdey's best sidelock easy opening ejector 12-bore game guns; apart from the unique design of the locks, an interesting feature is the wide drop that this allows the barrels which facilitates quick reloading.

2 The Dickson 'Round Action' mechanical, which combines strength with efficiency.

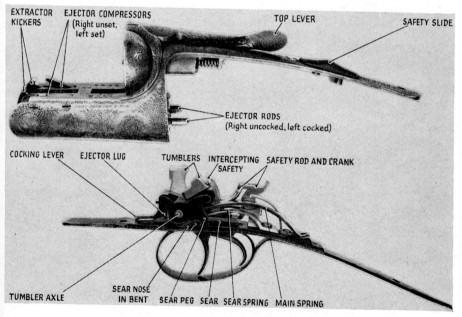

EXTRACTOR KICKERS

EJECTOR COMPRESSORS (Right unset, left set)

TOP LEVER

SAFETY SLIDE

EJECTOR RODS (Right uncocked, left cocked)

COCKING LEVER   EJECTOR LUG   TUMBLERS   INTERCEPTING SAFETY   SAFETY ROD AND CRANK

TUMBLER AXLE   SEAR NOSE IN BENT   SEAR PEG   SEAR   SEAR SPRING   MAIN SPRING

3 A barrel setter at work; despite many attempts to improve on this very simple hand-operated machine none has so far proved successful.

4 Three stages in the process of 'sleeving' barrels.

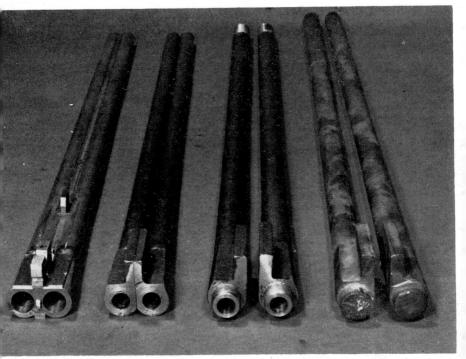

5   Four stages in the construction of a pair of chopper lump barrels, always the hallmark of a 'best' British gun, but employed by A.Y.A. throughout their range of Spanish made British-styled game guns.

6   Checking that the bores are clear before loading at a partridge drive.

7 'Overthrow' in action; point a is approximately where the shooter's eye said 'fire', point b where the bird was hit by the shot, point c where the bird is dead in the air and falling, and point d where the muzzles of the shooter's gun are pointing at the end of his swing. The wide angle through which the barrels have moved is due to the 'impulsion' coveyed by the hands in response to the dictates of the eye, and is probably much greater than is generally appreciated by the shooter himself.

emerges from the muzzle, the slits in the plastic skirting enable this to open like the petals of a flower and allow the pellets to spread normally. But because it obviates pellet deformation, all the pellets fly true, and in consequence slightly denser patterns are obtained in the 30 in circle at 40 yards, of around 5 to 10% above normal expectations. Although this is an undoubted asset to the clay pigeon shot, it is of more questionable value to the game shooter, as will be explained in the next chapter.

Another point concerning shot protectors is that when the shot charge reaches the constriction at the cone of the choke they make it harder for the charge to flow easily through. This results in a fractional pause with a consequent build up of pressure to force the charge through. In old guns with thin or weak barrel walls immediately in rear of the choke, this build up may be sufficient to cause a bulged barrel.

However, shot protectors do ensure that there is no leading of the barrel, and so make cleaning after firing easier.

Plastic wads are likely to be the most widely used in cartridges of the future, but despite their advantages, those incorporating a shot protector may prove a mixed blessing to the game shot.

Shot Pellets

Shot pellets are normally made of lead, alloyed with special hardening agents, by the conventional shot-tower method. Individual pellets should be perfectly spherical and absolutely uniform in size within a given shot size. The number of pellets in different standard shot charges is given in the table below; figures have been omitted which would have no practical interest.

The Cartridge Case

The cartridge case is made either of lacquered paper or of polyethylene plastic. The former is water-resistant, the latter waterproof. By no means all shooters have been won over to the plastic case since its introduction. It has obvious advantages to the wildfowler, and others whose sport involves the likelihood of their cartridges suffering from the wet. But the paper case is widely preferred by those who do not run much risk of this.

Plastic cases have been proven not to be harmful to farm stock if they are eaten, but they can seriously lame cattle if one becomes lodged in the cloven hoof of a beast. The makers play down the

THE NUMBER OF PELLETS IN DIFFERENT CHARGES OF SHOT

OUNCES

SIZE OF SHOT	$\frac{5}{16}$	$\frac{7}{16}$	$\frac{9}{16}$	$\frac{5}{8}$	$\frac{13}{16}$	$\frac{7}{8}$	$\frac{15}{16}$	1	$1\frac{1}{16}$	$1\frac{1}{8}$	$1\frac{3}{16}$	$1\frac{1}{4}$	$1\frac{1}{2}$	$1\frac{5}{8}$
BB	—	—	—	—	—	—	—	70	74	79	83	88	105	114
1	—	—	—	—	—	—	—	100	106	113	119	125	150	163
3	—	—	—	—	—	—	—	140	149	158	166	175	210	228
4	—	—	—	—	138	149	159	170	181	191	202	213	255	276
5	—	—	124	138	179	193	206	220	234	248	261	275	—	—
6	84	118	152	169	219	236	253	270	287	304	321	—	—	—
7	106	149	191	212	276	298	319	340	361	383	—	—	—	—
8	140	196	253	281	366	394	422	450	478	506	—	—	—	—
9	184	254	326	363	471	508	544	580	616	—	—	—	—	—

litter problem they represent, asserting it will only take a keeper a short while to remove all such cases from the gun stands after a day's shooting. In practice this remedy is not as simple as it is made to sound, and the fact is that many plastic cartridge cases litter the countryside where they remain an eyesore until they are ploughed in. The paper case, on the other hand, rots away and vanishes from sight in only a matter of weeks.

From a technical viewpoint the most important thing about the case is its closure. This may be accomplished either by means of a rolled turnover and a top wad, or a crimp. The latter is more widely used because it enhances pattern quality and density. But in certain circumstances a rolled turnover closure is obligatory, as with large shot over which a crimp cannot be formed.

Whichever form of closure is used it must be sufficiently firm to give a satisfactory pull-out strength, which must be exactly the same from round to round. This is necessary to allow the build-up of satisfactory and consistent pressures.

The bottom of the paper or plastic case is firmly secured between the base wad and metal head so that it does not 'separate' when the cartridge is ejected, as may happen if this is not done properly and the cartridge is a tight fit in the chamber due, for example, to a paper case having swollen from damp.

Just as the main wad provides obturation to the fore, so the cartridge case must provide obturation to the rear of the gases by effectively sealing the breech. Some old breech-loaders had small channels cut in the face in case of a blowback, but with good modern British cartridges this is an almost unknown contingency.

Ballistics—Pressure

Of the elements constituting the ballistics of a shotgun cartridge, pressure is of prime importance. Adequate velocities, reasonable recoil, and lethal patterns are all dependent on satisfactory pressures. Pressure is normally measured at 1 in from the breech face in a special 'pressure barrel'. In the case of an ordinary $2\frac{1}{2}$ in chambered 12-bore, the highest mean service pressure for which it is proved is 3 tons per square inch (t.s.i.). The pressure developed by the standard load $2\frac{1}{2}$ in cartridge has, therefore, to conform to this. In fact to avoid any risk of exceeding it, cartridge makers normally load their cartridges to give a mean pressure of about

2·6 t.s.i. A batch of cartridges giving satisfactorily consistent ballistics will vary from round to round up to ·3 t.s.i. above and below this figure.

Two typical hypothetical pressure/time curves for a standard load 2½ in 12-bore cartridge and a 'Maximum' 12-bore cartridge respectively are shown in Figure 17 below. The pressure developed by the 'Maximum' cartridge is kept within the prescribed top

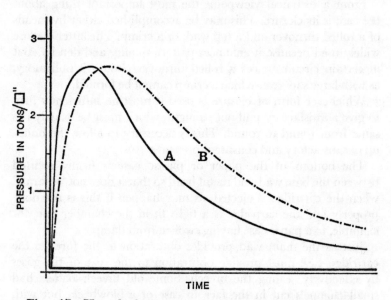

Fig. 17 Hypothetical pressure/time curves for shotgun cartridges

Curve A represents a standard load 2½ in 12-bore cartridge.
Curve B represents a 'Maximum' 2½ in 12-bore cartridge.

limit by employing what is called a progressive powder, i.e. one which burns at a slower rate. But having passed its peak, the pressure fades more slowly than in the case of the standard load. Thus, although pressure is not higher within the meaning of the term, it is over-all of greater volume.

When a cartridge is fired, the pressure of the expanding gases has first to overcome the inertia of the shot load and the counter pressure exerted by the closure of the cartridge case before the load itself starts moving on its way. The heavier the load for any given bore and the longer the shot column, the greater the inertia that has to be overcome. I have already mentioned the part played by the closure; if this is weak and gives way too soon, low pressures will result, whereas if it is too firm, a high pressure will build up. A precisely correct 'pull-out strength' has therefore to be estimated and incorporated in every cartridge case by the maker.

Cartridge makers have found that pressures are most manageable and consistent when what is known as a square load is used, i.e. one in which the length of the shot column in the bore is the same as the width of the bore. All the standard loads of the different gauges have been devised with this in mind. Longer shot columns tend to higher and more erratic pressures. Those of the 3 in ·410 cartridge, where the shot column is over twice the width of the bore, are exceptionally difficult to control so that they are satisfactory without being excessive. The same problem affects all magnum loads, but to a lesser degree.

Shot columns shorter than the width of the bore are also tricky because they tend to cause low pressures, which are variable on that account. The 'Two-inch' cartridge for use in 2 in chambered 12-bores is probably about as far as it is wise to go in this direction. Some people may therefore jump to the conclusion that such guns are to be avoided because their cartridges are 'weak'. From my own experience, I would assert that this is not so; I have seen as high pheasants killed stone dead in the air with these guns as were ever killed by fully fledged game guns with the standard load or a heavier one. This may in part be due to the fact that low pressures tend to improve pattern quality and density, whilst high pressures have a disruptive effect in both these respects.

So few people ever bother to pattern their guns on the plate that the damaging effects of high pressures, or those of greater volume, on pattern are little appreciated by the ordinary shooting man. Thus a man who uses a normal game gun with 'Maximum' cartridges for shooting driven pheasants, and a surprising number do, would probably be horrified to know that with an improved cylinder barrel this gives him a more open instead of a denser pattern. Yet this is the case on account of the greater volume of pressure developed by these cartridges. It may not be of much consequence at short ranges, but it can be decisive in failure to make a clean kill at 40 yards, as will be shown in the next chapter.

The question of when a high pressure also becomes a dangerous one is sometimes raised. Burrard, in his authoritative work *The Modern Shotgun*, gives clear guidance on this point, which, though it was written in the 1930s, is as valid today as it was then; he says, 'A pressure of $3\frac{1}{2}$ tons should be regarded as excessive and one of 4 tons as dangerous'. This, of course, refers specifically to game guns, but similar divergencies can be safely assumed to hold good in the case of guns proved to $3\frac{1}{2}$ and 4 t.s.i., respectively.

To obtain the best and most uniform pressures a cartridge case should match the length of the chamber of the gun in which it is used. If the case is markedly too short, as for example when a two-inch case is used in a $2\frac{3}{4}$ in chambered gun, some loss of pressure may occur due to the escape of gases in the interval between emergence of the charge from the case, and its entry of the bore. But when the modern, proprietary, crimped nominal $2\frac{1}{2}$ in cartridge, which when opened out is in fact $2\frac{3}{4}$ in long, is used in a $2\frac{1}{2}$ in chambered gun, it has not been found to give rise to any increase in pressure, which in theory might have been expected due to the extension of the case so far into the cone. On no account should this be construed to mean that a nominal $2\frac{3}{4}$ in cartridge can be safely fired in a $2\frac{1}{2}$ in chambered gun; it cannot; the powder charge and shot load are both too heavy.

Velocity

Velocity more obviously limits the effective range of a charge of shot than pressure, and is therefore, however mistakenly, of much greater concern to the ordinary shooting man. But it is of genuine importance because good penetration depends on satisfactory velocity.

Shotgun performance cannot be realistically evaluated in terms of muzzle velocity, as can that of rifled arms. This is because small pellets, such as No. 8's, lose their velocity so much more rapidly than larger ones, e.g. No. 3's, that in order to give the former a reasonably comparable effective range it is necessary to send them on their way with a higher muzzle velocity. It has been found in practice that the most satisfactory method of comparison is in terms of the mean velocity over the first twenty yards of their flight, and this is known as the 'observed velocity'. 'Standard velocity' is recognized to be an observed velocity of 1070 feet per second (f.p.s.) and 'high velocity' as one of 1120 f.p.s. A 'Maxi-

mum' cartridge has an observed velocity of 1090 f.p.s. Cartridges
for clay pigeon shooting are given an observed velocity of around
1030 f.p.s.; this is because penetration is not important, and to
ensure good pattern quality, since just as high pressure is
associated with dispersed patterns, so is high velocity.

The limits within which shotgun velocities can be raised without
seriously prejudicing consistent pattern quality and density are
very narrow. When observed velocities go above 1150 f.p.s.
patterning tends to become very erratic indeed, and recoil also
becomes unacceptable.

Some people use High Velocity (H.V.) loads because they
believe these cartridges help them to shoot better, and avoid
'tailing' their birds. But a normally fast, high pheasant at 40 yards
range will only have travelled a further four inches on its way
in the extra time taken by the standard load to reach the target.
So from a practical shooting viewpoint the benefit of H.V. loads
in this respect is negligible. Their true advantage lies in the better
penetration they provide for the shooting of heavily plumaged
quarry, such as the larger wildfowl. They will not transform an
indifferent marksman into a good one.

Recoil is measured in terms of momentum, i.e. of the mass in
pounds multiplied by the muzzle velocity in feet per second. The
mass in question consists of the shot charge plus the weight of
the powder and wadding expelled from the barrel, the former
being mainly in the form of gases, apart from fouling left in the
barrel. But the noticeability of recoil to the shooter, and indeed
its acceptability, has been found to depend not only on the overall momentum of the blow delivered, but on how it is delivered.
Thus a quick stab has been proved to be much less noticeable
than a more prolonged shove. A quick burning powder, as typified
by curve A in Figure 17, usually displays the first characteristic,
whilst a progressive, or slower burning powder, as typified by
curve B in Figure 17, usually exhibits the second. As far as provision of satisfactory ballistics allows, cartridge makers always try
and use a propellant that will keep the noticeability of recoil as
low as possible. This is obviously to the shooter's advantage, particularly when he is firing a lot of cartridges in a day, and even
more so when he is shooting over a number of consecutive days.
The old idea, still surprisingly prevalent abroad, that the more
punishing the kick developed by a cartridge the better its quality,

no longer holds good. In fact, unnecessarily noticeable recoil could be said to be the hallmark of a bad rather than a good cartridge.

As a guide, it has been found in practice that a minimum gun weight of 6 lb is necessary to handle a 1 oz standard velocity shot load. A gun of at least $6\frac{1}{4}$ lb is desirable for the full standard load of $1\frac{1}{16}$ oz, while the H.V. load of $1\frac{1}{8}$ oz will need a gun of almost $6\frac{3}{4}$ lb to allow a sportsman to shoot in equal comfort. Although the modern trend is to have as light a gun as possible, many sportsmen find it preferable to have a gun weighing an ounce or two more than the minimum required, as I do myself. For a general purpose game gun to handle the standard load for both driven and walked up game, I have found $6\frac{1}{2}$ lb to be the weight which suits me best; I do not enjoy a long day firing a lot of cartridges from a lighter gun.

In order to obtain best performance as well as minimal noticeable recoil, it pays the shooter to use the biggest gauge of gun to handle any given shot charge. Thus a 12-bore will handle a 1 oz load better than a magnum 20-bore, and $1\frac{1}{8}$ oz load better than a magnum 16-bore.

Cartridge Storage

Although, as already stated, modern powders are very stable and reasonably immune to changes in climate, it does pay to store cartridges properly, that is at normal living-room temperature and humidity. If cartridges are kept in the family airing cupboard, the powder may dry out, which will mean it will burn quicker and so give enhanced ballistics. If they are kept in an old cupboard in a chilly, damp passage by the back door, the powder may take up moisture with the result that ballistics will be lowered, and if the cases are of paper these may swell and no longer fit the chamber of the gun.

Cartridge Choice

Some shooting men are prone to boast that they use the cheapest cartridge they can buy. This is not, in my opinion, a sound policy. In one instance in my experience, a man had a noticeably high proportion of wounded birds down during the day; this, I am reasonably sure, was not so much due to faulty marksmanship as to the poor penetration provided by the brand of cartridges he was using, of which I had tested a sample some time previously and found them to give erratic and generally low ballistics. A good cartridge need not necessarily be the most expensive, but it will allow a shooter to do full justice to himself and, which is more important, to the quarry at which he shoots.

CHAPTER THREE

GUN AND CARTRIDGE IN THE FIELD

Introduction

THE last chapter should have made it clear that if a shooter is to obtain good results in the field he should use a properly matched combination of gun and cartridge. In particular, if he wants to shoot with a light gun he must be content with a light load, and if he feels a heavy load is required he must accept the need for a heavier gun. So that he does not encumber himself with unnecessarily heavy armament, he should have a sound appreciation of what is needful to deal effectively with the various quarry he sets out to shoot, just as does a rifleman for bigger game.

Small game is killed by being hit by a lethal pattern of shot. This means it must contain sufficient pellets to ensure that at least one strikes a vital part and that all of them have sufficient energy to give adequate penetration if they do so.

Lethal Patterns

Shotgun patterns are assessed by the number of pellets placed in a 30 in circle at 40 yards on a whitewashed steel plate. The amount of choke in a barrel will affect this. The percentages of the original number of pellets in a shot load which different choke borings should allow to be placed in the 30 in circle at this range are as under :

Full choke	70
Three-quarter choke	65
Half-choke	60
Quarter-choke	55
Improved cylinder	50
True cylinder	40

These figures should hold good for all gauges of gun and all sizes of shot. But the patterns shot by ·410s may quite often be found at variance, and I have never myself shot a gun of this gauge which gave a 70% full choke pattern, the highest pellet count I have ever obtained being a bare 65%. Some guns may display an aberration with one shot size; a gun once in my possession shot excellent quarter choke patterns except with No. 5s, with which it invariably shot half choke patterns.

Some gunmakers have special names for borings of their own, such as 'Modified Choke', but they do not always mean the same thing and it is advisable to stick to the recognized classification given above.

It is possible to have guns 'Super-choked' to shoot 75–80% patterns, but such tight borings are better suited to clay-pigeon guns than game guns.

Forty yards is regarded as the limit of sporting range and 45 yards as extreme range in game shooting. Beyond this patterns of small shot, i.e. Nos. 5, 6 and 7, deteriorate very quickly both in quality and density. Larger shot flies truer, but even with a well regulated full-choke magnum 12-bore the patterns obtained with Nos. 1 and 3 shot beyond 55 yards become quite unreliable, and I firmly believe that the corresponding range limits in wildfowling, despite the larger shot and heavier loads used, ought to be recognized as 50 and 55 yards respectively.

But, returning to the game shooter and his needs, it is sometimes forgotten that a shot charge travels through the air in the form of a column, which at 40 yards is about 12 feet long. About 90% of the pellets are in the first 6 feet of this column and only around 10% in the rear half. The increase in length of this column for a magnum load is insignificant from a practical point of view. The idea, therefore, that a bird is killed by flying into the shot column, rather than by being hit by the pattern as seen on the plate, has no real substance. But, in assessing minimum necessary pattern densities for various quarry, an allowance of 10% is usually made to offset the stringing of shot in this way.

The normal quarry of the game shooter vary in size from a snipe to a cock pheasant or blackcock, with the possibility in certain circumstances of a capercaillie or goose also having to be taken into account. This difference in size raises several important practical considerations. A pheasant is clearly better 'armoured' by bone and muscle than a snipe, so a smaller proportion of its total body area is vulnerable to lethal damage by shot. In fact out of a total body area of 40 sq in, only about a fifth can be considered to constitute a target on which a hit will result in a clean kill, and a large part of this comprises the head and neck. The need for adequate pattern densities to shoot snipe successfully is well understood by sportsmen, but where bigger gamebirds are concerned this need is often grossly underestimated, due to failure to appreciate just how small is the real target area.

Even the best quality shotgun patterns do not have the pellets distributed exactly evenly over the surface of the 30 in circle. Here and there three or four pellets may be grouped together, else-

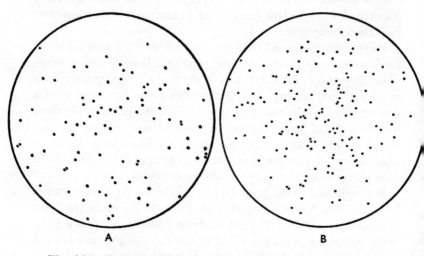

A   B

Fig. 18a   Pattern of a ·410×3 in magnum load at 30 yards, using full choke

A ·410×3 in load of ⅝ oz of No. 6 shot fired from a full choke barrel at 30 yards range. The pellet count in the 30 in circle is only 94, instead of an anticipated 135, or thereabouts, if the barrel had shot true to its boring. This is typical of the erratic performance of heavily choked ·410 barrels, a weakness aggravated in this case by the long shot column of the magnum load, and consequently high pressure.

Fig. 18b   A standard 28-bore load of no. 7 shot at 30 yards using an improved cylinder

This $\frac{9}{16}$ oz load has given a pellet count in the 30 in circle of 144, against an anticipated 136. This well illustrates the better quality and more reliable patterns shot by the 28-bore, which make it a better boy's gun than a ·410; it also shows the advantage of using the smaller shot size, i.e. 7's instead of 6's.

where there may be two or three spaces up to five inches in diameter which contain no pellets at all, and such irregularities may
occur in a good quality pattern, while one of poor quality may
have more clusters of shot interspersed with wider and more
numerous open spaces. So some allowance must be made for
these irregularities in assessing necessary minimum patterns for
game. Some typical patterns are shown in Figure 18a, b, c, d, e,
f, g, and h.

Striking Energy

Assuming that all pellets possess lethal striking energy, it is
reckoned that a hit from one only will suffice to knock out a snipe,

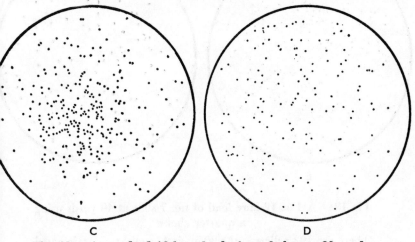

C   D

**Fig. 18c   A standard 12-bore load of no. 6 shot at 20 yards
using an improved cylinder**

This $1\frac{1}{16}$ oz load has placed 277 pellets in the 30 in circle, and
clearly indicates the danger of 'smashing' bigger quarry, such
as pheasants, if the body is centred in the pattern at such
short range.

**Fig. 18d   A standard 12-bore load of no. 6 shot at 40 yards
using an improved cylinder**

This pattern was shot with the same barrel as in 18c. There
are 146 pellets in the 30 in circle against an anticipated 144.
The pattern quality is good, and shows how lethal a well
regulated improved cylinder can be at this range.

but that at least two will be required to score a strike on a partridge or grouse to ensure that one finds a vital spot, the equivalent number for a pheasant being three, and for a bird as big as a goose four. I would stress that it is not the combined effect of these two or three pellets that is needed to prove lethal, but only the one that finds the vital mark.

Taking account of all these factors the following minimum patterns in the 30 in circle have come to be recognized as

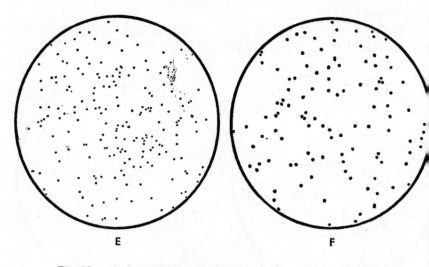

E   F

Fig 18e   A 1 oz 12-bore load of no. 7 shot at 40 yards using a quarter choke

There are 192 pellets in the 30 in circle against an anticipated 187. Pattern quality is good, and the effectiveness of this load for woodpigeon shooting is amply demonstrated.

Fig. 18f   A 'maximum' 12-bore load of no. 6 shot at 40 yards using an improved cylinder

This pattern was shot with the same barrel as in 18c and 18d. But there are only 113 pellets in the 30 in circle instead of an anticipated 160. It shows how these heavier loads are a handicap rather than an advantage when used in open bored game guns, unless specially regulated to handle them. It is noteworthy that the left, half choke barrel of the same gun gave a pattern density of 194, against an anticipated 193, when used with the 'Maximum' cartridge.

necessary, the estimated fraction of vulnerable body area being shown in brackets :

Snipe	290	($\frac{1}{2}$)
Golden Plover	220	($\frac{1}{2}$)
Woodcock and Teal	145	($\frac{1}{2}$)
Partridge and Woodpigeon	130	($\frac{1}{2}$)
Grouse	120	($\frac{1}{3}$)
Pheasant, Blackcock and Mallard	100	($\frac{1}{5}$)
Capercaillie, Goose	70	($\frac{1}{8}$)

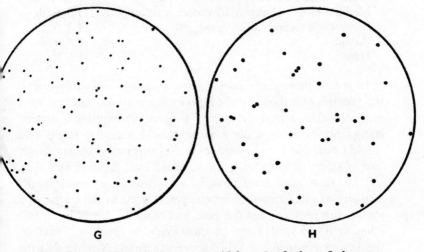

G   H

Fig. 18g   A 1¼ oz semi-magnum 12-bore load of no. 3 shot at 50 yards using a full choke

There are 82 pellets in the 30 in circle against an anticipated 85. Although pattern density is a shade light, quality is very good, and any grey goose correctly centred in the pattern should have been cleanly killed.

Fig. 18h   A 1½ oz 'magnum' 12-bore load of no. 1 shot at 60 yards using a full choke

There are 41 pellets in the 30 in circle against an anticipated 48. This was one of a series of shots fired at this range, all giving patterns of below par density, and illustrating how thin and unreliable patterns become at this long range despite the use of large shot and a well regulated gun. A grey goose correctly centred in the pattern could well not have been cleanly killed.

For some reason rabbits and hares are rarely included in this table, an omission which should be made good; minimum patterns of 100 and 70 respectively are suggested as appropriate.

Having obtained these figures it remains to establish minimum lethal striking energies needed by individual pellets. These have evolved mainly from empiric observation and experience, and for many years have been accepted to be as follows:

Very small birds: snipe, golden plover, etc	0·5 ft/lb
Small birds: woodcock, partridge, grouse, etc	0·85 ft/lb
Medium birds: pheasant, blackcock, mallard, etc	1·0 ft/lb
Large birds: capercaillie, goose, etc	1·5 ft/lb
Rabbit	1·0 ft/lb
Hare	1·5 ft/lb

In recent times some people have challenged these figures on the grounds that those for the bigger quarry are too low and have suggested that a bird the size of a pheasant requires a striking energy of 1·5 ft/lb while a goose should have 3·0 ft/lb. This would mean that a cock pheasant at 40 yards would be technically 'out of range' of guns using the standard load of No. 6 or 7 shot. Yet for those who have plentiful opportunities of seeing really well shown pheasants shot by competent guns in the course of a season, this is clearly not the case, and many birds will be cleanly killed at 40–45 yards range by these loads. In my view, therefore, the figures given in the table above are valid. A table showing the striking energies of various shot sizes at different ranges for the normal observed velocities is at Appendix 'A'.

But this does raise the question of whether, when a shooter has a choice of shot size, as is often the case, he should opt for additional pattern density or extra striking energy over and above minimum requirements. In the case of a pheasant, Nos. 7, 6 and 5 shot all meet the need for a minimum striking energy of 1·0 ft/lb up to 40 yards. A yard or so beyond that No. 7 shot ceases to be adequate, though No. 6 continues to be so up to almost 50 yards, and No. 5 to nearly 60 yards. However, the pattern density given by the standard load of No. 7 shot if used in conjunction with an improved cylinder barrel is sufficient up to and well beyond the 45 yard mark, as is that of a similar load of No. 6 shot, but fails with No. 5 shot at about 43 yards unless a quarter-choke boring is used instead of the improved cylinder, when it just holds good for the full 45 yards. Of these three the standard load of No. 6's is the most widely used, and rightly so, as it clearly offers the best combination. Of the other two, 5's were formerly favoured much more strongly than 7's, but during the last decade or so the reverse has become the case, and anyway for driven pheasants 5's are now seldom used. The reason for this swing to No. 7 shot is undoubtedly that the denser pattern appears to produce better results than the higher striking energy but consequently thinner pattern offered by No. 5's.

Woodpigeon have always had a reputation for taking 'a lot of shot'. To overcome this it was quite common up till the early 1950s to hear No. 5, or even No. 4, shot recommended for shooting them. But since then realization has grown that the denser patterns allowed by No. 7's have the greater killing power, and this shot size is now favoured by most experienced pigeon shooters.

The protagonists of large shot maintain that the greater 'shocking' effect of a blow from a large pellet, even though it may not be right on target in a vital spot, will quickly prove fatal, whereas a lesser blow from a smaller pellet may not even cause the victim to pause in his tracks and so allow him to escape and suffer. This contention is supported by medical/veterinary theory, but is otherwise misleading. Due to a variety of circumstances a shooter can just as easily fail to retrieve a bird which falls nearby as one which drops a mile away. The only way to ensure game is brought to bag is a clean kill. This requires a hit on a vital organ, the chances of which are enhanced by good pattern quality and density, but *not* by increasing striking energy.

Pattern Quality

Although a gun may be bored to shoot an improved cylinder pattern, i.e. one placing 50% of the pellets in the 30 in circle at 40 yards, or in other words 144 pellets out of a standard load of No. 6 shot, the actual figure will vary from round to round. In a really well-regulated gun shooting a good cartridge this may be by as little as 5%, in what might be described as a 'good plain gun' the variation could be up to 10% and in a poor quality gun higher still. Good pattern quality, i.e. a good even distribution of pellets throughout the pattern, is just as important as density in imparting lethal effectiveness, and particularly so when density is on the thin side.

C

As mentioned in the last chapter, high pressures and velocities tend to affect adversely both pattern quality and density. This is especially so with guns having what are called 'game borings', which are very susceptible to increases in pressure and velocity. If an improved cylinder barrel regulated to shoot the standard load is used for the H.V. 'Grand Prix' game load of $1\frac{1}{8}$ oz, it will, in my experience, produce patterns of nearer 40 than 50% density. A quarter-choke barrel may just hold this H.V. load together and shoot a 55% pattern, but this is likely to be the top rather than the middle figure of a series of shots fired on the plate. To be certain of obtaining patterns up to expectations with these heavier, faster loads at least a half-choke is usually necessary.

Choice of Boring

In Figure 19 a visual comparison of the total spread of improved cylinder and full choke patterns at various ranges is depicted, with a 30 in circle superimposed for easy reference. It will be seen that up to just under 35 yards range the greater spread of the improved cylinder pattern is a positive aid to the shooter and the tight pattern of the full choke at under 30 yards range an undoubted handicap. It follows from this that it pays the game shooter to have as little choke in the barrels of his gun as the needs of his sport dictate.

Those who will shoot almost nothing but driven game can hardly do better than have an improved cylinder boring in each barrel. But if one goes rough shooting, where a higher proportion of 'going-away' birds have to be shot, and the use of No. 5 instead of No. 6 shot is considered desirable towards the end of the season, then a quarter-choke may serve better, and certainly if opportunities for inland wildfowling call for the use of 'Maximum' loads. For the man who is principally a rough shooter with only an occasional day at driven birds a quarter-choke in the right barrel and a half-choke in the left seem suitable borings, while the man who is a rough shooter-cum-wildfowler and rarely shoots at all at driven game may find a half-choke in each barrel best.

Some people argue that it is beneficial to have more choke in the left barrel than the right, because the shooter then has the option of availing himself of the heavier choke for a long shot. In practice, except when shooting a stationary target such as a rabbit feeding alongside a hedgerow or a pigeon on the branch of

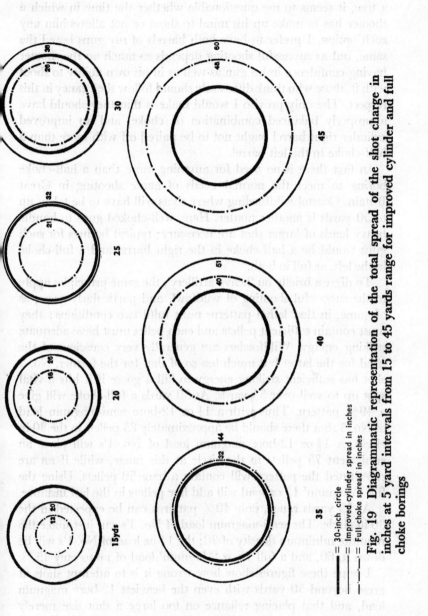

Fig. 19 Diagrammatic representation of the total spread of the shot charge in inches at 5 yard intervals from 15 to 45 yards range for improved cylinder and full choke borings

a tree, it seems to me questionable whether the time in which a shooter has to make up his mind to shoot or not allows him any such option. I prefer to have both barrels of my guns bored the same, but as successful shooting depends so much on the shooter having confidence in his gun as well as in his own ability to shoot with it, those who think differently should follow their fancy in this respect. The only proviso I would make is that they should have a properly balanced combination of choke, and an improved cylinder right barrel ought not to be paired off with more than a half-choke in the left barrel.

In fact there is no need for anything more than a half-choke boring to meet the normal needs of game shooting in Great Britain. Coastal wildfowling where shots will have to be taken up to 50 yards is another matter. Here, well-choked guns to handle heavy loads of larger shot are necessary; typical borings for such guns would be a half-choke in the right barrel and a full-choke in the left, or full in both.

To digress briefly on 'heavy artillery', the same principles apply to the successful shooting of wildfowl, and particularly geese, as of game, in that lethal patterns must fulfil two conditions: they must contain sufficient pellets and each pellet must have adequate striking energy. Wildfowlers are generally very conscious of the need for the latter but much less so of that for the former. No. 3 shot has sufficient striking energy to kill a goose if it hits a vital spot up to well over 55 yards. At 50 yards a full-choke will give a 49% pattern. Thus with a $1\frac{1}{4}$ oz 12-bore semi-magnum load of No. 3 shot there should be approximately 85 pellets in the 30 in circle. A $1\frac{1}{2}$ oz 12-bore magnum load of No. 1's will place an equivalent 75 pellets in the circle at this range, while if BB are substituted the pattern will contain a bare 50 pellets. Using the full 'Magnum' $1\frac{5}{8}$ oz load will add five pellets in the last instance.

At 55 yards range, only 40% patterns can be expected in the 30 in circle. The semi-magnum load of No. 3's can just make the requisite minimum density of 70; the $1\frac{1}{2}$ oz load of No. 1's will be down to 60, and a full $1\frac{5}{8}$ oz 'Magnum' load of BB to only 45.

I hope these figures show how wrong it is to attempt shots at geese beyond 50 yards with even the heaviest 12-bore magnum load, and that placing reliance on too large a shot size merely results in weak patterns, which even if correctly placed 'on target' will not ensure a clean kill. My own choice of gun for wildfowling has been a 12-bore semi-magnum weighing just under 7 lb, with which over the years I have been able to shoot consistently and reasonably successfully. But anyone preferring No. 1 shot for his geese would need a full 3 in magnum to obtain adequate pattern density.

Sportsmen when they grow older sometimes wonder if they might shoot more comfortably with a lighter gun or one with shorter barrels. A 20-bore with improved cylinder barrels, shooting the $1\frac{3}{8}$ oz standard load of No. 7 shot, will enable the user to compete on favourable terms up to over 40 yards range with a 12-bore owner using No. 6 shot. A 2 in chambered 12-bore with its $\frac{7}{8}$ oz load and No. 7 shot will put up a marginally better performance and some people find that, owing to the wider bore and rather softer pressures developed, the recoil experienced with these guns is a little kinder. For the same reasons they usually shoot patterns of exceptionally good quality. If, therefore, I were offered a choice, I would prefer a 2 in chambered 12-bore to a 20-bore.

When it comes to dealing with larger quarry, either of these guns will put up a satisfactory performance provided shot one size smaller is used than would be the choice with a full 12-bore game gun. If this is done there is no need for heavier choke, as is sometimes alleged. A 12-bore standard load of No. 4 shot contains only two more pellets than the equivalent 20-bore load of No. 5's, so for all practical purposes the former will give the same pattern densities, boring for boring, as the latter. It is not until the need to use larger shot becomes paramount that the limitations of these lighter guns with their lighter loads are significant.

As shown in the Table of gun weights in Chapter I, the 16-bore offers such a slight advantage in lightness that it does not really merit serious consideration in this role. Recognition of this may be the reason that demand for them in recent times has been steadily declining.

Choice of Gun

For many decades the ·410 has reigned supreme as a boy's gun. This is due in no small measure to the fact that old rook rifles rendered obsolete by the advent of the ·22 rifle could be converted to this gauge. In my view it is highly unsuitable as a gun for a young novice shot; it usually shoots poor quality and erratic patterns; even when used with No. 7 shot, pattern densities are too thin to be effective for small quarry, such as rats and grey squirrels, at a range much over 20 yards, which is very limiting. In fact it leads to a young shot doing all the things he has been told not to do, such as wounding quarry instead of killing them cleanly, shooting at excessive range, and so on.

A well regulated 28-bore will shoot good, consistent patterns. Even with only an improved cylinder barrel No. 7 shot will give effective patterns for small quarry up to just over 30 yards, which is a much more realistic range limit. The bigger and better pattern enables good practice to be made at clays. It is an eminently more suitable gun with which to start a young shot on his shooting career. It is to be hoped that, now sound and comparatively inexpensive A.Y.A. double-barrelled non-ejector guns of this gauge are available in this country, they will rapidly replace the ·410 in popular favour. But I would stress that in order to obtain the best results with a 28-bore it is essential to use a small shot size, preferably No. 7. The temptation to try and compensate for poor shooting by resorting to heavier shot must be resisted; it will only exacerbate the condition it is hoped to cure.

Short barrels do not cause any significant loss of performance, and for practical purposes a 25 in barrelled gun will kill just as efficiently as a 30 in barrelled one. The real importance of choice of barrel length is more in the sphere of gun fitting than ballistics in that it has been found that as a rule tall men shoot better with long barrels, and short men with short ones. This is probably why the majority of shooters of around 5 ft 10 in to 6 ft in height favour 28 in barrels.

Some tall men do of course shoot very well indeed with 26 in barrels. But all I have known have been experienced shots. I have myself in recent years changed from 28 to 26 in barrels and discovered that they do definitely call for sharper reflexes and nicer judgement to handle successfully. In fact it is not unlike riding a spritely little horse after a bigger, staider creature; unless one keeps alert and concentrates one can easily lose touch! I do not, therefore, believe that the modern trend to short barrels is a fashion everyone should slavishly follow if they want to shoot their best.

There are one or two technical points about them worth bearing in mind. When a gun is fired, in addition to the barrel flexing over all, a wave effect is created as the charge moves down the bore. The result in a 30 in barrelled gun is that the charge is centred at 40 yards appoximately 10 in below the point of aim, and with a 25 in barrelled gun an equivalent distance above it. This means that if a change is contemplated to a shorter barrelled gun, it may be necessary to alter the bend of the stock.

Some people find that the more noticeable muzzle blast from shorter barrels has an unpleasant effect on their ears and hearing. Although I have not found this myself, I have noticed that the discharge of a 25 in barrelled gun sounds quite distinctive from that of one with a longer barrel.

Gun Cleaning

There are thus many factors to be considered in choosing a gun, quite apart from the price one is prepared to pay for it, and having gone to all the trouble of obtaining the gun best suited to one's needs for whatever that price may be, one should clearly know how to look after it and keep it in good working order. Modern cleaner/lubricants, sold in aerosol packs, have taken all the hard work out of cleaning after firing. The gun should be taken down into its three principal components of fore-end, stock and barrels. The cleaner/lubricant is sprayed down each barrel from the breech end. The barrels are then left for ten minutes or so. In this interval they can be dried on the outside if necessary after shooting in the rain; a piece of an old flannel shirt does well for this, and the edge of a piece of blotting paper should be run down the channel on each side of the rib afterwards to ensure no moisture is left there. The stock and fore-end should then each be wiped dry, and the metal parts gone over lightly with a little '3-in-One' oil, which is still as good as any for the locks. The barrels should now be ready for attention; I normally use a pullthrough on the end of which is a bristle brush followed by a sufficiently big wad of 4 × 2 flannelette to fill the bore reasonably. Usually no further action is necessary except to oil up the bores with the cleaner/lubricant by means of a wool mop kept specially for the purpose. But sometimes streaks of leading may be apparent in the barrels, generally either just beyond the cone of the chamber or in the bore just short of the choke. This should be tackled with a phosphor-bronze brush to which the cleaner/lubricant is liberally applied. This treatment should be continued until, after wiping clean with a mop, the leading is seen to have been removed. The barrels can then be oiled up as already explained.

After rain it may be advisable to remove the extractors by unscrewing the extractor stop pin in the forward lump with a suitable screwdriver. This will enable any moisture to be mopped up with a rag. The extractors can then be lightly oiled and returned, the stop pin being screwed home again.

Oil on the metal and working parts should always be applied sparingly. Although the new cleaner/lubricants are excellent and, it is claimed, do not congeal as older gun oils, such as Rangoon oil used to, they do still collect dust and grit which can have an abrasive action if it gets between two working surfaces.

There are various ways in which the wood of the stock can be treated to keep it in good order, and a good stock on a well-cared-for gun should have a shine of which any dining-room table could be proud. I still find the old-fashioned method of buffing in a little boiled linseed oil with the heel of the hand gives the best finish, after any mud or dirt in the chequering has been brushed out with an old toothbrush. A good wax furniture polish also serves well, as does rubbing with a silicone-impregnated cloth.

In the case of sidelock actions it may be desirable from time to time carefully to remove the pins securing the locks with a screwdriver, lift the locks out and make sure they are free from moisture. I lightly coat the edges of the lock plates with a little mineral jelly every now and again to help prevent moisture penetrating and especially so with the semi-magnum I use for wild-fowling.

Proprietary abrasive pastes for removing corrosion in the bores are best avoided, and if this is necessary the gun should be taken to a qualified gunsmith. However, minor abrasions suffered by the stock can often be satisfactorily made good by being carefully rubbed down with ordinary domestic wire wool such as Brillo.

But, however conscientiously a gun may be maintained by its owner, a regular annual overhaul by a qualified gunsmith is desirable to ensure that its mechanical state is as sound as its good appearance and that it is a really mechanically safe and fully operational gun when taken out in the field for the first time next season.

Having attended to the well-being of his dog and gun, in that order, at the conclusion of a day's shooting, a sportsman may then in good conscience look to his own creature comforts. If this drill is always followed it will save a gun being put away in its case and forgotten for several days, in which time extensive corrosion can occur.

c*

CHAPTER FOUR

HOW TO SHOOT YOUR BEST

Gun Fitting

TO be able to shoot his best a man must have a gun which fits him. It is helpful if he understands the reasons for this.

The purpose of gun fitting is to make the centre line of the barrels, when the gun is correctly mounted to the shoulder, coincide with the shooter's line of sight. This is necessary because a shotgun is directed on to the target by the eye, unaided by any sighting apparatus as in rifle shooting. The muzzles must, therefore, point at the same spot as the eyes are looking in order to be 'on target'. To describe the eyes as the backsight of a shotgun, as is sometimes done, is misleading because it suggests a similarity with rifle shooting which is non-existent. More exactly, they can be regarded as an optical instrument, which actuates a computer, the brain, at the critical moment when it appears that the shot will hit the target if all the other instruments involved, such as the gun, the hands and the feet, are properly synchronized and function correctly.

The Eyes

This entails in the first instance that the eyes should be correctly positioned in relation to the gun. They should be level, which means the shooter's head must be upright, and not canted over to meet the stock. When seen from a target's eye view, they should be a fraction above the centre of the breech, as depicted in Figure 20.

Both eyes are used in shotgun shooting because binocular vision enables distances to be judged, which monocular vision cannot do. However, it is perfectly possible to shoot with only one eye, though as it also inhibits vision in depth, one-eyed shots often have difficulty in correctly selecting the leading or nearest bird in a covey, especially when they are shooting in country either lacking in landmarks or in which these are unfamiliar.

Fig. 20 The target's eye view of a properly fitting gun for a right-eyed shot

Actually to determine a shooter's line of sight the *'Master Eye'* concept is employed. This is based on the belief that a person's line of sight is determined by whichever eye is the stronger and therefore exerts the greater influence. As it is generally acknowledged that people usually have one arm stronger than the other, as also one leg, it seems both logical and reasonable to assume that one eye should be so as well.

When combat pistol shooting is taught in the Services, which is popularly, but incorrectly, known as 'shooting from the hip', the marksman looks at the target and shoots from hip level, the hand instinctively pointing the weapon where he is looking. But it is noticeable that the hand is always brought slightly across the body, so that not only the muzzle but also the barrel is aligned on the target. In other words the firer instinctively brings the pistol barrel into lateral alignment with his own line of sight.

A shotgun is pivoted at the shoulder, so the barrels cannot be moved at will into the shooter's line of sight. A golfer knows that if, after he has addressed the ball, he moves his head while making his swing, he will fluff his shot. A shooter has the same problem : if he moves his head after he has 'addressed' his target and started to mount his gun, he too will fluff his shot. He must not, therefore, move his head so as to adjust his line of sight to the centre-line of the gun barrels; it is the latter that must be made to coincide with the former. This is precisely what the master eye concept seeks to achieve; it is why gun fitting is necessary, and what might be described as 'body fitting' is not a satisfactory substitute, despite what certain medical men, who from time to time take it upon themselves to deride the idea of the master eye, may assert to the contrary.

Stock Measurements

Fitting a gun is dependent on the assessment of three measurements, which are *stock length, bend* and *cast off*. Stock length is the most important, and is taken from the front trigger to the centre, toe and heel of the butt as shown in Figure 21. Unless length is correctly estimated, it may result in incorrect bend and cast off. If a stock is too long, it will mean the butt will not come up on the pectoral muscle as it should, but on the point of the shoulder or even the biceps of the arm; if this occurs painful bruising will result when the gun is fired. If the stock is too short it will cause generally erratic gun mounting.

A stock for a young shot is often left rather on the long side because he will 'grow into it'. This is a great mistake, as it prevents the young novice from mounting his gun properly, and may mean

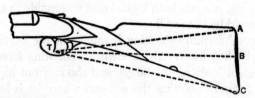

Fig. 21   How stock length is measured

TA is the length from the front trigger to the bump or heel; TB is the length from the front trigger to the 'middle' of the butt, and is normally the measurement referred to where one only is given; TC is the length from the front trigger to the toe of the butt.

that in trying to overcome this handicap he will develop all sorts of other faults in technique, some of which, having become habitual, will later be difficult to eradicate. A stock on a boy's gun can always be lengthened, as he grows up, and the fact that such an alteration to a man's gun is thought rather to spoil the look of the stock should be treated as a very secondary consideration compared to the importance of the boy learning to shoot properly right from the start.

Heavy guns will require shorter stocks than lighter ones. Thus if a man has a magnum for wildfowling weighing a pound or so more than his game gun, the former may need a stock at least a

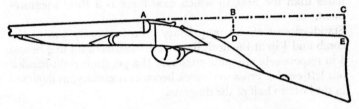

Fig. 22 How bend on a stock is measured

Bend is the perpendicular distance between the top line of the stock and the centre line, i.e. the top rib, of the barrels, represented by the lines DE and ABC above respectively. Measurements are taken at the comb, BD, and at the heel, CE.

¼ in shorter. The reverse will be the case if he has a light 28-bore or ·410 for his own use for shooting rabbits or just pottering around as some people do.

Bend is measured as shown in Figure 22, and provides for correct elevation. When the butt is properly bedded home on the shoulder, the line of the top of the stock, BD, should rest against the shooter's cheek midway between jawbone and cheekbone. Generally speaking a tall man with a long neck will need more bend on his stock than a small man with a short neck.

Cast off is the lateral adjustment made to the stock to bring the top rib of the barrels into the shooter's line of sight, and as with the bend consists of two measurements, one taken at the comb and the other at the bump, as depicted in Figure 23. The amount of cast off required depends on width of shoulder as well as line of vision. For a left-handed person a stock is cast on. If a person

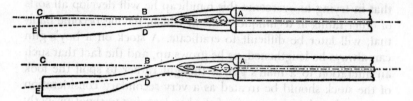

Fig. 23   How cast off on a stock is measured

Cast off is the divergence of the centre line of the stock,
ADE, from that of the centre line of the barrels, ABC. It is
measured at the comb and heel, i.e. at BD and CE respectively.
It is sometimes desirable to cast off the toe of the butt a little
more than the heel, in which case there is a third measurement.

Standard cast off on proprietary guns is usually $\frac{1}{8}$ in at the
comb and $\frac{1}{4}$ in at the heel; but measurements of up to $\frac{1}{4}$ in and
$\frac{1}{2}$ in respectively are quite common. If a person is right-handed
but left-eyed a 'crossover' stock becomes necessary, as depicted
in the bottom half of the diagram.

is right-handed but left-eyed, as can happen, what is known as
a cross-over stock will have to be fitted, as shown at the bottom
of Figure 23.

Shooting Style

The correct fit of a gun depends very much on a person's style
of shooting. Various different styles are taught, just as they are in
golf or cricket. Thus if a person goes from one shooting coach to
another, he may well end up with two or three different sets of
measurements each of which is claimed to be correct, and
probably is for the style to which it relates. It is important, therefore, that a shooter first of all settles into a definite style of shooting and then makes sure that his gun fits. This applies particularly
to a novice who is a grown man by the time he takes up shooting.

A person's needs in this respect may also change with age, as
sight and physique alter. For example, sportsmen quite often find
that in later life they need a shorter stock. So anyone who suffers
an inexplicable loss of form, as opposed to merely having an off
day, may well find if he has the fit of his gun checked by a quali-

fied instructor at a shooting school that it needs altering in some way.

The whole concept of gun fitting is sometimes ridiculed by clay pigeon shots on the grounds that if they can shoot effectively with straight-stocked guns so ought game shots. But the only form of competition clay pigeon shooting that is really comparable to game shooting is Skeet, and in this the aim is to break the clay at 20 yards range. The guns used in this sport are open-bored, and fire heavy charges of 8 or 9 shot, with a view to compensating for any minor inaccuracies in the centring of the pattern. If all game shooting consisted of similarly short range work, whether or not a gun fitted would indeed have less significance; it is not until shots have to be taken at over 30 yards that inaccuracy due to lack of fit usually begins to show and quarry to be hit by the fringe instead of the centre of the pattern, while at 40 yards they are missed altogether. Criticism on these grounds is not, therefore, valid.

Effective Shooting

Having obtained a properly fitting gun, the novice can then settle down to learning to become a really effective shot. Successful shotgun shooting is just as much a matter of good co-ordination of eyes, hands and feet as is good golf or cricket. Similarly the shooter must keep his eye on the target and shoot at it. He must not allow his eye to be distracted by the movement of his gun muzzles any more than a golfer is by the head of the club or a cricketer by the blade of the bat. Just as a cricket ball is hit by swinging a bat, so a shooter hits his target by swinging his gun, though there of course similarity ends. But I think this analogy with golf and cricket is worth taking thus far because it helps the novice to understand and master the basic technique of shooting.

A problem which worries many a young novice is how, if he shoots *at* a moving target, can his shot possibly hit it. It is important to know the answer to this at the very start of one's shooting career to dispel the temptation to aim off at points ahead of the target. If the gun is mounted and swung through the target correctly, as described later on, when the muzzles bear on the target, the eye sends an impulse to the brain, indicating that the moment to fire has arrived. As a result the trigger is pulled. But there is a momentary delay between the shooter's eye saying 'fire', and his finger actually pulling the trigger. This is known as personal reaction time and in a normally healthy person is about ·25 of a second. In this brief interval the gun muzzles swing fractionally onwards, or 'overthrow' as it is called, and so ensure the shot charge arrives on target, instead of at the point where the eye said 'fire'. It is, therefore, as important for the shooter to trust his eye and always aim at the 'ball' as for the cricketer or golfer.

How the eye should be positioned has been explained earlier; the paragraphs immediately preceding should make it clear how

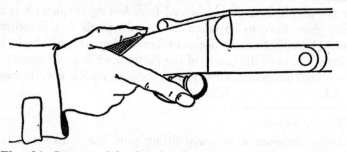

Fig. 24 Correct right hand grip at the 'ready' position, prior to firing

The forefinger of the right hand should be laid along the trigger guard, and the side of the thumb should rest on the back end of the safety catch, so that it can easily thumb it forward as the gun is mounted to the shoulder for a shot.

it ought subsequently to be used. A proper understanding of this, and of how it is the eye that calls the shots, is, I believe, a key factor in the making of a competent shot. The hands and feet play an important but supporting role.

Correct hand holds on a shotgun are no less necessary than on a golf club. The left is the aiming and main motivating hand, playing a part equally as important as that of the right, which in addition to pulling the trigger must also do its share of lifting and swinging the gun. As shown in Figure 24, the right hand should grasp the 'hand' of the stock, so that the top joint of the forefinger can comfortably reach the front trigger when the gun is to be fired. The left hand should be in the region of the top of the fore-end, with the thumb pointing straight down the left side

8 Take care when carrying guns at the 'slope' that the barrels do not clash, and cause denting.

9 If you must 'light up' when walking with a gun over your arm, avoid raising the muzzles like this because they can easily come to bear on somebody in front.

10 If you carry your gun over your shoulder it should always be with the trigger guard uppermost and the butt held well down, so that the muzzles do not point at somebody behind you, as could well happen here.

11 Nothing is more disconcerting tha sitting next to someone at a drive wh holds his gun like this! Always hold it s that the muzzles either point up in th air or down at the ground.

12 When shooting partridges with a pair of guns remember they are low flying birds, comparatively speaking; the loader must keep down out of the shooter's way, and pickers-up should either stand right up with the guns, as in this instance, or be right back 250 yards behind, out of shot.

13 When walking up in line make sure it is straight line, as shown here.

14 A typical walking gun's view of partridges flushing in front of him, in this instance from a snow covered field.

15 A safe, accomplished change, when shooting with a pair of guns calls for well rehearsed teamwork, as the shooter will generally be picking his next target during the change, and will have eyes only for that.

16 A brood of young redlegs on a farm track. The vivid markings of the adult show up clearly.

17 Young pheasant poults in an intensive brooder unit; note that it is well lit so that they can see to eat and drink.

of the barrels. The fingers of the left hand should not be curled over the top of the barrels or they may obscure the rib, and the shooter's eye will then subconsciously be caught by the centre line of the left barrel instead of that of the rib when the gun is mounted, and an error in aim will result.

Balance

When a gun is correctly held it should feel nicely balanced, with each hand taking an equal share of the weight. A shooter will soon appreciate the difference in feel between a well and a badly balanced gun, and the lively response of the former compared to the sluggish behaviour of the latter. In fact good balance in a gun is in my view a virtue second only in importance to the excellence of its shooting characteristics. The term 'balance' in a shotgun embraces its dynamic handling qualities as well as its static point of balance which is normally in the region of the crosspin at the knuckle.

Gunmakers seek to achieve good balance by 'concentrating the weight between the hands'. In particular this means the inertia of the barrels in front of the left hand is kept down. A noticeably muzzle heavy gun is certainly one to be avoided, but some people find that they shoot erratically if the forward section of the barrels does not have sufficient inertia, and exactly what suits each person best in this respect is a matter of individual taste. The heavier a gun, the more need there is to see that there is not an over-concentration of weight between the hands. On one occasion I handled a 25 in barrelled, 3 in chambered 12-bore Magnum, which weighed over 8 lb and felt just like a lump of lead. Proper distribution of weight is, therefore, as critical a factor as concentrating the greater part of it between the hands and in heavy guns longer barrels allow greater scope for this.

Engineers sometimes prefer to try and describe the phenomena of balance in the more technical jargon of their trade, in particular by reference to the radius of gyration of a shotgun. I deplore this, not only because many laymen have no idea what they are talking about but because it implies that a shotgun is rotated about its axis when it is mounted to the shoulder, which if it is mounted correctly is precisely what should not happen. Also I feel that final judgement on balance lies in a shooter's hands, rather than an engineer's sums.

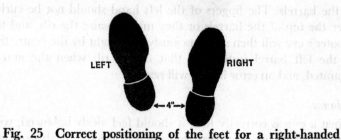

Fig. 25 Correct positioning of the feet for a right-handed shot

The Feet

Correct positioning and use of the feet is to the game shooter what a good gun platform is to an artilleryman; it allows him the widest scope in his shooting. The feet for a right-handed shot should be placed as in Figure 25, with the right foot slightly withdrawn to the rear, and the heels for a man of average height about four inches apart. A taller man may need a slightly wider stance and a shorter man a rather narrower one. While awaiting a shot, the shooter's weight should be equally balanced on both feet. Having come to the 'ready' position, described below, the shooter, in order to take a shot to the right, places his weight on the right

Fig. 26 Correct use of the feet for a shot to the right
As the shooter pivots about the hips, and his arc of turn increases, so his left heel must rise.

foot and pivots his body about the hips. As his angle of turn increases it will become necessary for him to raise the heel of the left foot and pivot on the toe, as shown in Figure 26. If he is young and supple he will be able to cover a wide arc to his rear in this way. But if he fails to raise the left heel, it will become necessary for him to bend at the waist in order to increase his angle of turn which will cause his gun muzzles to move through an arc, known as 'rainbowing', and make his shot go low and behind the target, as depicted in Figure 27.

To shoot a bird going to the left the procedure is similar except that the weight is put on the left foot and the right heel raised

Fig. 27 'Rainbowing' caused by failure to use the feet in turning for a shot

If the shooter stands flat-footed, he limits his degree of turn, and can only get further round by bending at the hips, which causes the gun to cant, and the muzzles to describe an arc, or 'rainbow', instead of moving in a straight line coinciding with the flight path of the quarry.

Fig. 28   Correct use of the feet for a shot to the left

This time the shooter must raise his right heel as his angle
of turn to the left increases, in order to avoid 'rainbowing'.

Fig. 29   Correct use of the feet for a shot low in front

The weight should go forward on to the front foot, and for
a real 'downhill' shot, such as may sometimes be required
when shooting low flying grouse in Scotland, the heel of the
right foot must be raised.

as the angle of turn increases (see Figure 28) and most shooters find that this happens more naturally, and they are less inclined to become rooted to the spot than when taking a shot to the right.

To deal with ground game or a low bird in front the weight should be placed on the left, or forward, foot and if necessary the right heel raised, as in Figure 29.

Fig. 30 Correct use of the feet for the high overhead shot
The weight should flow smoothly back on to the right foot, the left heel coming off the ground as the backswing increases.

To shoot a high bird overhead the weight should be allowed to come back on to the right foot and as the gun is swung to the vertical and beyond, the heel of the left foot should be raised to allow the maximum rearward swing to be obtained, as may be necessary to achieve a successful second barrel shot (Figure 30).

If time allows, it always pays to turn and face your target, so that the feet are in the position shown in Figure 25 when you shoot.

Gun Mounting

I have mentioned what I call the 'ready' position above. The shorter the distance the butt has to travel to the shoulder, the more consistently it can be correctly bedded home there. To enable this to be done as a drill the shooter, as soon as he makes up his mind to fire at a target, should adopt a position with the butt tucked between his upper arm and chest with the muzzles pointing towards it, as shown in Figure 31. If the gun is held in a vertical position with the butt at approximately waist level, and mounted from there straight to the shoulder, it will mean it has to be cartwheeled, with the result that the butt is likely to come to the shoulder after the muzzles bear on the target, as in Figure 32. The reverse will be the case if the gun is mounted from a position where the muzzles are pointing at the ground, when the butt is likely to bed home on the shoulder before the muzzles are on the target. In either case it will mean the shooter will have to make an adjustment before he fires, which may well lead to a miss.

Fig. 31   The 'ready' position when awaiting a shot

In anticipation of a shot, the shooter should come to the 'ready' position as depicted, with the stock tucked well up under the arm, and the gun muzzles pointing where he is looking, i.e. either at the target, or where it is expected to appear.

Fig. 32 Incorrect positions of the gun when awaiting a shot

If the gun is held with the butt either materially below or above the muzzles when awaiting a shot, the stock will have to be cartwheeled to the shoulder. This is a common cause of the butt either mounting too high so that the muzzles bear too low, or vice versa.

After the shooter has brought his gun to the ready position he should keep his eye firmly fixed on the target until he sees the moment has arrived to mount the gun and shoot. This should be done in a brisk, fluent movement, during which the safety catch is pushed forward, so that the trigger can be pulled the instant the butt comes to the shoulder. If everything has been properly co-ordinated, he should kill every time.

The most common cause of missing is head movement during gun mounting. This is usually induced either by failure to mount the gun high enough on the shoulder so that the head has to be bobbed down to meet the stock, or by starting to mount the gun too soon, hesitating, and then pressing the head down on the stock to 'improve' the aim. I would unhesitatingly assert that more middle height and high pheasants are missed due to premature gun mounting accompanied by an attempt at conscious aiming than any other single cause. This is particularly so with the inexperienced, who want to give themselves plenty of time and to 'make sure' of their bird; as with so many good intentions, these are a passport to failure!

The shooter will obtain all the swing he needs if he allows his hands to obey the dictates of his eyes. It is the impulsion provided by the movement of the gun from under the arm up into the shoulder which gives the 'overthrow' that ensures the shot hits the target. If this impulsion is lost by first mounting the gun and then starting the swing, so that what should have been one smooth, smartly executed movement is divided into two separate ones with a momentary pause between them, then a miss behind is inevitable. People rarely fail to hit a bird which takes them by surprise, because they snap their gun to the shoulder and shoot instinctively; they don't have time to dither around as they do when a pheasant comes into view long before it arrives in shot.

Practice

As with golf, cricket, tennis or any other game, there is only one way in which a person can master the art of shooting to the full extent his natural ability permits and that is by practising under the supervision of a qualified instructor. Many golfers begin their season by having a round or two with the club professional and sometimes, if they go off their game during the season, return to him to have any faults they have developed in their play straightened out. Similarly an increasing number of shooting men, especially those who rate as good shots, nowadays start off the season with an hour or more's practice at a shooting school under the eye of an instructor.

Some people aver that shooting at clays is bad for their game shooting, because a clay is slowing up while a gamebird is usually accelerating. This is a fallacy. Shooting clays over a well-organized 'game layout' is excellent practice and it is immaterial to the perfecting of co-ordination of eyes, hands and feet whether the target is slightly decelerating or accelerating. But just as partridges require a different timing from pheasants and a sportsman can find after shooting a lot of partridges that it takes him a day or so to adjust to pheasants, so a man after practising a lot at clays will take a little while to adjust his rhythm to the pace of whatever quarry he next pursues.

Conclusion

As recently as thirty years ago it was generally held that good shots were born and not made. I can remember experienced shooting men giving this as their unequivocal opinion. But today it is widely realized that this is not so, and that anyone, except the most abject natural duffer, can hope to become a competent shot if he takes a course of lessons at a shooting school and equips himself with a properly fitted gun. The sooner a young shot can start having such lessons, after he has learnt the rudiments of gun handling and elementary shooting at home, the better. Also if more newcomers to the shooting field in later life were to take advantage of the facilities at these schools, not only would a much better standard of game shooting generally prevail but those concerned would probably obtain much greater enjoyment from their sport.

CHAPTER FIVE

SAFETY IN THE SHOOTING FIELD

THE prime ambition of every shooter should be to become a safe shot. If he can also earn himself a reputation as a crack shot it will undoubtedly stand him in good stead. But every shooting man should understand from the earliest moment he handles a shotgun that this is the second, *not* the first priority.

Mechanical Safety

There are two aspects to safety in the shooting field : one concerns shooting with a mechanically safe gun, the other how to handle and use it safely. I have already referred in Chapter III to the need to look after a gun properly and have it serviced annually by a qualified gunsmith. It is generally acknowledged that a well-maintained car is a safe car and this applies with equal force to a shotgun. I have several times seen good quality guns, as well as others of more doubtful repute, discharged inadvertently in the shooting field due to mechanical failure. Luckily, because the weapon was being handled correctly on each occasion, no harm came to man or dog. But it is an unnerving experience both for the person to whom it happens and those in whose company he is shooting. For the peace of mind of everyone, the right thing to do when such a misfortune occurs is to pack up shooting for the day and have the offending gun repaired as soon as possible.

Proof

The Law, by virtue of the Proof Acts, and Rules of Proof relating to them, seeks to prevent the manufacture and circulation of unsafe firearms. Every gun in course of construction has to pass two stages of Proof, the first designed to see that the barrels on their own are sound, and the second to ensure that the barrels and action together are properly jointed and up to their job.

Having passed Proof the barrels are marked accordingly on their flats, the London and Birmingham Proof Houses each having their own identification symbols which are added to the prescribed Proof marks. Examples of guns marked according to the 1925 Proof Act by the London and Birmingham Proof House respectively are shown in Figure 33. Similar markings in accordance with the current 1954 Act are given in Figure 34. Guns proved before 1925 do not have the nominal length of cartridge case, e.g. $2\frac{1}{2}$ in, included. 'NITRO PROOF', or 'N.P.', indicates that the gun has passed nitro-proof, but very old guns may have no such mark, which will mean they have been proved for Black Powder only and are not safe to use with modern nitro powders.

It is illegal to sell, offer for sale, exchange or pawn a gun which is unproved or out of proof. A gun is held to be out of proof if, despite bearing apparently valid proof marks, the bores have become enlarged beyond the stipulated limit for the gauge of gun in question, or the action or barrels have otherwise become materially weakened. I would stress that the presence of proof marks is no guarantee that a gun is still in proof; they merely show

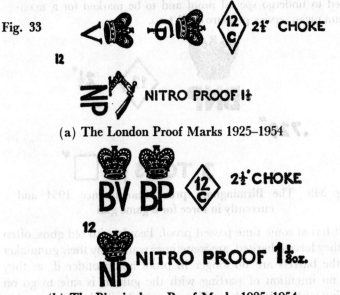

Fig. 33

(a) The London Proof Marks 1925–1954

(b) The Birmingham Proof Marks 1925–1954

Fig. 34a   The London Proof Marks since 1954 and currently in force

These are the proof marks for a $2\frac{3}{4}$ in chambered gun, or semi-magnum; the equivalent pressure shown for a 3 in chambered magnum would be $3\frac{1}{2}$ tons. A gun to fire the 3 in 'Magnum' cartridge with a $1\frac{5}{8}$ oz load of shot would need to have undergone special proof, and to be marked accordingly for a maximum mean service pressure of 4 tons. A semi-magnum to fire the $2\frac{3}{4}$ in 'Magnum' load of $1\frac{1}{2}$ oz would also need to undergo special proof and to be marked for a maximum mean service pressure of $3\frac{1}{2}$ tons.

Fig 34b   The Birmingham proof marks since 1954 and currently in force for a game gun

that it has at some time passed proof. People with old guns, often ones they have inherited, are sometimes warned by their gunmaker that the barrels are no longer in proof and wonder if, as they have no intention of parting with the gun, it is safe to go on shooting with it themselves. They seem to fear, when a gunmaker has gone so far as to recommend rebarrelling, that he is out to make a 'fast buck' at their expense. A car owner who is told by a qualified mechanic that his vehicle needs a new engine usually accepts the advice without reservation. But for some reason a gunmaker has only to suggest a gun needs new barrels to be thought a rogue! In fact the repair side of a gunmaking business is the most time-consuming and least profitable and I would unhesitatingly say that if a reputable gunsmith recommends a customer to have new barrels for his gun then it assuredly needs them and that if he feels he cannot trust his gunmaker he should find a new one whom he can. As a guiding rule it is unwise to continue shooting with a gun which is no longer in proof, however superficially safe it may look.

By reciprocal agreement the proof marks of some foreign countries are valid in this country and British proof marks in theirs; they are Austria, Belgium, Czechoslovakia, France, West Germany, Italy, Spain and Southern Ireland. However, the pressures shown in kilogrammes do not allow of direct comparison with British pressures shown in tons per square inch; they are not the same, and are also taken at a slightly different point in the barrel.

Sleeved barrels, which as far as experience has shown are a cheaper and perfectly satisfactory way of having a gun rebarrelled, have to be stamped with the word 'SLEEVED' in addition to the other proof marks. Some foreign guns have chrome-lined barrels. The advantages claimed for this are debatable and there are certainly some disadvantages when, for example, dents have to be raised in a barrel. Special instructions have been issued by the Proof Houses regarding their treatment.

Proof is the foundation on which gun safety in Britain is built. For those who wish to know more, Burrard has written very fully on the subject in the third volume of *The Modern Shotgun*. There is also a booklet published under the auspices of both Proof Houses and entitled *Notes on the Proof of Shotguns and Other Small Arms*, which costs pennies rather than pounds and is more up to date.

Correct Gun Handling

Safety in gun handling and usage in the shooting field is largely a matter of following certain well-established drills. If asked to

summarize the salient points as a code of behaviour, I would
suggest the following Golden Rules:

1 Prove if a gun is loaded or not as soon as you lay hands
on it.
2 Only point a gun at quarry you wish to shoot, never at
people.
3 Check that the bore(s) of your gun is/are clear before you
load at the beginning of a day, drive, walk up, or after any
significant interval between shots and invariably after a
misfire.
4 Never put down or leave a loaded gun.
5 Carry a gun with the barrels pointing either up in the air
or down at the ground, except when you come to the 'Ready
position' to take a shot, when they should point where you
are looking.
6 Learn to shoot in good style; polished performance promotes
safety.
7 Don't shoot where you cannot see; small shot can travel
over two hundred yards, and may also ricochet off hard
ground, water or the branches of trees.
8 Always unload your gun when crossing an obstacle, or
entering a car or building, and make it a drill always to
check it on these occasions.
9 Don't be a greedy shot; observe proper safety angles and
never swing through the line of guns or beaters.
10 Only use cartridges which you know give ballistics within
the limits for which your gun has been proved.
11 Make sure your gundog is always kept under proper control.
12 Don't take other people on trust as safe shots.

When to carry a gun with the breech open is, in my view, really
a matter of good sense and good manners. If you carry your gun
in company with other people with the breech closed only you can
know that it is empty. If the breech is open everyone can see for
themselves that it is empty. I therefore believe it is right that as
a rule a gun not needed at instant readiness should be carried
with the breech open. However, there are occasions on which
exceptions are justified, and to pretend that these invalidate the
general rule, as do some died-in-the-wool adherents of the 'closed
breech' school, is being a little silly.

Fig. 35   How to carry a gun safely with the breech open

Fig. 36   Carrying a gun safely in the 'slope arms' position
When carrying a gun in this position the trigger guard should
be uppermost, and the butt held well down so that the barrels
are almost vertical.

If carried over the arm with the breech open, the gun should be held as in Figure 35, or if with the breech closed in the 'slope arms' position, as in Figure 36, the trigger guard being uppermost, and the muzzles pointing well up in the air. In this latter position care must be taken if walking alongside a companion with his gun carried similarly, because the barrels may easily collide with each other and be dented. Two positions in which guns should not be carried are shown in Figure 37a and b, as the muzzles will point straight at a companion to the flank or in rear.

Fig. 37 Two potentially dangerous ways of carrying a gun

a It is always disconcerting walking in line on the left of a man carrying his gun like this, and especially if you know it is loaded!

b Don't carry a gun like this; nobody following behind will enjoy looking down the muzzles!

When loading a gun, always close it by raising the stock, so that the muzzles remain pointing at the ground, as depicted in Figure 38.

Safety Range and Radius

Because the effective range of a shotgun is limited to between 40 and 50 yards, it is easily overlooked that small shot, e.g. 5's, 6's and 7's will travel over 200 yards before becoming spent. Even a pellet which has ricochetted may have sufficient force remaining to penetrate a man's eye at a range of 100 yards and cause

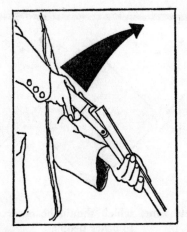

Fig. 38   The correct method of closing a gun

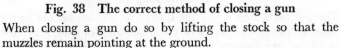

serious injury. Many shooting accidents are the result of ricochets rather than direct hits, and comparatively few people fully appreciate how real this danger is, and how, even when the greatest care is taken, a ricochet through some quite unforeseen angle may cause an injury. Sir Ralph Payne-Gallwey proved conclusively that ricochets can come off a gamebird's plumage. This unpredictability of ricochets is the principal reason it has become customary to observe rather wider safety angles in game shooting than formerly prevailed. Typical safety zones at a covert shoot are shown in Figure 39; the same angles should apply when walking up, or shooting in the vicinity of anyone. Low flying birds and ground game should never be shot in the shaded zones. High birds may be shot in these zones, but I like to see them at a vertical angle of at least 45 degrees before they are. Birds flushed at the end of a beat should always be allowed to rise clear of the treetops before they are shot at, owing to the danger of a ricochet hitting a beater.

Pickers Up and Stops

At some shoots pickers up are left very much to their own devices and to use their own discretion in positioning themselves. This is slack management, but it does happen, particularly with syn-

D

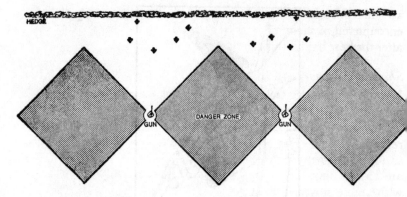

Fig. 39 Safety zones which should be observed in relation to other people

Ground game and low flying quarry should not be shot in the shaded 'Danger Zones'. The unshaded area in which it is safe to shoot can usually be assessed on the ground by picking out eye-catching features in a hedge, e.g. a gap or prominent bush, or further afield, e.g. a cottage or pylon, when a shooter first takes up position.

dicates. Except where special circumstances dictate otherwise and some feature of the ground offers protection, pickers up should either be stationed right up with individual guns, or else at least 250 yards in rear of the guns. This is particularly important when normally low-flying birds, such as partridges, are the principal quarry, and the ground is open. In covert shooting it may be necessary if there is thick woodland behind the guns for pickers up to go to work at closer quarters, in which case it is essential that the guns are informed accordingly, so that in the excitement of a woodcock flashing by, one of them does not take a shot low and behind. Equal care must of course be exercised should stops be present and it is the duty of every gun, walking and standing, to know where they are.

End of Drive Drill

At the end of a beat I like to see all guns unloaded, and each placed in a canvas cover from which it is not removed until its owner arrives at his stand for the next beat. However, this may not always be practicable and walking guns have to be taken into account. But whatever is the arrangement, the practice sometimes encountered of shooting at stray birds flushed by dogs picking up after the beat has finished should not be permitted.

Shooting Manners and Discipline

Nothing is more aggravating than spending a day next to another gun who is always trying to shoot your birds before you do. An almost sure way of putting a stop to this deplorable habit is to retaliate in kind. But one thing can easily lead to another and so to an accident; unhappily the worst offenders in this respect are usually singularly difficult to impress in any subtler fashion with a sense of wrong-doing.

In my experience the standards of safety observed at a shoot are a direct reflection of the quality of its management. With syndicates, maintaining 'discipline' among the guns is a difficult exercise, calling for greater diplomacy than in the case of the owner who is lord of all he surveys and can, if he so wishes, banish a dangerous shot completely and for ever. Such rough justice is rather frowned upon nowadays, but I am quite sure the fact that it could be, and was on occasion, invoked made the need to do so rare.

The modern businessman who takes up game shooting in middle age and buys a gun in an expensive syndicate sometimes seems to think that this gives him the right to behave as he likes regardless of established protocol. Shooting is a recreation, but it is only an enjoyable one as long as it is conducted in safety. No one, therefore, can be exempted from observance of the rules of the game, and the most important of these is that everyone should know how to behave as a safe shot, and meticulously observe the disciplines which this imposes.

Duties of the Host

The host or manager of a day's shooting has many responsibilities. Before the day he must arrange the various beats in consultation with his keeper, and in particular decide where the guns are to stand, and any limitations on their field of fire, due to the presence of stops, etc., of which they must be informed. On the day itself, it should be the host's job, not the keeper's, to place the guns and see that each receives any necessary briefing as to the whereabouts of other people. This is often specially necessary when shooting in hilly, wooded country, where a high bird to a gun in the glen may be only knee high to a fellow gun out of sight among the trees further up the hill. Simple plans, well supervised in their execution, will do much to minimize the chances of an accident, the most common cause of which is somebody being where they ought not to be at the critical moment. When walking up, it must be a golden rule for all concerned, beaters as well as guns, to keep in line; the pace must be adjusted to that of the slowest over the heaviest going. (See Plate 13.)

Automatic and Repeating Shotguns

So far I have purposely not mentioned repeating and automatic shotguns, because except for solitary occasions shooting pigeon either coming into decoys or to roost, they are not in my opinion suitable or safe weapons to use in the British shooting field. This is because they are slow to unload and reload and neither the breech nor magazine can be checked at a glance to see if cartridges remain in it. Also, the bore of the barrel cannot be easily inspected to see that it is clear.

Conclusion

Safety should be the concern of everyone who shoots. We may live in more easy-going times than when our grandfathers went shooting, but the best way to prevent accidents is still strict compliance with the safety procedures and etiquette which became largely an established part of shooting lore in their day. Every accident which has been brought to my notice over the past twenty-five years has, on investigation, been found attributable to some failure in some way in this respect.

CHAPTER SIX

CLOTHING AND EQUIPMENT

THERE is nowadays a great variety of excellent ready-made clothing available in the better shops, which is specially designed to meet the shooter's needs. When I was young, at any reasonably good shoot a bespoke tailored tweed plus-four suit, or riding breeches instead of plus-fours, was practically standard dress in fine weather, and if it rained one donned a riding mackintosh. Footwear consisted either of brogues or boots and gaiters; to wear gumboots was all right for the young, but considered slightly undignified by grown ups. Although this rather stereotyped form of dress had its good points, it also had many disadvantages which have now to a great extent been overcome.

Footwear

In my view, the most important item of a shooter's clothes is his footwear. The gumboot has been so universally adopted that it may seem a trifle heretical to suggest that it in any way falls short of the ideal. But at the beginning of the season and especially when walking up I find even the best of them too hot for genuine comfort unless it is a really wet day. More comfortable by far is a pair of well-studded veldtschoen-type brogues. Some people complain that walking a moor in shoes allows bits of heather and other debris to fall in the top, so that the wearer has continually to stop and empty them out. Leather boots, worn with well-fitting leather or canvas anklets, overcome this handicap and also provide better support for the ankles. But shoes on a warm August day are cooler, and I prefer them for the limited amount of walking required on a driven grouse day. The same holds good for a fine September day walking up partridges in the South of England. But one important point which applies equally to brogues and boots is that the heels must be adequately studded as well as the soles, or the wearer is liable to slip and go flat on his back when walking down a steep grass bank; not all bootmakers realize this and it is advisable when having a pair of boots or shoes studded to see that they are instructed accordingly.

There are many types of gumboot from which a shooter can choose, some of which lace up, or partially lace up, others which just pull on, some which come only halfway up the calf and others the full length of the calf. My own choice is the 'Hunter' type boot with the studded composition sole, which gives one a good grip on slippery ground. It is also light in weight and cut reasonably narrow at the top so that, when one is walking through tall cover, debris does not fall down inside. If the boot is bought in a size sufficiently large to enable a nylon innersole to be worn, the deadly disadvantage of gumboots, namely chilled feet, is overcome. I have tried many other different styles and brand names but have found none as satisfactory as the 'Hunter' which, although an expensive boot, does last well.

The Coat

Next in importance to me is a comfortable shooting jacket. I have found that by far the most satisfactory for general game shooting is the standard Grenfell cloth jacket. It is windproof and showerproof, but equally important, it is very light and supple, allowing the shooter great freedom of movement. But for shooting in really rough country and wet weather, a Barbour thornproof is unsurpassed, as it is also for coastal wildfowling.

For shooting on fine autumn days, when the problem is to keep cool rather than warm, my preference is a light tweed jacket, but it must be loosely cut across the shoulders. If it is, then I have found little to be gained by having fancy pleats inserted at the back to allow the arms still greater freedom of movement, though some shooters set great store by them.

Trousers

As regards one's breeks, what are called nowadays 'plus twos' rather narrowly cut, have always seemed to me the most serviceable and comfortable. They do not constrict movement of the legs in crossing fences and so on, as do riding breeches, and they also fit snugly under waterproof overtrews, whereas old-fashioned widely cut plus fours are very bulky when so worn. To finish dressing one's legs, I have always found thick wool stockings the most comfortable irrespective of the time of year.

Some people prefer waterproof leggings, others overtrews; a light pair of the latter made of good quality, tough nylon cloth, when not worn can be carried in the pocket, and has the advantage over leggings of allowing the wearer to sit down, if at any time he wants to, without fear of getting a wet behind.

Headgear

Many people like to shoot without a hat or cap, others invariably wear headdress of some sort or other. On most occasions this can well be left as a matter of personal choice. However, in driven grouse shooting the head of a hatless man with a high forehead and fair hair, or possibly none at all, shining in the autumn sunshire as he peers over the top of his butt can be quite sufficient to turn grouse short of the line, especially in drives where they have a tendency anyhow to swing away to one flank or the other. I think, therefore, that the wearing of some form of headdress by guns shooting driven grouse is desirable. When shooting woodpigeon over decoys or at evening flight a hat of some sort is an almost essential item of dress.

The ordinary peaked cap is splendid in fine weather, but in heavy rain merely ensures that the water pours down your neck. A much more satisfactory garment is a tweed 'Connaught' hat which, with its all-round rim that extends slightly into a peak fore and aft, carries the rain off. These hats can be rendered virtually waterproof if they are treated with one of the proprietary silicone aerosol sprays.

The Hands

A major problem the shooter has to deal with on a really cold day is that of keeping his hands warm. Some shoot happily in gloves, others prefer mittens. But there are so many well-designed and well-made proprietary brands of both available in most good gun shops that everyone should readily be able to find an answer to this problem to suit himself.

Cartridge Bags

Turning now from clothing to equipment, a major consideration is a good cartridge bag. Except for boys, who have small hands and are using 28-bore or ·410 cartridges, I can see no point in having a cartridge bag smaller than the 100 × 12-bore size, as otherwise a man with normal sized hands has difficulty in extracting cartridges quickly. Also there is no need to fill it, if it has to be carried on a small day.

The materials of which bags are normally made are pigskin, cowhide and waterproofed canvas, though more fancy ones of zebra skin and other exotic materials can be obtained at a considerably higher price. Pigskin bags are the most expensive of the three ordinary ones and probably the most durable and serviceable. My own after twenty years' reasonably hard service still comes up almost like new with the help of a little brown boot polish. But to keep it company there is also a plain hide bag which is older and in good shape, and a canvas one which is even older still, but in perfectly good order apart from one small tear which has been mended. In my opinion leather cartridge bags have a social cachet, rather as did the solid leather luggage of our Victorian ancestors when they travelled, but waterproofed canvas ones will serve the needs of most shooters entirely adequately and are half the price.

To be seen wearing a cartridge belt at a shoot of any standing used to be considered rather a social solecism. This is no longer so and I have come to find that a cartridge belt, worn under one's shooting jacket, is the most convenient and comfortable way of carrying a reserve of cartridges on one's person, irrespective of whether I am shooting driven or walked-up game. I prefer the open-ended leather loop type with a strip of leather added to prevent the cartridges being pushed too far through. The only complaint I have about my present belt is that when I bought it, the salesman peered over the counter and said, 'Ah, I thought you'd be able to manage the 30-size, sir!' I have often since been thankful that vanity did not dictate that I changed it for the more usual 25-cartridge size.

The Cartridge Extractor

A cartridge extractor used to be carried as a matter of course by most shooting men, but with the improvements which have been made in modern cartridges the services of one are now seldom required. However, as a result, any half-dozen shooting men picked at random would be lucky if they could muster a single cartridge extractor between them. When this implement is needed there is really no adequate substitute for it; I always carry one, though in thirty years I have only used it twice, and then to rescue others, once to remove a jammed case, and once a separated case. It is a wise precaution to keep one permanently in one's cartridge bag, attached by a light cord to the buckle, so that it won't get pulled out by mistake, and lost, when the shooter helps himself hurriedly to cartridges.

Shooting Sticks

For those who need a shooting seat, the qualities to look for are comfort and convenience. My own preference is for a leather sling seat, an adjustable shaft, and a kick-over plate to stop it sinking too far into the ground. The 'Hill' shooting seat is both comfortable and stable, as it has three legs instead of one, but it is bulkier and not so convenient to carry, and so is not my first choice, especially as most of my shooting involves me carrying all my own kit. Shooting sticks to be avoided are those with wooden shafts, which may snap with painful consequences, and those with a removable plate, which when sunk in heavy ground may pull off and be lost.

Other Equipment

A good gamebag with a hempen proofed net is an undoubted asset to the rough shooter, though it is a mistake to have one larger than really needed, as you can then easily find yourself carrying what everyone else has shot as well.

Medical opinion strongly favours the wearing of ear plugs by shooters to prevent damage to their hearing. For clay pigeon shots I think this is an entirely valid and sensible precaution. Except for those game shots who regularly fire a lot of cartridges in a day throughout the season, I am not so sure that it is. However, for those who feel the wearing of ear plugs will be beneficial, there are a number on the market, those sold by the Game Conservancy under the trade name of 'Gunfender' being the only ones I have myself tried and for which I can vouch.

There are a number of other gadgets with which a shooter may encumber himself to some fairly good purpose, but if he has to carry all his kit himself it is wise to keep the load as light as possible. For some types of shooting, such as decoying wood-

D*

pigeon or ferreting rabbits, additional specialized equipment is required which will be dealt with in the appropriate chapter. From my own experience the main thing is to be comfortably and adequately clothed, and to have the equipment you really need; in particular always try to make sure you have sufficient cartridges and a suitable means of carrying them.

CHAPTER SEVEN

FACTORS IN SHOOT MANAGEMENT

Introduction

GAME shooting is the harvesting of a game crop. The first concern of shoot management lies, therefore, with the production of this crop. There are five principal aspects to this; they are :

a The management of habitat, which could well be described as making the best provision for shelter and food that resources allow.
b Winter feeding.
c The protection of game from its enemies.
d Prevention of, and protection against, disease.
e Stocking with reared birds, in the case of certain species only.

In this and the next chapter it is proposed to deal with *a*, *b*, and *c* above, while *d* and *e* are covered in later chapters.

Habitat

Abundant game populations will only thrive in a congenial habitat. Thus it is a complete waste of time and money to embark on lavish pheasant re-stocking programmes if the birds have subsequently to be released into an unsuitable environment, because they will either languish and die, or go elsewhere in search of better conditions.

All gamebirds require cover of varying kinds to meet different needs, such as roosting, nesting, concealment from predators and so on. Also, just as human beings dislike eating in draughty dining-rooms, so do gamebirds; they prefer places sheltered from the wind in which to feed. After rain, birds will seek sheltered, sunny open spaces in which to dry out, and adequate provision of these is just as important as that of suitable cover.

But the pattern of the countryside is primarily dictated by the requirements of farming and forestry, with which those of game have to be reconciled as best they may. This is especially true in the case of the partridge and pheasant; the grouse enjoys a rather more privileged position.

Neither partridges nor pheasants flourish in bleak, prairie-type farming conditions, and the wholesale removal of hedges has unquestionably had an adverse effect on the wild population of both. However, it is becoming increasingly evident that too few hedges can lead to serious soil erosion, and that the hedge can play a more valuable role even in purely arable farming than was at one time recognized. From the game conservationist's point of view, little harm is done until field size becomes larger than 50 acres. So where fields can be restricted to this size, and hedges, instead of barbed-wire fences, form the boundaries between fields, the problems of sustaining high game populations are greatly alleviated. Where such conditions do not prevail there are, however, other measures which can be taken to try and remedy deficiences in cover, of which more later.

Hedges and Hedging

The two most cogent arguments advanced by farmers in favour of hedge removal are that it reduces the problem of controlling couch grass and eliminates that of hedge maintenance. The encroachment of couch on a crop from the hedgerow can be a scourge and unfortunately a really satisfactory and economic way of dealing with the problem has yet to be found. But the bottom of a permanent barbed wire fence can also provide a source from which couch may spread, though the fence can of course be removed, and replaced after the couch has been dealt with.

As regards the economics of hedge maintenance, if a hedge has been properly cut and laid to make it stockproof, subsequently keeping it in good order with modern tractor-mounted machinery, which is excellent, is really a very minor item on the farm balance-sheet. It is doubtful if, over a period of years, the cost would amount to more than would have to be expended on a similar length of barbed-wire fencing.

There seem, therefore, reasonable grounds for hoping that the rate of hedge removal may tail off and that some new hedges may one day in the foreseeable future be planted.

But meantime those who manage shoots have to deal with things as they are. If a critical eye is cast over any farm, some waste or not fully utilized ground will almost certainly be found somewhere, and the larger the farm the greater the number of such places there are likely to be. They can vary in size from a boggy depression in the corner of a field, a few square yards in extent, to a half-acre strip of bank too steep to be ploughed, or a bit of 'short work' in a field sandwiched between a wood and a track, which always takes longer to 'work' than it is worth. These are the sort of plots which, it can be fairly claimed, when fenced off, planted up and utilized for the shoot will have a far greater value than they ever will as farmland. They are the areas which a good shoot manager with a keen eye for country should be picking out and utilizing; with, of course, the farmer's consent where necessary.

Game Crops

Farmers take as much pride in reviewing their serried ranks of wheat, barley, roots and so on as any general ever has in inspecting the massed regiments under his command. But if certain crops especially attractive to game, such as kale and roots, can, instead of being sown in one massive block, be spread round the farm in, say, a number of five-acre strips adjacent to various coverts, they will serve the shoot much better and also be easier to tackle on a shooting day. In fact, if farm crops generally can be organized in a patchwork pattern rather than large single units, it will be beneficial to game.

From the point of view of game, the land should be disturbed as little as possible from the middle of March to mid-July. But towards the end of April and in early May cattle will be intensively grazing the early bite; at the end of May silage-making starts and continues into June when hay-making also starts. All these operations can play havoc with nesting gamebirds. Cocksfoot is often the first of the grasses to make headway in the spring, and as soon as the tussocks grow sufficiently to offer minimal cover they become favourite nesting sites for both partridges and pheasants to whom the centre of a field seems as good a choice as a hedgerow. Nests out in a field are almost bound to be lost before the brood can be hatched off and escape. It does no harm to quarter a dog over grass and forage crops in late March and early April, so that any hens intent on nesting in them are chased off, or if any nests are found the eggs can be removed and the nest destroyed. German short-haired pointers or English setters are ideal for this work.

The practice of planting small acreages of special game mixtures, either to expand small existing coverts or improve the holding qualities of bigger ones, is growing. Various crops can be used for this; maize or mustard is excellent for the purpose and flourishes in the South of England, as do sunflowers; there is the Game Conservancy's recommended mixture which contains maize, sunflowers, canary seed, buckwheat, caraway seed, American sweet clover, marrowstem kale and Nida rape; but two crops which always seem to give good results and can be left *in situ* for a number of years are Jerusalem artichokes and marrowstem or thousandhead kale.

Jerusalem artichokes should be sown in drills at 5 ft spacing, with a potato planter, the space between plants in each row being not less than 2 ft, and the seeding rate about half a ton to the acre. On all soils except the very lightest it is important that they are ridged up, so that pheasants in due season can scratch at and expose the tubers off which they feed. The ridges should run in the direction in which the crop is to be driven so that beaters can walk down the drills. In any reasonably good soil this crop will thrive and can become very dense unless it is kept under control by annual inter-row cultivations and periodic thinning of the rows with a potato spinner. Once a shoot has established a patch of these artichokes it need never lack for seed to plant others, which is a compensation for the high initial price of seed unless this can be obtained from a well-disposed sporting neighbour.

Mustard is much used as a game crop in the South of England, as well as an ordinary farm crop. It is specially favoured by partridges, but being only an annual, must be renewed each season.

The further north one goes, and especially from Yorkshire onwards, the more rigorous climate severely limits the shoot owner's choice of game crops. But in Scotland, kale, either marrowstem or thousandhead, seems to give such unfailingly excellent results when used as a game crop, that a visitor may be forgiven for wondering if the more exotic mixtures used in the south are really worth the additional expense and trouble. For the sporting farmer who likes to keep things simple, a policy of relying solely on strips of kale and artichokes respectively has a lot to commend it, as the chances of crop failure are minimal, which can happen all too readily in a bad summer with maize and some game mixtures. However, this is in no way to denigrate these mixtures which, when successful, can undoubtedly attract and hold game in large numbers.

The Economics of Game Cropping

The moment it is suggested that an acre of genuine farmland be devoted exclusively to the interests of game a farmer begins to worry whether he may not be taking the first dread step on the road to bankruptcy. It is worth considering, therefore, what is actually needed in this respect, and the financial implications thereof.

For this purpose let us take the case of 1500 acres of land of which 200 are woods, and out of which a good shoot could be made if an appropriate proportion of farm and woodland could be developed in the interests of game. The Game Conservancy has found from practical research and experience in shoot management that 1% of cultivated land and 5% of woodland will suffice to meet the needs of game. On our hypothetical farm this would mean 13 and 10 acres respectively.

A well run farm on good land may hope (in 1972) to make a net profit of around £25 an acre. So the 13 acres required by the shoot will cost the farmer £325 net a year. Few farms make much if anything at all out of their forestry, but let us say in this case that a net income of £5 an acre is obtained. The sacrifice of the 10 acres of forestry will therefore cost the owner £50 net a year. This puts a total annual charge of £375 on the requirements of the shoot.

Shooting rents vary enormously but, considering the top rather than the bottom of the scale, potentially good land with an uncooperative owner might fetch 150p an acre per annum, while similar land with a co-operative owner could well command 200p an acre. So, returning to our hypothetical shoot, the latter by giving up his 13 acres of farm and 10 of forestry at a loss of £375 per year, could make £3000 out of letting the shooting rights instead of only £2250 if he was uncooperative—a net gain of £375. Most farmers, if it is explained to them, find a proposition of this kind attractive.

Sporting Assets

Although deer and their management are outside the scope of this book, the presence of roe and/or fallow deer on a shoot can be a pleasant additional sporting asset. In the case of the farm we have considered, the acreage of forestry, taken in isolation, is too small to anticipate any sizeable resident deer population, unless there happen to be extensive woodlands nearby. But wherever there are deer in reasonable numbers a properly planned annual culling policy should be put into effect to keep numbers under control and prevent untoward damage to forestry, gardens and farm crops, although unless Red deer, Fallow or Sika are concerned the risk to the last named is small.

Scrub and rough grazings, such as may be found on Scottish hillsides, and on the steeper slopes of the Downs in Southern England, are invaluable assets to the game preserver. Wild populations of both partridges and pheasants always seem to prosper in such places. But since the demise of the rabbit, scrub quickly becomes so dense as to be impenetrable to beaters and dogs alike, and areas of this kind need to be tackled from time to time with a 'Swipe' so that the dense cover is kept in small manageable clumps from which game can be readily flushed by beaters, and just as importantly retrieved after it has been shot. On rough grazings it has been found that if swaths are cut by making one run with a forage harvester or 'Swipe' at about 50-yard intervals, and some phosphate if available is then spread on the swath, the resultant growth of young grasses and clovers encourages insect life; these strips are much sought after by young partridge broods in their early days, when they need the high protein diet with which only insect life can provide them. Old grass is not normally rich in insects.

The management of woodland for pheasants, and the catering for the detailed needs of other species in respect of habitat are dealt with in the appropriate chapters.

Winter Feeding

Let us now turn to winter feeding. To realize what a bleak, hungry prospect faces game on the land one has only to cast an eye over the bare acres of seemingly endless plough in a hedgeless landscape in East Anglia on a February day, with an overcast sky, and a biting east wind blowing, which makes even a hardy Labrador's teeth chatter as it waits at heel for master to finish surveying the scene and head for home. On such days it is easy to appreciate why winter wastage of partridges in a hard winter can be as high as 75%, if no effort is made to winter feed.

Some of the crops planted specially for game and mentioned earlier, such as maize, artichokes and some of the special mixtures, provide food as well as cover, but a lot of this will be cut back when the first frosts strike and by the year's end most of these resources will be eaten out. The more severe the weather, the more likely other species of birds as well as game are to utilize them. Undersown stubbles may still provide a little food and some may be gleaned in what are principally cover crops, e.g. kale and mustard. In well-maintained coverts there may also be pickings among the fruits of the forest, in the form of nuts and berries. But, generally speaking, from the beginning of the New Year until the spring growth gets under way, winter feeding is necessary to sustain game populations.

The aim of winter feeding should go beyond merely trying to ensure survival, important though this is; it should also be directed at launching the birds into the breeding season in good physical condition, so that they can rear strong, healthy and numerous broods. This plays a material part in keeping disease at bay. It is a great mistake, therefore, to stop winter feeding too early. The date for this should be left open, so that in a cold, late spring feeding can be continued well on into April if need be.

The three species with which winter feeding is mainly concerned are pheasants, partridges and wild duck. Experiments in providing winter food for grouse have been made and continue to be made, but nothing really satisfactory has yet evolved.

Strawed Rides

The traditional and still one of the most satisfactory methods of feeding pheasants in covert is the strawed ride. This entails placing a carpet of straw on a woodland ride, which should be at least 8 feet broad, and the longer it can be made for a given number of birds the better. The ride selected as the site should be wide and open to the sky so that it enjoys the midday sun. It should not be too straight, or the wind will blow straight down it, and its exit from the wood should be screened from both the wind and prying eyes by a barrier of bales or natural growth. Avoid at all costs a narrow ride with an overhead canopy of branches, or in bad weather there will be a continual drip of rain off the branches which the birds dislike and soon causes the straw to go mouldy.

The straw on the ride should be raked up, removed and renewed at intervals as the weather dictates. On no account allow mouldy straw to accumulate on the ride; straw which is removed should be taken away and burnt. As this type of winter feeding is an extension of in-covert feeding from the time pheasants are released, it is a good plan to arrange with the farmer to stack a supply of straw bales handy to the ride when he is baling up after harvest. The stack must be protected from the weather by being covered either with a tarpaulin, polythene sheeting, or if nothing else better is to hand, cut open plastic fertilizer bags. Whatever covering is used must be secured by either a layer of bales, a net or some other means.

Feed should be scattered on the straw at regular times each day, normally first thing of a winter's morning and again late in the afternoon. Don't be too generous; the more birds have to scratch about in the straw and work for their meal, the less time they will have to devote to straying elsewhere. Always use good, clean, sound grain; not only is it more nourishing but it will reduce the risk of disease. As regards choice, pheasants normally prefer wheat to barley, and barley to oats; but some keepers like to ring changes in the diet, and successfully intervene a week on barley at intervals throughout the winter.

Scratching heaps are still sometimes used; these consist of a trailer-load of builder's sand, with which a quantity of grain has been mixed, and the whole tipped in a sunny clearing. It is surprising how quickly pheasants can demolish the heap in their search for the grain, and about once a week it will be necessary to mix in a fresh supply of grain and shovel it all together again.

Hopper Feeding

Hopper feeding has been increasingly used in recent times. As the name implies, this consists of some sort of weatherproof container to hold the grain, when the pheasant or partridge either pecks directly at it through some form of grille, or pecks at some kind of agitator which, when moved, allows a few grains to fall to the ground.

There are many forms of self-feed hopper, some of the best of which can easily be made from old 5 gallon oil drums. A variety of these are shown in Figure 40a, b, c, and d. Where oil drums are used they must first be cleaned; it has been found that the most convenient way to do this is to swill a little paraffin around inside them, insert a lighted match and stand well back! When the paraffin and old oil have burnt out, the inside of the drums should be scrubbed clean with a weak solution of detergent in hot water. To substitute petrol for paraffin can be highly dangerous!

Next, the means of dispensing the food should be built in. The disadvantage of slots cut in the side or base is that they need to be varied in size according to the type of grain used. In my view the most satisfactory method is the small wire-mesh dispenser

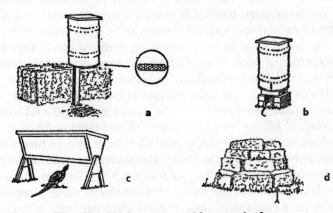

Fig. 40   **Various types of hopper feeder**

a A very successful 5 gallon drum-type of home-made hopper, with a wire mesh grille insert in the bottom for dispensing the grain, which has the advantage of being sparrow-proof.

b Another 5 gallon drum-type with slits cut in the side near the base; it is mounted on bricks, which allows a rat baiting point to be incorporated in the base, as shown.

c A good type of proprietary hopper made from resin bonded plywood, with a wire mesh grille along the underside.

d A hopper made from straw bales; a waterproof cover of some kind must be provided, and a piece of plastic sheeting held down by the top layer of bales serves very well in this respect. Note that rat baiting point incorporated at A.

depicted in Figure 40a; this means that small birds, such as sparrows, cannot get at the grain and the flow of grain is not impaired by damp. The bottom of a hopper so constructed should be set at about fifteen inches from the ground for pheasants, a straw bale should be placed behind it, and the ground immediately under it strawed. If the outside of the hopper and its lid are painted a neutral green or brown it will help to preserve them.

Hoppers with slits at the bottom of the side, as in Figure 40b, can be very wasteful unless these are cut to the right size. The slits are also liable to clog in wet weather due to the grain swelling and forming a paste with any dust or other foreign bodies.

Partridges will make use of hoppers placed on the edge of coverts, and where they are so sited for this purpose the height must be adjusted so that these smaller birds can reach the grain.

Wherever hand-feeding is practised rats are liable to become a problem, and this is especially so with hoppers. So every feeding point should have its own rat-baiting point, which is kept regularly supplied with Warfarin; an example of how this can be conveniently arranged is shown in Figure 40.

Hoppers should be inspected and refilled at least once a week. To facilitate this a series of 'silos' consisting of old milk churns, galvanized bins or 40-gallon drums should be established at convenient points beside tracks around a shoot, where they can be handily replenished by a tractor and trailer or a Land Rover.

A recent advance in hopper feeding is the Parsons Automatic Feeder. In this a single feeder or a number of feeders are linked up to an electric time-clock worked off a car battery, and feed is dispensed once or twice a day in quantities according to how the time-clock is regulated. A spinner is used, similar to that employed on a fertilizer distributor, so the grain is spread over quite a wide area. The hopper on these feeders holds approximately 1 cwt of grain. An example of this feeder is shown in Figure 41.

Hopper feeders of one sort of another are ideal for the rough shoot where the shoot manager/amateur keeper cannot feed on a daily basis. They can also play a useful role on the more sophisticated shoot if placed in outlying coverts which it is inconvenient for the keeper to have to visit every day. But however they are used, placing them to good advantage is important. One

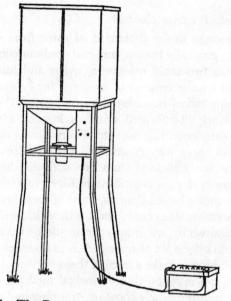

Fig. 41 The Parsons automatic feeder

This admirable feeder works on the 'spinner' principle, similar to a fertilizer distributor, and is operated by a time-clock, powered by an ordinary car battery. Full operating instructions are provided by the makers, and several of these hoppers can be run off the one time-clock.

shoot I know had a major outside covert, some 50 acres in extent; in this the owner, in conjunction with his keeper, carefully sited and set up 50 hopper feeding points with a bale of straw behind each, as described above. This covert had previously failed to hold many birds later in the season, but after this action had been taken it was transformed into one of the best January coverts on the shoot.

On rough shoots the siting of hopper feeding points in the areas most favoured by the birds is crucial. The better the arrangements that can be made in this respect, the greater the chances not only of holding birds but of attracting others in from outside. Lack of proper attention to this very important aspect of management is one reason why many rough shoots experience such poor sport towards the end of a season.

Pest and Predator Control

So we come to the protection of game from its enemies, or as it is more generally known, pest and predator control. These enemies fall into two main categories, avian and mammalian. But first let us be quite clear as to the need for control. There is a lot of nonsense talked nowadays about upsetting the balance of nature and much ill-informed criticism levelled at shoot owners and their keepers on this account. Every time a new housing estate is built or motorway constructed the balance of nature suffers a far greater upheaval than probably all the shoot owners and keepers in Britain contribute in fifty years! If game populations are to multiply and flourish, those of their predators must be kept under reasonable control, or it is they that will do the multiplying and flourishing, quite apart from the fact that it is obvious nonsense to offer a lot of reared birds as hostages to a host of enemies just waiting to make a meal of them.

Control relies on three principal methods as far as the keeper is concerned, namely shooting, trapping and snaring, and poisoning. I will deal with control by gun and rifle first. On estates where a keeper always carries one or other with him on his rounds they may account for up to 40% of the pests and predators disposed of annually.

Shooting

As the bullets of a ·22 rifle can carry up to a mile, and that of higher velocity weapons further still, even greater care is necessary in the use of rifles than shotguns. A police firearms certificate is required to legalize their ownership and use, and some chief constables exhibit an almost pathological reluctance to issue such certificates. Also rifles are really only suitable for dealing with stationary, or near stationary targets, so opportunities for their effective use are limited. A ·22 rifle fitted with telescopic sights and firing the 'long rifle' cartridge will give excellent results up to 75 yards, but to be equally effective at longer ranges calls for more skilled and practised marksmanship than the ordinary shooter is capable of, and can lead to unnecessary wounding. To ensure clean kills a head or heart shot is necessary and with a creature the size of a mink, for example, the target area this represents at 50–75 yards is extremely small and calls for very accurate shooting. However, for a keeper who can learn to become a competent marksman, a ·22 rifle is a valuable adjunct.

The ·22 'Hornet' with its higher velocity cartridge allows accurate shooting by a skilled marksman up to about 150 yards, while the higher muzzle energy of the bullet makes it more suitable for dealing with larger quarry such as foxes, as is necessary on the grouse moors of Scotland. But in my view it is unwise for the normally 'good shot' to attempt targets at over 100 yards.

Where roe or other deer are present, and numbers have to be kept under control, this should be done with a rifle in preference to a shotgun. By law the weapon used must be of a calibre of not less than ·240 in, and the bullet fired have a muzzle energy of not less than 1700 ft lb.

It is sometimes argued that rifle shooting is bad for shotgun shooting and vice versa. Certainly instances of men being outstanding performers with both weapons are rare. But, as this requires mastery of two different and in many respects conflicting, techniques, this is hardly surprising. It is more important for a keeper to be a good man with a shotgun than a rifle, but this should not preclude him attaining a reasonable mastery of the latter, so that he can put it to effective use when the need arises. Most Scottish keepers seem to strike a happy balance in this way and I can see no reason why others should not do the same.

The shotgun almost universally used by keepers is an ordinary 12-bore double-barrelled game gun. With this he will be expected to deal not only with avian pests and predators but also with mammalian ones varying in size from possibly a rogue badger to a weasel. He should, therefore, have a sound working knowledge of the shot sizes and ranges suitable for dealing with the quarry which he may meet. As a guide some recommendations in these respects are given in the Table overleaf, average body weights of creatures concerned being shown in brackets, the female of the species being normally somewhat smaller.

In practice many encounters will occur which cannot be catered for in a table of this kind. For example one may come face to face with a fox at a range of 15–20 yards and shoot it stone dead with a charge of No. 6 shot, the lethal effectiveness of which is beyond dispute at such close range. As with the shooting of game, effective striking energies must be matched with adequate pattern densities to ensure clean kills. It will be readily understood that

PREDATOR OR PEST		RECOMMENDED SHOTGUN GAUGE	RECOMMENDED SHOT SIZE	MAXIMUM RANGE
Badger†	(30 lb)	12	BB or 1	30 yd
Otter	(25 lb)	12	BB or 1	30 yd
Fox	(15 lb)	12	3 or 4	30 yd
Wild Cat	(10 lb)	12	3, 4 or 5*	35 yd
Feral Cat	(6 lb)	12	4, 5 or 6*	35 yd
Mink	(4 lb)	12	5 or 6*	40 yd
Pine Marten	(3½ lb)	12	5 or 6*	40 yd
Polecat	(2¾ lb)	12	5 or 6*	40 yd
Grey Squirrel	(1¼ lb)	12	6 or 7*	40 yd
Rat	(1 lb)	12	6 or 7*	40 yd
Stoat	(¾ lb)	12	6 or 7*	40 yd
Weasel	(¼ lb)	12	7 or 8*	30 yd
Hedgehog	(2¼ lb)	12	6 or 7*	30 yd

NOTES

1. The cartridge on which the data is based is the 12-bore standard load.

2. The performance of a 16-bore so nearly matches that of a 12-bore that for practical purposes it can be considered equivalent.

3*. A 20-bore is suitable provided it is used only with the smaller shot sizes marked with an asterisk, so that pattern density is adequate. If used to shoot either of the three larger animals shown in the table not only should the smallest recommended shot size be used, but the maximum range reduced by 5 yards.

4. If it is used with a shot size no larger than No. 7, and to a maximum range of 30 yards, a 28-bore is suitable for shooting grey squirrels, and the creatures listed subsequently in the table.

to try and shoot a weasel at over 30 yards with a charge of No. 5 shot would be as great a folly as if the target were a snipe. The same applies to the shooting of larger quarry; thus if a standard 20-bore load of BB, which will place only approximately 40 pellets in the 30 in circle at 30 yards with a quarter-choke barrel, is used to shoot at a fox in retreat, so that its stern is presented to the shooter, it is more likely to be wounded than killed by such a weak pattern.

So, although the Table above is intended to provide a sound guide, commonsense and experience must be the final arbiters in

† But see page 335 for the latest legislation on badger control.

any given situation in deciding whether it is right or wrong to shoot.

Avian pests and predators which a keeper may wish to tackle with a gun include :

Carrion and Hooded Crow	Greater Black-backed Gull
Rook	Lesser Black-backed Gull
Jackdaw	Herring Gull
Magpie	Cormorant
Jay	Shag

All the crow family shown in the left-hand column can be satisfactorily dealt with, with No. 5, 6 or 7 shot at normal game ranges. Heavier shot, preferably 3's or 4's, should be used to deal with the gulls and cormorants in the right-hand column.

All eagles, buzzards, kites, falcons, hawks and owls are at the time of writing fully protected.

Trapping

Turning now to trapping; the use of traps for predators, particularly avian ones, is strictly regulated by law, some relevant provisions of which are set out in Chapter 32. But it will not come amiss here to remind readers of some salient restrictions. The use of pole traps, i.e. a spring trap set on top of a pole, gatepost, cairn or some similar elevated position has been illegal in Great Britain since 1904. The Protection of Birds Act 1954 prohibited entirely the use of spring traps, gins and snares for the killing or catching of winged predators. The use of the gin trap became prohibited in Scotland, as well as England and Wales, in 1972 by virtue of the Agriculture (Spring Traps) (Scotland) Act 1969.

In fact the use of spring traps for small vermin is now limited to those of a pattern approved by the Ministry of Agriculture, of which there are currently three, the Fenn, the Lloyd and the

Fig. 42a   The Fenn trap in the set position

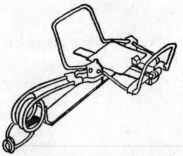

Fig. 42b   The Lloyd trap in the set position

Both these are Ministry 'approved' traps, the Fenn for small vermin, the Lloyd for rabbits as well.

Sawyer. Examples of the two former are shown in Figure 42a and b. Both are very effective but the Fenn, being the lighter, is probably the more popular.

A well-organized network of traps on a shoot should be the key-stone of the predator control campaign. Traps may not legally be set in the open and so are placed in natural or artificial tunnels, typical instances of which are shown in Figure 43a and b. On a 1000–1500 acre shoot one keeper should be able to operate up to 70 traps. These have by law to be inspected once daily between sunrise and sunset. There may therefore be times of the year, such as during the rearing season, when a keeper's other commitments necessitate a reduction in the number of tunnel traps actually operative. But at other times the more traps that can be kept in action the better. Nevertheless, 70 is about the largest number one man can tend properly and 1500 acres about the biggest area that can reasonably be covered by this number. Some keepers nowadays have beats of 2000 or more acres; unless parts of such an area can be virtually ignored as far as trapping is concerned, the best plan is to divide it into sections each of which is systematically and thoroughly trapped in turn, paying particular attention always to the best coverts.

Various 'catch-'em-alive' box traps can be used for taking the bigger mammalian predators such as mink, feral cats and so on. Examples of these are depicted in Figure 44a and b. They can be set in stone walls, along river banks, and in similar sites. (See Figure 45.)

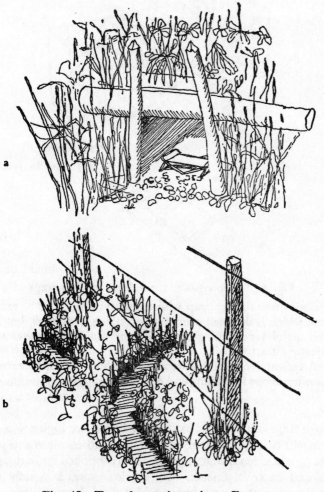

Fig. 43 Tunnel trapping using a Fenn trap

a Shows how the trap should be set, and dug in so that it is flush with the level of the ground in the entrance to the tunnel.

b Shows how the headland furrow of a ploughed field can be diverted so that an artificial tunnel can be constructed in which traps can be set.

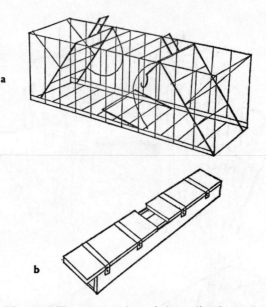

Fig. 44 Two types of catch-'em-alive box traps

a Shows a wire cage trap with a spring-loaded door at each end, which is designed primarily for taking feral mink, but is also useful for catching feral cats, for which fish proves an equally attractive bait.
b A typical double-ended wooden box trap with a sliding roof allowing access for baiting and removing captives.

Cage traps of the letterbox or funnel type (see Figure 46a and b) can still be legally employed for taking crows, rooks and jackdaws, provided food, water and shelter are supplied for both decoy birds and captives. Success with carrion crows is usually very limited, even if the trap is baited with a dead sheep or some other carrion. However, great success can be had in catching rooks and jackdaws, especially where these birds are a nuisance round a rearing field, and I have known 50–80 taken from such a trap each morning for a week.

At present there is no trap of an approved pattern to catch or kill foxes. As a result, since the abolition of the gin trip increasing recourse has been made to snares for the purpose of dealing with foxes and badgers. Such snares may or may not be self-locking. To ensure they kill with a minimum of suffering they need skilful setting; the noose should be pear-shaped and measure 8 in long by 6 in wide; the height at which the bottom of the noose should be set above ground level should vary from about 4 in in cover, such as a run through a hedge, to 8 in in an open run; it should be held in position by a tealer, as is a rabbit snare. If set in an open run in country where there are deer, a deer-leap of three ash or hazel wands should be built over it. (See Figure 47.)

The law relating to snaring is not so precise as that concerning trapping. However, humane considerations should ensure that all such snares are firmly secured to a peg or post in the ground, and that they are inspected no less frequently than traps, i.e. at least once a day.

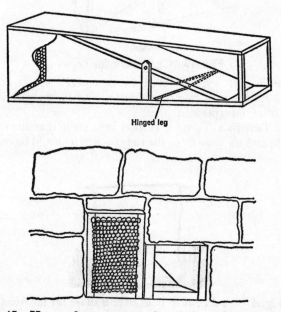

Hinged leg

Fig. 45 How a box trap can be set in a dry stone wall

In this case two traps are used so that access is given to prey using either side of the wall. The top diagram shows the trap in the set position; when the weight of the victim tips the pivoted floor over, the hinged leg swings down and prevents it swinging back again.

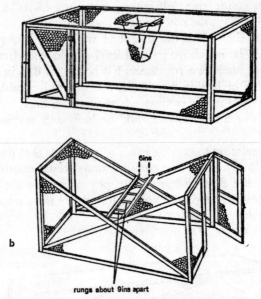

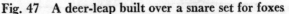

Fig. 46   Cage traps for crows

a The Funnel Type, with a wooden perch set across the
funnel entrance. A funnel at ground level in one side is also
quite often incorporated.
b The Letterbox Type; it is most important that the size of
the slit, and the spacing of the rungs across it should be correct.

Fig. 47   A deer-leap built over a snare set for foxes

Such a snare will usually be set in a 'run' in a wood leading
off a footpath. If a deer-leap is not built over it, a deer can
catch its leg in the snare, and painful injury with prolonged
suffering result. This is another reason why snares of this kind
should be regularly inspected, at least once a day between
sunrise and sunset.

Poisoning

The use of poisons for pest control in Britain is rightly very strictly controlled. Generally speaking they may only be used against rats, mice and other small vermin, and precautions must be taken to prevent harm resulting to domestic animals and other wild creatures which are protected.

Cymag gas, as used in the control of rabbits, may be legally used against foxes in their earths, but not against badgers.

Order of Villainy

A question often asked is what is the order of villainy, so to speak, of the various predators mentioned in this chapter. On a grouse moor I would unhesitatingly give pride of place to the fox and hooded or carrion crow in that order. But on a lowland shoot the rat must undoubtedly head the list; of the various keepers I have questioned over the years, all have agreed that they catch more rats in their traps in the course of a year than any other single species, several estimating the figure as high as 70–80% of all animals trapped.

A creature which is spreading steadily over the face of the countryside is the mink. Its favourite habitat is in the vicinity of streams, rivers and lakes, but wherever it is found it is a ruthless killer and justly rated as a pest.

The magpie is little less of a menace than the carrion crow and should be tackled with the same determination. Unfortunately reliance now has to be placed entirely on the gun for legally dealing with both these species, and unless a keeper can obtain assistance, ambushing crows and magpies at their nests, or other sites, can be a time-consuming task.

Rooks and jackdaws in excessive numbers are inveterate egg stealers and nest robbers.

Greater and lesser black-backed gulls can do considerable damage on a grouse moor and no opportunity of reducing their numbers with a gun should be missed.

Feral cats can unquestionably become a scourge if they are allowed to take up residence in a covert; the best remedy is to make sure they don't!

Grey squirrels, stoats, weasels and hedgehogs all do some harm, as do jays, but can probably be better tolerated than the species already mentioned.

But a word in favour of the badger and otter; if a member of either species develops a taste for game, it can indeed do a lot of damage and the only way to stop it is to bring it to book as quickly as possible. But the badger otherwise does a considerable amount of good and is little trouble to the game preserver, who can well afford to let him go his way in peace; and the same applies generally to the otter.

With the exception of the rat, the carrion crow (and hooded crow), and the mink, all of which should be pursued relentlessly with every means available, the aim of the game conservationist should not be annihilation, but reasonable control of predator populations. This can best be achieved by good planning between shoot manager and keeper to ensure every possible legal means is utilized to the fullest extent.

CHAPTER EIGHT

MORE FACTORS IN SHOOT MANAGEMENT

The Gamekeeper

A GAMEKEEPER is the chief executive of a shoot, responsible for putting into effect the policies and plans of the owner or manager. To many people, including some shooting men, mention of a keeper conjures up an image of a large, red-faced man in a plus-four suit, better blessed with brawn than brains. Yet almost everyone, if asked what sort of character they would themselves seek to fill this post, would stipulate a man with all the sterling personal attributes, professional expertise and dedication of a first-class Guards' sergeant-major. If pressed further as to what wages such a man should receive for his services, many would probably suggest a figure no higher than that paid to a farm worker. It is a curious paradox, and high time the realities of the sort of man a modern keeper ought to be, the job he is required to do and the reward he merits were considered in the light of present-day circumstances, instead of in a kind of Victorian twilight, or good young keepers will become even harder to find than they are already.

To aspire to a place at the top of his calling, a keeper does indeed need to possess the qualities of a good sergeant-major. He holds a position of responsibility. A lot of his work must be done on his own, unobtrusively, and some at hours which other men normally devote to leisure or sleep, so detailed daily supervision is impracticable. He will probably have equipment in his charge valued at thousands of pounds. He must therefore be trustworthy and reliable. Building and retaining the goodwill of farmers, farm workers, foresters, tradesmen and other local personalities can make or mar the smooth running of a shoot. The days when the laird's or squire's word was law and his keeper could afford to disregard other people's susceptibilities are a thing of the past. His modern counterpart must be something of a diplomat, obtaining by negotiation many things his forebears had only to demand as of right. He must be a good organizer and possess qualities of leadership which on shooting days not only ensure beaters do their job well and willingly, but enable him to keep walking Guns 'in line', both literally and metaphorically, with equal facility.

A modern farmer requires a far greater knowledge and wider range of skills than his predecessors, so does the modern keeper. Also, like the farmer, the years since 1950 have seen dramatic changes in the tools and techniques of his trade.

As explained in the previous chapter the importance of making the best possible use of available resources of habitat on a shoot has become absolutely paramount. To enable him to play his part in this, the keeper today requires some of the knowledge and skills of both farmer and forester to complement those of a Game Conservationist. As already indicated, a keeper should not allow a state of armed neutrality to arise between himself and farmer or forester, as often used to happen in the past. A modern estate, run on proper business lines, literally cannot afford such frictions. Where good co-operation exists, farmer and forester will help out the keeper by doing various jobs to improve habitat or keep it in order. But often these have to be done at a time of year when the farmer, for example, is heavily committed to his farming and cannot spare any man or tractor power. In these circumstances a keeper should be able to step into the breach, and carry out straight forward ploughing, cultivations and sowings of game mixtures. He should also be able to operate a normal range of grass-cutting machinery to control the growth of grass in forestry rides and elsewhere. He should be able to work a 'Swipe' for cutting beaters' tracks through scrub, etc.

Where forestry is concerned, he should have a sound working knowledge to enable him to plant up small areas with shrubs and trees as game spinneys, to improve flushing points by planting low cover, such as *Lonicera nitida* or box, and effect other simple operations, like coppicing and brashing up.

He should use his knowledge of these matters to promote good relations with both farmer and forester, and be prepared in his turn to assist them when, for example, woodpigeon decimate the farmer's young clovers, or grey squirrels the forester's nursery trees.

But work of this kind raises the question, with what sort of vehicle is a keeper best equipped for his task? A few years ago the answer would almost without exception have been a Land Rover. But these are expensive vehicles to buy and to run and, although they have a power take-off, can only operate a very limited range of farm machinery. On some of the best-managed shoots in the South of England the keepers have a tractor and trailer each, which enables them to work farm machinery as required and to get things done independently of the good offices of farmer or forester. A tractor and trailer may not be so 'comfortable' as a Land Rover, but from a practical point of view it has undoubted advantages and, although no less expensive, probably shows a saving on running costs.

On a grouse moor a keeper's needs are rather different and in some cases the balance of advantage may lie with the Land Rover.

As indicated in the last chapter, a keeper should be master of the art of trapping and snaring, and practise it just as assiduously as his forebears. He should also be a competent shot with a gun and a reasonable one with a rifle. He should have a sound knowledge of the practical usage of both weapons, especially in matters relating to safe handling in the field and in addition a rudimentary technical knowledge of them and their ammunition. In this last respect most keepers are woefully ignorant. Some keepers take up competition clay pigeon shooting and, within reasonable limits, this is probably to be encouraged rather than the reverse. However, a gamekeeper's work is demanding, and it cannot be properly done by a man who is, in everything but name, a professional clay pigeon shot.

Much the same applies to dogs and dog-training; a keeper ought to have a good working dog and be able to handle it competently. But by no means all keepers are natural 'dog' men, and a small minority would be better never allowed near a dog. Those who have the ability should certainly be encouraged to train dogs for their own use and possibly for the owner. They should not be allowed to become dog-trainers rather than keepers. Those keepers whose gifts are limited to handling rather than training are much better presented with a dog trained elsewhere at the expense of the estate.

Prevention of poaching is still one of a keeper's duties. In the neighbourhood of industrial towns this can be a real problem.

A lone keeper has little chance of effectively tackling a gang of poachers and apprehending them; in fact he may get severely beaten up if he attempts to do so. Where this problem exists for a single-handed keeper, either counter-measures must be co-ordinated with neighbouring keepers or the co-operation of the local police secured. For reasons unknown, this latter is not always as readily forthcoming as might be hoped.

Most lowland keepers rear pheasants, some also wild duck, or partridges, or both. As will be explained in due course there are various methods used for rearing these birds. But however it is done, the success of the operation depends a great deal on a keeper's skill and initiative. Modern incubating and brooding equipment is costly, and where several thousand birds are reared on an estate in a season, its total value may well amount to £6000 or more. Unless the equipment is used correctly not only may it be damaged but losses of birds may be numbered in thousands.

It requires a man of considerable natural ability and versatility properly to master all these skills, also one of robust physique and temperament to deal with day-to-day vicissitudes due to the weather and other causes. It has long been customary for a keeper to be given a rent-free house and to receive certain other perquisites, such as an annual suit, food for his dogs and so on. But keepers' cottages are usually remote from main roads, and many young wives are not prepared to lead a life so cut off from shops and social life, quite apart from the difficulties of getting children to school. There seems therefore a strong case for a modern keeper to have a small car paid for by the estate for the use of himself and his wife, and particularly so where his work vehicle is a tractor and not a Land Rover. But although it is undoubtedly time to bring a keeper's fringe benefits more into line with the needs of the times, the same applies with even greater force to his wages. A keeper's position is one of authority and responsibility and, if the right sort of man is to be attracted to such employment, his basic wage should in my view be at least a third as much again as that of an ordinary farm worker.

The Shoot Owner or Manager

We now come to the part a shoot owner or manager should play. Much can be safely left to a good keeper, but no shoot can be really efficiently run on a 'Carry on, Sergeant-Major' basis, where a keeper is left entirely to his own devices between the end of one season and the beginning of the next. In one instance I knew of where this state of affairs prevailed, it led eventually to three mishaps occurring in one day : a beater was peppered, a window was shot out of a cottage and a loaded gun was placed on the ground by its owner and promptly discharged itself, fortunately not injuring those in the vicinity. It seems to me a typical sequence of disasters which slack management can precipitate.

Good shoot management requires the acquisition and application of knowledge and skills, just as does business management or command in the services. It calls for an all-the-year-round interest, and supervision of every aspect of the work on a shoot. During the shooting season whoever is running a shoot should spend as much time walking with the beaters as standing in the line of guns. As trees, shrubs and undergrowth mature in a woodland, its attraction for gamebirds changes, possibly for the better, but also maybe for the worse. In the latter case, apart from failing to hold birds as well as formerly, it may also mean they adopt different flight lines due perhaps to the growing attractions of some other covert. These sort of things become noticeable in the course of several seasons rather than merely one. But the sooner they can be recognized for what they are the sooner measures to counteract them can be taken, either by altering the direction of a drive or by improving the holding qualities of the covert in question.

After the shooting season is over it is a salutary experience to walk a shoot in company with the keeper in order to appreciate just how bare of food and shelter the coverts and the rest of the land are. At the same time his trapping round can be inspected; he should be given every encouragement to start his spring campaign against pests and predators in January. If rabbits are a problem, he should also start dealing with this in January.

In many areas, special hare shoots have to be arranged in February. These are dealt with in detail in Chapter 26. Suffice it to say here that to leave their organization solely to the keeper is wrong. They are, together with backend days at 'cocks only', an opportunity to ask pickers-up and others who have contributed to the season's sport to a day's shooting. Their invitation should come from the 'host', not from the keeper, and he should be there himself in charge of the day's sport to see that it is properly run. It is because some hosts think it beneath their dignity to be present on such occasions and leave everything to their keeper that a happy-go-lucky atmosphere prevails and accidents happen. If a host really cannot attend he should at least ensure that his apologies for absence are conveyed to the guests and it is understood by them he is there in spirit if not in person.

The advent of the rearing season throws a heavy responsibility on a keeper. This is a time when a good shoot manager, having made plain his active interest, should be unobtrusive but always available to help or consult when needed. If necessary he may arrange for the keeper to receive assistance with some of his other tasks, for example, for a retired keeper, or some other suitable person, to take over responsibility for the trap line, or his own teenage son, home for the school holidays, to ambush some carrion crows or magpies at their nesting sites.

He should at all times see that his keeper is kept supplied with game food and everything else he needs. Subject to any advice his keeper may give, he should be responsible for all major decisions in the running of the shoot, such as the siting of the rearing field, release pens, and so on. As the new shooting season approaches he should consider with the keeper the organization of all the beats to see whether any modifications are necessary in both the handling of the beat itself and the placing of the guns. He, not his keeper, should be the shoot's principal public relations officer, and, apart from any formal social occasions at which he and the tenant farmers on the shoot may meet, he should contrive to see each of them for an informal chat every now and again to ensure that, if local difficulties have cropped up, they are aired and resolved. In the case of a shooting tenant he should remember the owner, or his factor or agent may also appreciate an occasional visit. As soon as a shooting season is properly under way, he should see that each tenant farmer is given a brace of birds, and if this gesture can be repeated at Christmas time so much the better; where applicable, the shoot owner or his factor should not be forgotten.

Securing the services of a team of pickers-up and beaters for a shooting day is usually the task of the keeper, though sometimes the former may be reinforced by personal friends of the owner or manager who have useful retrievers. Much depends on the personality of a keeper in getting and keeping together a good team of beaters, but his task is made immeasurably easier if the owner or manager ensures they are paid a fair wage, beer is available for them at lunchtime and that a place is set aside for them to eat their lunch where they can be dry and warm on a cold, wet day.

Over-all responsibility for a day's shooting rests with the owner or manager, who should be personally in charge of the 'gun end' of the proceedings. This will involve the placing of the guns at each stand, seeing they receive all necessary instructions relating to the position of other guns, stops, pickers-up, the approach of the beaters and any special features of the ground, etc., and deploying the pickers-up. The keeper should be responsible for organizing the beaters, siting stops, the briefing and control of walking guns and seeing the beaters' transport knows where to go. Each beat should start on a prearranged signal given by the manager.

Disposal of Game

A point which often receives less attention than it merits is the disposal of shot game. Frequently it is merely thrown on the floor of either Land Rover or tractor trailer, where it is subsequently trampled on by both dogs and humans. As a guest gun it is always more pleasing to receive a handsome-looking brace of grace birds at the end of the day than a couple of dishevelled objects decidedly the worse for wear. Also, where surplus game is sold to a poulterer, it will fetch a better price if it is and looks in good condition. Only on a big shoot where the day's bag is 300 or more head will the sole use of a Land Rover and trailer as a gamecart be justified. But some provision for the hanging of shot game in a Land Rover or trailer ought to be made at every shoot of any size. Special racks for this purpose are manufactured and can be bought for fitting to the sides of Land Rovers, but any competent estate handyman should be able to design and fit just as serviceable a rack.

Tipping

Tipping by guest guns is a controversial subject. Sporting writers argue endlessly about it. At an excellently run shoot I knew some years ago, the host at the end of the day quietly went round each guest and told him what the keeper was to be given. It may sound an unusual, rather dictatorial way of organizing matters, but it was so admirably done that nobody could have taken offence or failed to comply with the request. If the practice were more general, tipping would cease to be any problem. It is often difficult to assess what is appropriate; this can be especially so when at the end of a big day, where three to four hundred head has been shot, the wealthiest gun present is seen carefully to extract one £1 note from his well-filled wallet and press it into the keeper's hand with barely a word of gratitude. When I mentioned this some years ago to a friend who ran a first-class shoot of his own, he capped it by telling me that he knew of three big businessmen who regularly shot as his guests one day each season and always tried to get away without tipping the keeper at all!

I normally tip on the basis of £1 per hundred head, or part of a hundred head in the bag. Some may consider this a little on the low side, but it seems at the present time to conform with general practice in Scotland and England. However, special factors, such as a day prematurely curtailed by rain, or a day's bag adversely affected by a storm the previous night, should all be taken into account. Experience is a considerable help in judging what is right. But whatever you decide fits the occasion, a word of thanks and appreciation for the sport you have been shown, as it is handed over will have a value of its own beyond anything which can be expressed solely in terms of money.

How members of a syndicate should reward their keeper is a slightly different matter. In my experience one satisfactory way is for each member to contribute an agreed amount, which is then given in a lump sum as an *ex gratia* payment to the keeper by the syndicate secretary or manager at Christmas time.

CHAPTER NINE

MANAGEMENT OF ROUGH SHOOTS

A ROUGH SHOOT normally implies one which does not have a full-time keeper, where game is usually walked up instead of driven, and such game rearing as is done is on a small scale. In fact it is a much more modest establishment in every respect than a keepered shoot, relying for its sport almost entirely on such stock of wild game as the land will support. But a well-run rough shoot on reasonably favourable ground can often offer a wide variety of very enjoyable sport. This is particularly true of such shoots in Scotland.

The principles on which a rough shoot should be managed do not differ materially from those obtaining to a big shoot but their application does, and it is his ability to turn slender resources to good account which distinguishes the skilful rough shoot manager.

Work Planning

Clearly the more constructive work which can be done on a rough shoot the better it will flourish. If such work is well planned so that the right thing is done at the right time and in the right place, it is surprising how part-time or amateur keepering can improve the sport. The key figure in this should be somebody living in the vicinity, who can visit the ground regularly, and ideally the man running the shoot. If this is not practicable, it may be possible, if funds permit, to find a retired keeper or a retired person with some knowledge of keepering, such as a former policeman or farm worker, who can fill the role. But if this is not feasible, the members of a shoot should arrange between themselves to do the best they can to help themselves. One way of achieving this is for each gun, in addition to the money he pays for his gun every year, to undertake to contribute a stipulated number of hours of work during the close season. For those who live too far away, or are too busy, arrangements can be made for their share to be done by proxy, for which they pay.

The three things which will show the best dividends are selective habitat improvement, winter feeding and predator control. There is a slogan in service life to the effect that one should always reinforce success and not failure. This is particularly applicable to rough-shoot management in that it is most profitable to ascertain those areas or parts of coverts most favoured and frequented by game and to do everything possible to make them better favoured still. In my experience it is a complete waste of time and effort trying to convert bad cover into good, because the task is normally quite beyond available resources.

Habitat Improvement

Improvements must be tailored to suit available means as well as money. Thus it is no use trying to plant up strips of game cover of a size which will require a tractor and farm machinery, unless by arrangement with a farmer these implements are forthcoming. However, with initiative and perseverance, much useful work in this way can be accomplished with a spade and other garden tools and a patchwork of allotment-sized plots of game mixtures created on a shoot in the course of a few years.

On some shoots, and especially Forestry Commission lettings, the large size of the coverts is a major problem, making it extremely difficult for a small shooting party of five or six guns to cope successfully. Large blocks of woodland containing alternate rows of conifers and hardwoods, spruce and beech are a common combination, unbrashed up, and, intermingled with ash coppice and other natural growth, can become impenetrable jungles from which even if a dog is stout enough and agile enough to flush a pheasant, a gun will seldom get a real chance of a shot because a bird is no sooner on the wing than it is lost to sight. Coverts favoured by game have, therefore, also to be considered in relation to their size and manageability on a shooting day. Priority should be given to those which are long and narrow, or form the apex of a triangle or which otherwise allow a small number of beaters with dogs to drive them effectively.

Improvements to habitat should include, by arrangement with the owner or forester where necessary, provision for cutting snake-like paths through the undergrowth in late summer, so as to allow walking guns a reasonably clear passage, which will enable them to concentrate on their shooting instead of having to disentangle themselves from the clutches of endless briars. At the same time the aim should be to divide the area into manageable clumps of cover from which birds can be readily flushed and retrieved. This last aspect is all too often overlooked. In consequence shot birds fall in cover so dense that even the best of retrievers has little chance of making a successful unseen retrieve because it has to work entirely out of sight and control of its handler, or else it has such a struggle to wrench the quarry free of the thorns and brambles into which it has fallen, provided, that is, it can reach high enough to retrieve it at all, that the softest-mouthed dog is almost bound to return with a badly torn corpse and as a result earn itself a completely unjustified reputation for being hard-mouthed. From a gun's point of view, nothing is more maddening than having brought off a very pleasing shot and killed a bird stone dead, to find that because of the contours of the ground it has fallen a hundred and fifty yards away, and due to the thickness of the cover no dog is able to get out to it. This is particularly true when the day's bag is so small anyway that everyone is shooting for his own grace bird!

Winter Feeding

Winter feeding can play a significant part in holding game in those parts of a rough shoot where they are wanted. Unless feeding can be done daily, any attempt to do so on the basis of strawed rides should be forgotten. But a good system of hopper feeding with, say, up to half a dozen hopper feeders in each area in which it is hoped to hold birds, can be very rewarding, if the hoppers are regularly tended, and grain replenished as necesasry. It is absolutely useless tipping grain from a sack on to the ground once a week, and leaving the sack with a number of others at the site under cover of a tree, or in some similar situation; they merely become gradually sodden and the grain goes sour; rats are attracted to the spot and the whole exercise is a complete waste of valuable game food and money.

Predator Control

As intimated in Chapter 7, traps and snares should be inspected at least once a day. Unless, therefore, the manager of a rough shoot, or somebody specially employed by him, is able to do this, this very important aspect of predator control has to go by default. However, a great deal more can usually be accomplished with a gun than is in fact attempted. If a careful reconnaissance is made when the trees are bare in February or March it should be quite easy to detect old carrion crow and magpie nests, particularly the latter because of their domed roof of twigs. Later in the season watch can be kept on these to see if they are occupied. If they are, an ambush can be set by a member of the shoot with time to spare at a weekend, the parent birds dealt with and the nest shot out with a charge of No. 3 shot, specially provided for the purpose and used in conjunction with a choke barrel. The Game Conservancy reckon that every nesting pair of carrion crows disposed of saves at least one partridge's or pheasant's nest on a shoot. It is, therefore, well worth while for members of a rough shoot to make a serious effort to deal with these pests.

Foxes are a more difficult problem. Unless the local hunt, if there is one, really does its stuff in due season, other means must be used to control them. Although I wish nothing but well to fox-hunting and have no desire whatever to impair their sport, after thirty years of running shoots of various kinds in different parts of the United Kingdom, I am in absolutely no doubt as to the need to control fox populations in the interests of game. Where pheasants are reared in their thousands it is all very well to maintain that the presence of a fox or two in the coverts makes little odds to the overall number of birds shown. But on a rough shoot where every wild brood successfully reared adds considerably to the sport in the following season, the presence of a litter of fox cubs in a covert in early spring should not be tolerated, especially as for every one detected in a heavily afforested area there will probably be at least one other that is not. Fox earths can be gassed, but otherwise control on a rough shoot is dependent on the gun.

Where there is a river or other waterway on a rough shoot, mink may well prove a menace. If they do, the wisest course is to make an all-out effort to exterminate them by trapping and every other available means.

In all these matters the co-operation of farm workers will be invaluable and no effort should be spared by those running rough shoots to gain and retain their help.

Unless pests and predators are systematically controlled, and on most rough shoots this is not practicable, it is a waste of time and money to attempt lavish rearing schemes. However, small, well-laid plans to release, say, two or three score pheasant poults under suitable conditions or a clutch or two of wild duck if there is a pond on the shoot can show a good dividend. But restocking should normally be given lowest priority in a rough shoot manager's plans.

Conclusion

It is not difficult on any rough shoot to pick out a hundred and one things that need to be done. But the art of good management lies in selecting those which can be done with the available resources and seeing that they are well done. In this way a shoot can be progressively built up over a number of years, so that a great deal of good sport is had, every bit as enjoyable in its own way as that shown by more lavishly endowed establishments. It is all too easy to be overcome by how much needs to be done, and in consequence do nothing; this is a council of despair. Not only is every rough shoot capable of improvement, but if such improvements are well and realistically planned in accordance with available means, it need only be a season or two before they are amply justified by better sport and bigger bags. Successful rough shoot management probably requires an even better understanding and application of basic principles of game conservation than management of a big shoot, because failure in these respects cannot be concealed by merely rearing another thousand or so birds next year.

CHAPTER TEN

SYNDICATES AND THEIR
ORGANIZATION

THERE are several recognized ways in which a shooting syndicate can be organized. The cost of running a good shoot has escalated dramatically since the late 1960s. Many owners have found that to continue doing so as a private amenity is prohibitively expensive. In consequence, the practice of letting guns out to selected friends, in order to recoup part, anyway, of the cost, has become quite widespread, with the owner continuing to manage the shoot over his own ground and employing his own keeper(s) as before. This is, in my view, the most satisfactory form of syndicate, as the owner and keeper work closely together as a team, both know the land intimately and the former has control of the farming and forestry operations on it. However, some landowners have more land than they require for themselves as a shoot and some are not interested in shooting. With the present high values shootings can command it is an important part of estate management to see that they are let to best advantage. Thus there are keen shooting men who, owning no land themselves, combine together to rent ground over which to shoot.

Compatibility

In such circumstances, the first and most important consideration is that all who band together to form a syndicate should be 'birds of a feather', because if they are not all sorts of differences and petty squabbles will arise and make it impossible to run a happy and efficient shoot. A first-rate covert shoot, with a keeper's wages to be paid over and above the rental of the land, may cost £2 an acre or more in 1973, and the price is rising. Even quite a modest rough shoot, unkeepered, and comprising the remoter 'outsides' of an estate may cost 50p an acre. According to the type of shoot, the price of a gun can vary from around £2000 for one in a good covert shoot, where shooting is with a pair of guns

142

early in the season, to about £100 for one in a good rough shoot, or less where sport is a correspondingly tougher and more problematical proposition. But as I have indicated in the last chapter, much can often be done with the latter if a band of enthusiasts combine together and work hard to make improvements in accordance with a carefully thought out plan. In any case those who rent land to shoot over should make sure they have a lease of sufficient length to enable them to reap the reward of any improvements they make, and as a result of which the rental is likely to be subsequently increased.

Shooting Tenancies

A shooting tenancy should be for not less than five years, with an option on both sides to terminate at the end of the first season if either finds it unsatisfactory or if the conditions of the lease are not properly fulfilled. There should also be an option for the tenant to be able to renew the lease for a further term, subject to satisfactory conditions being agreed.

Rental

Such is the demand for shooting that 25p an acre would now be considered a low rental. Let us consider the case of a 1000 acre rough shoot let at this figure, and see approximately the total outlay a syndicate taking the letting would have to meet annually. The bare rental will amount to £250. On top of this a tenant is normally required to pay rates, say an additional £50. Provision must be made for certain expenses, which might include cost of work done on improving the shoot, a supply of winter feed, purchase of equipment, possibly wages for a couple of beaters, etc.; if it was decided to limit expenditure in all these respects to a further £100, the total outlay for the shoot would be £400 per annum. If the syndicate comprised eight guns, this would mean the price to each would be £50. It will be noted that over half this figure is attributable to rental, and only a quarter is spent on the actual running of the shoot.

For comparison, let us now look at the finances of a good covert shoot of, say, 2000 acres let at £2 per acre per year. Rental will be £4000 and rates about a further £500. There will also be a keeper's wages, his National Health Insurance, his usual perquisites in kind, the depreciation and running costs of his vehicle, plus the costs of winter feed, equipment, casual labour, rearing expenses, beaters' wages and so on. Contrary to what many people believe, the sale of game may possibly pay the beaters' wages in a season but that is all. It will not, therefore, be excessive to estimate these outgoings at a net figure of at least £4000. So with an eight gun syndicate the charge per head will have to be a minimum of about £1100, of which approximately half is spent on rent and rates and the other half on actually running the shoot.

These rough figures should show quite clearly that game shooting is an expensive sport. Unless the person who undertakes to act as the manager of a syndicate is really capable of running a shoot efficiently, the gross cost per bird in the bag by the end of a season can quite easily work out at over £10. Comparatively few shooting men seem properly to appreciate this. As a result the standard of management of many syndicates is much lower than it ought to be, as is the return obtained in terms of game brought to bag.

It should perhaps be made clear that the figures shown in respect of rates in the two examples above are nothing more than intelligent guesses of what typical costs might be. Assessment of rates is based on the annual value of the sporting interest, which is not simply the rent, but the rent reduced in respect of any services which the landlord provides. Keepers' cottages are rated separately.

Keeper's Status

It is important that the status of the keeper of a syndicate shoot is clearly defined. Whatever detailed arrangements are made, he must know to whom he is answerable and for what. In my view he should be an employee of the estate, which pays him, gives him his usual perquisites, looks after the maintenance of his cottage, provides his vehicle, etc., and recoups itself financially in these respects from the syndicate. The latter should be responsible for paying directly for everything else, such as rearing equipment, winter feed, traps and so on. The syndicate manager and estate factor or agent must maintain a close liaison, and the initiative in this rests with the former. In this way the siting of rearing fields, release pens and other things can be agreed amicably with tenant farmers also a party to the arrangement where applicable.

8 Cutting the primary wing feathers of a pheasant poult prior to transfer to the release pen.

9 Brailing a hen pheasant prior to placing in an aviary for breeding.

20 Debeaking pheasant poults prior to release.

1 Bitting, an alternative to debeaking, which is gaining favour with many keepers and shoot managers.

22 A corner of a release pen of a kind found on smaller shoots; it is covered with 'Ulstron' netting to keep out winged predators.

23 An example of good low cover into which pheasant poults can be let out in a release pen.

In fact, although the estate remains directly responsible for the keeper's pay and administration, the syndicate becomes responsible for control and supervision of his daily work and routine, and the keeper himself should know exactly where to turn for assistance or advice in any particular respect.

Where a good working relationship is struck up between the syndicate manager and the owner or his factor few causes of friction should arise due to the keeper not being able to get hold of the right person in an emergency, such as when, for example, he suspects an outbreak of disease among his reared birds. This sort of three-sided management of a shoot certainly calls for greater give and take than a direct owner/keeper relationship, but where the problem is tackled intelligently and with goodwill on all sides, there is no reason why it should not work perfectly satisfactorily.

Sometimes a syndicate may be a keeper's employer in every sense and be responsible for his housing and everything else. This means a keeper's continued employment is dependent on renewal of the lease and he lacks the security of tenure he has as an employee of an estate. Also, on a big estate where other keepers are employed, and other estate functionaries such as forester or warrener operate over 'his' shoot, he may feel himself at a disadvantage, and relations between shoot and estate become 'difficult' in consequence. So although this may seem a more clear-cut arrangement, it does have undoubted drawbacks in practice, though these may not be so significant where the shoot and estate are one entity, which the owner has in hand himself.

Legal Aspects

The days when an informal verbal agreement between the parties concerned sufficed as a 'lease' are very much a thing of the past. However friendly the relations between syndicate manager and landowner may be, a shooting lease should always be in writing and should cover essential points such as :

a The area over which shooting rights are granted, best defined on a map or plan attached, and for how long.

b Details of any buildings or other facilities placed at the syndicate's disposal and consequent responsibilities for same.

c What rental is to be paid and when.

d Responsibility for payment of rates.

e That the exercise of the rights assigned shall be in a proper and sportsmanlike manner.

f The conditions in which any part or the whole of the rights may be sub-let, if at all.

g Provisions relating to the shooting and rearing of game, and control of pests and predators. (N.B. Some landlords, notably the Forestry Commission, prohibit the taking of certain predators, such as otters and pine martens.)

h Conditions governing the employment of a keeper, if applicable.

i Indemnification for damage caused in the exercise of shooting rights.

j Details of insurance policies which the syndicate is required to hold for indemnification against personal, public liability.

k An undertaking by the lessor to conduct farming, forestry and other operations on the land with reasonable consideration for the welfare of game, and to see that his farming tenants do so.

l Details of mutual responsibilities for prevention of poaching and trespass, and apprehension and prosecution of poachers.

m The conditions under which the lease may be lapsed by either party, together with any penalty clauses appropriate.

n Conditions governing renewal of the lease.

Although a set form of shooting lease is sold by some sporting papers, drawing up a lease is in my opinion a job for a solicitor so that it is properly tailored to the prevailing circumstances in each case. The signatories to the lease are usually the shoot owner or his agent, and a named member of the syndicate, normally the senior member or manager of it.

Syndicate Rules

Prior to 1939 it could be reasonably assumed that all those who ventured into the shooting field were aware of the precepts of safety as well as the ethics of sportsmanship, having acquired both in boyhood. This is not now so. Increasing numbers of businessmen take up shooting in middle age with no background of country knowledge, let alone game shooting, on which they can call. No syndicate of which I have ever been a member has had a written constitution or set of rules. But my fellow guns have always been countrymen and there has been an obvious understanding of the accepted code of behaviour in the shooting field, which has made anything in writing unnecessary. But nowadays I think a syndicate is well advised to have a written code of conduct to which members agree to adhere. This ought to include clauses disposing of the following matters :

a Every member should have a valid insurance policy to cover himself against indemnity to any third party in the event of a shooting accident for which he is held responsible.

b Every syndicate member and any guest gun of such member should obey without question on a shooting day the orders of the syndicate manager, or person otherwise appointed to manage a day's shooting, and should any such member or guest be considered by the said manager or other person acting for him to be shooting dangerously, he should, if requested to do so, stop shooting for the day and quit the field without demur.

c In the case of somebody who is considered by the syndicate manager habitually to shoot dangerously, he should, on a majority vote by other members of the syndicate, be required to forfeit his gun forthwith, and any monies already paid or owing for his gun for that season.

d The amount each gun has to pay and when it has to be paid should be stipulated.

e How the bag is to be disposed of after each shooting day should also be set down.

f An agreed method of payment of gratuities to the keeper should be adopted.

g There should be a policy regulating the asking of guest guns by members to shoot either in addition to, or instead of, themselves on shooting days. Syndicates differ widely in this respect; most allow a member to nominate a substitute for himself on days when he is unable to shoot, and some permit each member to ask one guest gun on any agreed day in each season.

h Syndicate members may only be accompanied by dogs on shooting days with the consent of the syndicate manager.

Every member should be given a copy of the rules, and required to sign a master copy indicating that he understands and accepts them.

The rule about dogs may seem to some superfluous. But I have seen so many potentially good shoots spoiled by dogs over which their owners had no control that this is to me one of the most important rules. On rough shoots where the bag may in a large degree be dependent on the ability of the dogs to find and flush game, a dog that is not under proper control can well mean that the day's sport is ruined, and because everything has been put up out of shot the bag is virtually empty at the end of it. At a covert shoot a wild dog which runs in on every hare or bird down can at least be tied up so that its activities are curtailed until a drive is over. But at a rough shoot this is not practicable and the need for well-trained, good, steady working dogs which will find and retrieve game, while under proper control of their handlers, is even greater than at a covert shoot.

Conclusion

Finally, two other important matters which are the lot of a syndicate manager. Firstly he must keep an accurate record of game shot, a copy of which is usually required each season by whoever is running the estate. Secondly he must not only keep an accurate account of income and expenditure but be able to budget ahead and foresee the need for capital expenditure on equipment, for example, which may require an increase to be voted in the annual subscription. As I have suggested earlier in this chapter, successful management calls for a combination of knowledgeable shooting man, competent businessman and diplomatist—in fact in Service terms an ideal Commanding Officer! This is often far from being fully appreciated by those who take on the job, and as a result there are a lot of poorly managed syndicate shoots in this country.

CHAPTER ELEVEN

PARTRIDGES: NATURAL HISTORY

Introduction

EVEN in these days when partridges are not as numerous as they used to be in Great Britain, every sportsman should be familiar with the grey, or common, partridge, as many will also be with its cousin, the red-legged, or French, partridge. However, owing to the widespread decline in partridge populations in the 1950s and '60s, the fairly detailed knowledge of these birds and their habits, which many shooting men formerly acquired as a normal part of their sporting education, can now no longer be taken for granted. In fact some youngsters may have to wait several years before they even get a shot at a partridge.

Shoots place more and more reliance on reared gamebirds for their sport. Rearing partridges has proved a more complex operation than rearing pheasants. As a result comparatively little rearing of partridges is done, and on shoots where reared pheasants now provide the main sport of the season, wild partridges are increasingly left to find their own salvation. This trend is reflected in contemporary shooting books, in which the rearing and releasing of pheasants, and sometimes partridges, are dealt with at length, but only rarely is any substantial mention made of management of wild stock. This seems to me a sad omission and a major one in any volume purporting to be authoritative. For if we do not have a good understanding of the habits and needs of game in its wild state then we shall certainly not be able to provide adequately for our reared birds after they have been released. The difficulties experienced in rearing partridges successfully have highlighted the considerable shortcomings in our existing knowledge. This makes the research projects into wild partridge and pheasant populations undertaken by the Game Conservancy of supreme importance to the future of these gamebirds in Britain.

It is proposed, therefore, in the following chapters to deal at some length with the natural history of each species and the management of its wild populations, as well as going into details of rearing and release where these are applicable.

I. THE COMMON OR GREY PARTRIDGE

The partridge is much more of a family bird than the pheasant in that even when the young of the year are grown up they remain together with the parent birds, going about their daily lives as a family group or covey, which only breaks up on the approach of the following breeding season. This normally takes place towards the end of January or in February, though in exceptionally mild winters pairing has been known to start in late December.

The plumage of a partridge at a distance appears a warm brown colour, but on closer inspection it can be seen to comprise a pattern of varying shades, from the rich chestnut flecking of the wings and upper parts to the grey of the throat and pale buff of the underparts. The cock is usually quite readily distinguishable from the hen by his obvious 'cockiness'; also the chestnut horse-shoe on his breast is usually more pronounced; but the only infallible way of distinguishing between the sexes is to examine the wing coverts, those of the male having a light longitudinal stripe, while those of the female have in addition light transverse barring, as depicted in Figure 48.

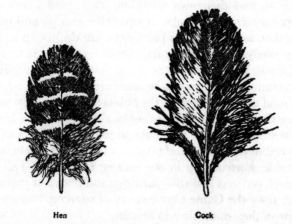

Hen   Cock

Fig. 48   The median wing covert feathers of adult female and male grey partridges

The average weight of a cock partridge is around 14 oz, and that of the hen about an ounce less. Average body length from tip of beak to tip of tail is 12½ in and wing span about 15–16 in. The beak is a greenish horn colour, and the legs and feet are grey, though in young birds of the year both the latter are yellowish.

On the ground partridges walk or run. They fly in typical gamebird fashion, a series of rapid wing beats alternating with periods of gliding on set wings. They only very rarely perch in trees, though they may occasionally do so on a vantage point, such as a stone wall or building. At night they roost, or 'jug', on the ground; it is generally held that a covey adopts a circular formation for this purpose so that an all-round watch can be kept against predators. Some authorities maintain that all the birds face outwards and others that they face inwards when jugging; in fact, precise information on this point has yet to be obtained.

Although not considered to be 'territorial' birds in the same way as grouse, partridges do definitely take up residence in an area over which they roam by day, though there is a certain amount of overlapping in that a number of coveys can often be found feeding in the same fields at the same time. This continues after birds have paired and in a 30-acre clover field in early spring three or four pairs, for example, may be found feeding in different parts of it. On really first-class, well-keepered partridge ground it is possible to obtain a breeding density of one pair of birds per 5 acres or even as little as 3. However, a density of one pair to 10 acres can be considered very satisfactory and nowadays a man who finds he has one pair per 20 or 30 acres may count himself fortunate.

Breeding

A partridge nest consists of a hollow scraped in the ground by the female, lined with dried grass and dead leaves. The site is usually the bottom of a hedgerow, the edge of a plantation, rough grass under barbed wire fences separating arable fields or any sort of rough grass cover on marginal land, waste ground or bank. In the past partridge nests have been found in such unlikely sites as haystacks, but modern farming offers fewer opportunities for such eccentricities.

Egg-laying begins around the end of April or early May. A

complete clutch may number anything from 9 to 20 eggs, 15 being about average. The eggs are normally olive-brown in colour and are laid at daily or rather longer intervals. As soon as the clutch is complete incubation by the hen starts and takes about 24 days. The chicks all hatch within a few hours, the cock often helping to brood those first off. Both parent birds assist in the rearing of the family until the chicks are fully grown and able to fend for themselves. The young start to fly when about 16 days old.

Young Birds

During the first three weeks of their lives the chicks require a high animal protein diet for which they rely on insects. Thus, warm spring weather in April and May to encourage the emergence of insect life which has lain dormant during the winter is a critical factor in promoting a high rate of chick survival. Also, up to fourteen days old young partridges are very prone to the chill; to escape falling victim to this they must be able to extricate themselves from wet vegetation and find an open space in which to dry off within a matter of a few minutes. The increased size of modern fields and the greater density of modern cereal, forage and grass crops has considerably aggravated this problem, and particularly so if there is wet weather during the period of the main partridge hatch between 7 and 30 June.

Food

In former times ants and ant-eggs comprised a large part of the partridges' animal food. However, it has been found that the warmth of the sun shining directly on an anthill is necessary for the incubation of ant eggs. With the widespread demise of the rabbit from 1953 onwards, due to myxomatosis, the grass and other vegetation on and around anthills, which the rabbits used to eat down, has been allowed to grow unchecked, with the result that anthills have become shaded from the sun and the eggs inside have not hatched, thus causing a substantial decline in ant populations. However, recent research has shown that other insect life, such as the larvae of the sawfly, which is harmless to agriculture, is an adequate substitute for the lack of ants, provided it is available in sufficient quantities.

After the first three weeks of its life, the young partridge adopts an increasingly vegetable diet, until by the time it is **adult** this comprises approximately 90% of its food. An extensive range of grain, grass and weed seeds is eaten; occasionally the leaves of kale, brussels sprouts, cabbage, sugar beet, turnips and other vegetables are also consumed. But generally by its consumption of harmful insects such as aphids and a large variety of weed seeds the partridge can truly be considered a friend of the farmer.

Distribution

The grey partridge is widely distributed throughout the British Isles. It specially favours such areas in England as East Anglia, the downlands of Sussex, Hampshire, and Wiltshire, and is numerous locally in parts of Scotland, notably Morayshire and some of the eastern counties. Partridges have been recorded in recent times as far north as Wick in Caithness, and also in the Outer Hebrides and Orkneys; there are none in the Shetland Isles. In Wales they are generally sparse. In Southern Ireland they are rare indeed, having been almost exterminated due to the failure in that country to make and enforce properly effective game laws and implement realistic game conservation policies.

Some people assert that there is a distinct sub-species of the common partridge which frequents the marginal lands of the Borders and elsewhere in Britain, and which they refer to as the 'hill partridge'. Although the partridge is always associated with stubbles and cultivated land, it is surprising how well the birds can thrive in areas of uncultivated land, such as around the slag heaps of the Durham coal mines, Army training areas in southern England, the lower slopes of the hills in Berwickshire and so on. The partridges in some such areas, particularly in the North, do often seem to have rather darker plumage and, because they lead a somewhat hardier life, may be a trifle smaller in size. But the plumage of grouse also varies quite extensively from district to district and, as far as it is possible to ascertain, there are no genuine grounds for believing the so-called 'hill partridge' differs in any material way from his lowland cousin except that he lives in a harsher habitat.

When assessing the bag at the end of a shooting day, and making gifts of birds to friends, it is important to be able to differentiate young from old. Early in the season the yellowish colour of the legs will readily distinguish the young ones, but later

Old   Young

**Fig. 49   The difference in shape of the outer wing primaries
of old and young partridges**

it will be necessary to examine the two outer wing primaries. In
young birds these will be pointed, while in older ones they will
be rounded, as shown in Figure 49.

II. THE FRENCH OR RED-LEGGED PARTRIDGE

The red-legged partridge is not indigenous to Britain. The date
of its introduction to this country has been settled conclusively
by the discovery, *circa* 1921, of two letters in the *Bibliothèque
Nationale* of France, dated 1673, relating to permission being
requested and granted for the catching up of red-legged partridges
for transference to England. Except that the request for these
partridges was written by the gamekeeper to King Charles II and
so presumably they went to one of the royal estates, there is no
information as to where or how many were released. In the years
following 1673 there is some documentary evidence to show that
red-legged partridges existed in England, though they would seem
to have been rare, as in one instance they are referred to as
'curious outlandish partridges'.

However, in 1770 or 1790, probably the latter, red-legged
partridges were successfully introduced into Suffolk by the then
Marquess of Hertford and another nobleman and it is from this

introduction that the spread of the red-legged partridge is generally held to stem.

It is a slightly larger and heavier bird than the grey partridge and, with its more vivid and brightly coloured plumage, quite distinctive from it. However, its field characteristics are very much the same, except that its covey discipline is less strict, and when pursued on the ground individual birds will often run forward and take wing on their own, or in two's or three's, instead of as one covey.

Although the plumage of cock and hen is the same, the former can be distinguished by a rudimentary spur or knob on each leg.

Nesting and breeding habits are also very similar to those of the grey partridge but there are some important differences. The average number of eggs in a clutch is only about 11, instead of 15; however, one hen may lay two clutches in separate nests, the second one being incubated by the cock. It was suspected that this happened many years before it was actually proved in 1952 by observing the behaviour of tagged birds on the Game Conservancy's experimental estate. It is still not known how frequently

Fig. 50   Map showing distribution of the red-legged partridge
in the British Isles

it occurs. Where only a single clutch is laid the cock also sometimes helps with the incubating.

Its food and feeding habits are also much the same as those
of the grey partridge, though adult birds tend to eat an even
higher proportion of vegetable foods, which may include beans,
peas, roots, acorns and beech mast as well as cereals, grass and
weed seeds, etc.

Although red-legs generally favour the traditional partridge
areas of England, there appears to be a 'line finely drawn' beyond
which they will not willingly advance. This is as noticeable in
Europe as in this country. Thus red-legs are found in the south
of Yorkshire but not further north; they have spread westwards
as far as the boundary between Devon and Cornwall, but no
further. They have spread into North Wales, albeit sparsely, but
not into the south of the Principality. Figure 50 shows the limits
of their distribution in Britain. Whether or not red-legs could be
settled successfully in some of the good partridge areas in Scotland
is a question that has yet to be answered.

The red-leg is a most interesting bird which will sometimes
thrive in circumstances and places where the grey will not. It
certainly deserves further study and encouragement in the British
shooting scene.

CHAPTER TWELVE

PARTRIDGES: CONSERVATION AND MANAGEMENT

Introduction

ALTHOUGH partridges are widely distributed throughout Scotland, England and Wales, only certain regions are recognized as first-class potential partridge ground, where in the past their value as a sporting asset has been rated on a par with that of the pheasant. Almost without exception these areas are prime arable land, where the problems posed by modern farming methods have to be faced in their most acute form. On some shoots these problems have been tackled reasonably successfully, and the sport shown today is of a very similar standard to that which formerly prevailed, though the methods by which this is achieved have changed dramatically.

However, there are other places which in former times always produced a fair showing of partridges, but now do not. They provided sport which was acknowledged to be of secondary importance to the covert shooting, to which it was regarded as no more than a pleasant overture, probably consisting of a few informal days, mainly walking up, in September and October. But the decline of the partridge, accompanied as it has been by the growth of a seemingly overwhelming preoccupation with pheasant rearing, has almost completely put an end to them. The idea seems to have gained currency that nothing can be usefully done to try and repair the partridge's fortunes and consequently nothing is done.

Management

Successful management of wild partridges is largely a matter of knowing and applying basic keepering skills, and is often referred to as 'hedgerow keepering'. It is time-consuming in that it requires a keeper to spend a good deal of his day out on the ground finding exactly where his partridges are nesting, and thereafter maintaining a check on every nest right up until hatching time. It is not, therefore, a task which can be taken on by a keeper committed to looking after pheasants penned in an aviary, and the collection and setting of their eggs for hatching under broodies or in incubators. However, as will be explained in Chapter 15, there are ways in which the pheasant-rearing burden on a keeper can be lightened so that a shoot may benefit in other respects, of which the partridge stock is one. According to the time a keeper can spare from his pheasants, there are various practical measures he can take to improve the lot of his partridges short of full scale management, which is only worthwhile in the best partridge districts.

The Euston System

On big partridge shoots the 'Euston System' of nest management used always to be practised. Although essentially simple, it involves a lot of work. At the end of April or in early May a keeper should set out to find every possible partridge nest on his beat. Each as it is found is marked on a large-scale ordnance map and given a serial number. The latter is also entered in a notebook together with the date the nest was discovered and any other relevant information, e.g. the number of eggs already laid.

Each day every nest should be visited and as soon as six eggs have been laid these are removed and replaced by dummies, details of this with the date being recorded against the appropriate serial number in the notebook. On succeeding days, whenever a real egg is found, it is removed and a dummy substituted, until each nest has a clutch of twelve dummy eggs, after which additional eggs laid are removed but not replaced with dummies.

The real eggs are placed in trays to set, and then under broodies for incubation. For partridges the bantam makes a better foster-mother than a chicken, and twenty eggs in one clutch is quite enough. As soon as the eggs start to chip, the keeper selects a nest from his notebook in which the eggs would be due to hatch, and when the hen is off the nest, removes the dummies and replaces them with the chipping eggs. It has been found that a hen partridge will sit for a few days longer than her normal full incubation time of 24 days on eggs which have not chipped, and also will take quite happily to chicks which appear to have hatched any time after about twelve days' incubation. This allows a keeper a generous measure of latitude in disposing of chipping eggs among suitable nests.

The system also gives him flexibility in controlling the size of broods, one of ten or twelve chicks being much more manageable for the parent birds even in a fine season than one of twenty, while in a bad season an average-sized one of fifteen may prove too many to look after properly. Another advantage is that the hatch can be spread over about an additional fortnight beyond the normal three weeks. Also, if a sitting hen should fall victim to a fox, feral cat, prowling dog or any other predator, as some invariably do, at least her eggs are saved.

As will be appreciated, operating the Euston System is a whole-time job. So for the man who is primarily concerned with pheasants but wants to do something for the partridges as well, it will have to be modified. Thus a keeper, whose pheasant-rearing duties properly begin with the purchase of day-old chicks in late May or early June, should be able to devote a good part of May to work in connection with the partridges.

Nest Protection

Where barbed-wire fences border arable fields, tufts of cocksfoot will probably be the first to grow under them in the spring. In consequence, partridges often choose these tufts as a site for a nest. But although the grass gives excellent protection from the prying eyes of carrion crows and magpies, it gives none against cattle grazing the early bite who always seem to find the grass under a fence as well as on the other side of it greener than that of the field they are in. Also, when cattle are being moved from field to field one animal sometimes breaks away and runs down the head-land of a field; if a partridge is nesting in the grass there, the beast seems invariably to pick that precise spot either to stop and graze or put its foot down on the nest. So when nests are found under barbed-wire fences, it is a wise precaution to provide them with some extra defence in the form of branches of quickthorn cut and strategically laid to shield them. If a nest is found beside a grass or forage crop it is better not to remove the eggs and destroy it, because it is likely that a second nest will be made actually in the crop, and so be doomed to certain destruction. However, where nests are in patently dangerous situations, such as beside public rights of way or on roadside banks, and trying to give them added protection is obviously a waste of time, they should certainly be destroyed after the eggs have been removed, in the hope that a safer site will be chosen for a second nest.

In years when spring growth is late partridges seem much better able to make good use of such cover as there is than pheasants. In such years nests of the latter with eggs in them can quite often be found wide open to the heavens and the eyes of any passing winged predator. Although it is rarer for partridge nests to be so exposed, it can happen and the best answer when they are found is to remove the eggs for hatching under bantams or in an incubator.

It has been estimated by the Game Conservancy that on a well-keepered shoot approximately one third of the partridge nests will be lost due principally to predation and farming activities. Where no effort at all is made to help the partridges there is every reason to believe that the proportion of nests lost is much higher. How much a keeper can do is something he alone can judge in relation to his other work. But if he can only give added protection to nests in need of it and remove and hatch under bantams the eggs from those in dangerous places he will have made a positive and useful contribution to partridge conservation on his ground.

Broodies

Any keeper concerned with partridges ought to keep a small flock of bantams from which broodies can be obtained in due season. Generally speaking Silkies, Wyandottes, Orpingtons and Sussex are good strains for this purpose, as are crossbreds of all kinds. Ordinary chickens are not so satisfactory on account of their size, and a clumsy hen can cause wholesale slaughter among a brood of very young chicks by treading on them.

If more shoots could arrange to do more in this way for their partridges and improve their winter feeding arrangements for them, then we might indeed be able to look forward to better and more widespread sport with partridges in this country in the future.

Rearing Partridges

The modern partridge shoot relies to a large extent on reared birds. But, as already mentioned, rearing and releasing partridges is by no means such a straightforward operation as it is with pheasants. However, it has become evident in recent years that the red-leg is not such a tricky customer in these respects as the grey partridge, and in consequence has come much more into favour at the expense of the latter.

Thanks to the work of the Game Conservancy most of the early difficulties experienced with the rearing of partridges have now been largely overcome, but those concerning release have proved more intractable. If partridges are reared *en masse* like pheasants and then released they do not break up of their own accord into convenient little coveys of ten to twenty birds, but remain together as one big family group of a hundred, or whatever number of birds it was that was reared together. Also it has been found that artificial coveys of this kind are very apt to be taken over by any barren pair of old birds which happens to come across them after they are released, and not in the least perturbed by adopting a family six to ten times bigger than they might normally have expected, the old birds sometimes take their new-found family right away off the shoot altogether. At my first attempt to rear partridges this actually happened; we released some sixty birds in a field of kale adjacent to a meadow, three broodies in coops being spaced along the headland to hold the birds and also, we hoped, to keep them in the three separate coveys in which they had been reared. But almost at once the three all joined up together and after a week a barren pair appeared and within twenty-four hours our treasured partridges had vanished for ever.

Anyone taking on the rearing of partridges must possess that rare quality of 'sympathy' with his charges. Unlike pheasants, which readily respond to set routines of management, partridges are much more individualistic, temperamental, and erratic in their behaviour. Anyone who has not an instinctive understanding of them and their ways will soon become infuriated and frustrated by their seeming waywardness. This intangible quality, irrespective of the excellence of the rearing equipment employed, can make all the difference between success and a total loss of every chick hatched within the first few days of their lives. Most keepers are loath to admit they cannot do something, so before embarking on even a modest partridge rearing scheme, it is advisable to have a trial run with one or two settings of eggs to confirm that he is the man for the job.

F

As with pheasants there are four principal methods of rearing partridges, namely :

a The open field.
b Movable pens with broodies.
c Brooder units.
d Intensive systems.

The Open Field Method

The Open Field Method is only suitable for rearing partridges in large numbers. It is basically similar to that used for pheasants (see Chapter 15) with broody bantams confined in coops of slightly different design, which should be more widely spaced with at least 40 yards between each. A keeper must be in attendance all the time from when the chicks are let out first thing in the morning until they are shut in again in the evening. In the light of other methods which have been developed it must be considered obsolescent.

Possibly the most convenient method for those who want to rear partridges in a small way as an 'extra', without prejudice to the pheasant-rearing programme, is that with movable pens and broodies.

The Movable Pen System with Broodies

The Game Conservancy has pioneered an excellent low-silhouette type of pen as shown in Figure 51 (in which chicks can be reared to six weeks old). Novel features of this are the dusting tray in the sun parlour at one end which is roofed with Claritex, or some other transparent plastic, and the fact that the bantam broody is not confined in a coop, but allowed to move around freely with her chicks. The other end of the pen is roofed with plywood or some other suitable material. These pens are easily made by an estate carpenter or handyman, but it is important that the roofing of the sun parlour is made waterproof, so that the sand or fine soil in the dusting tray keeps dry.

Owing to the small size of partridge chicks in their infancy, the pens must be sited on close-cropped level grassland. A density of only twenty pens to the acre is necessary to allow for moves; the Game Conservancy recommended routine is for one move to be made after the first week, two during the second, three in the

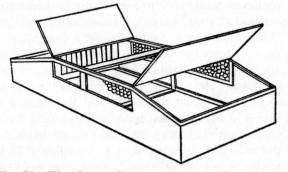

**Fig. 51   The Game Conservancy low-silhouette type
partridge rearing pen**

This is an excellent type of pen for rearing partridge chicks
to 6 weeks old tended by a foster mother bantam broody. The
hinged roof at the opposite end to the hutch should be covered
with Claritex, or some other transparent plastic material, so
that when closed it provides a sheltered solarium, a facility
much appreciated by young partridges.

third, and then daily after the twenty-first day until the end of
the sixth week. When moving the pen special care must be taken
to see that chicks are not crushed. If irregularities in the surface
of the ground make it necessary, any gaps under the sides must
be blocked with turf.

As the chicks grow so will the grass on the field; from the age
of three weeks onwards it has been found they show a marked
liking for wild white clover, so a ley containing plenty of this is
beneficial.

Brooder Units

Partridges can be successfully reared in various kinds of brooders,
heated by paraffin, electricity or gas; but judging from the experience of many users quite the most reliable results seem to be
obtained with what is known as an 'electric hen', as depicted in
Figure 52. However, there are other brooders that also give good
results, in particular the small Cotswold Game Farm brooder,
incorporating an 'electric hen'-type heater primarily designed for
indoor use and for broods up to 25 in number, and the well known
'Rupert' brooder which is heated by paraffin.

But, whatever source of heating is used, overcrowding in brooders must at all costs be avoided. It has been found in practice that 60 chicks in one unit is quite enough; though 70–75 have been successfully reared on occasion, to put as many as a hundred in one unit, which a standard brooder will readily accommodate, is to court disaster. Heat should be provided in the brooder until the young birds are about five weeks old; they should then be allowed access to the unheated brooder house for a further few days before it is removed altogether, and they are left with shelter only in the pen. The full procedure to be followed in brooder rearing is fully set out in the Game Conservancy booklet entitled *Partridge Rearing*.

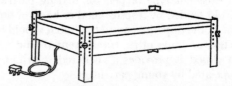

Fig. 52 A typical electric hen with adjustable legs

This excellent electric heater is ideal for both partridge and pheasant brooder units. It was pioneered by the Cotswold Game Farm, and is both safe and robust. The young birds are able to roost on it as well as under it.

The same procedure in brooder rearing should be followed for red-legs as well as grey partridges. All reared partridges in pens should be approached cautiously so that they do not take fright and possibly damage themselves by flying up against the roof of the pen; this precaution is even more necessary with red-legs than greys.

Intensive Systems

Intensive partridge-rearing systems call for the greatest skill in management and are really only for experts who want to rear birds in large numbers. However, there are several big shoots in the country which have devoted a lot of study and work to perfecting such systems, though these seem to vary quite a lot in detail. One, which I know has produced consistently good results over a number of years, is basically an adaptation of the deep litter method employed with domestic poultry. In this, groups of sixty chicks are penned together, each in a separate partition of the brooder house, with heat provided by an electric hen. But the success of these systems lies in following meticulously the drill prescribed, and those who wish to attempt intensive partridge rearing on their own account should find someone already 'in business', and arrange to go and learn his technique at first hand. For those who may contemplate adopting a system of this kind it is again stressed that they do call for very competent management, and comparatively trifling mistakes in routine can cause catastrophic losses.

A point on the credit side when partridges are reared in brooders or intensively is that they seldom indulge in feather picking unless too many are placed together in one unit or in too small a space.

Feeding Young Partridges

The correct feeding of young partridges is of great importance, and nearly all the major game food suppliers now publish their own recommended feeding schedules covering every need from day-old to release and thereafter. The composition of these foods varies slightly from one firm to another but all have obviously gone to considerable trouble to produce what they believe to be a properly balanced diet to meet the needs of partridge chicks at different ages. Some keepers prefer the foods of one firm, others of another, and for practical purposes it probably pays to follow a keeper's fancy in this respect. However, for those who are not committed, my own recommendation would be to give the foods sponsored by the Cotswold Game Farm a trial, as they have done a great deal of practical work over many years on improving all aspects of partridge management and in particular have made a close study of the nutritional needs of penned and brooder reared birds. I therefore have complete confidence in their advice on game foods, which in making a choice is really the critical factor, because a keeper 'forced' to use the products of a firm of which for some reason he does not approve will lay every mishap on the rearing field at their door. Although one would hesitate to say these are ever contrived, they do sometimes seem to follow one another in as remorseless a procession as the plagues which beset the Egyptians of old.

Eggs

In case it should appear that the partridge has come before the egg in this chapter, this is because it is pointless considering how to obtain eggs until a partridge policy has been decided.

For the big genuine partridge shoot, eggs can either be obtained from a game farm, from penned breeding pairs, or a combination of both. It has been found that caught-up wild stock birds seldom lay well, and that the only really satisfactory way of obtaining eggs by this means is from reared birds. This, of course, entails penning, over-wintering and pairing-off of breeding stock, all of which is quite a major operation which has been studied in detail by the Game Conservancy, and those who wish to undertake it cannot do better than follow their advice as set out in their booklet on partridge rearing already referred to.

For those merely interested in trying to improve their stock of partridges and who wish to gain a few pleasant sporting bye-days in so doing, there are three principal sources of eggs, which should provide a keeper for whom partridges are a sideline with all that he has time to deal with; they are :

- *a* By taking eggs from nests found by dogging grass and forage crops.
- *b* By removing the eggs from nests in dangerous situations and then destroying the nests.
- *c* By collecting eggs from early nests, which are then destroyed.

On only moderate partridge ground an observant and active keeper may well find he can easily get two hundred or more eggs in a season by these means.

Release

Though certain guide lines can be laid down for releasing partridges, success in this difficult operation depends much more on improvisation, imagination and initiative than slavishly following a set routine (although where large numbers are concerned scope is naturally more limited). As stated earlier in this chapter arbitrarily created coveys of reared birds released in too close a proximity to each other tend to pack straight away. Also subsequent winter wastage among reared partridges appears to be exceptionally high, with only a small percentage surviving on the ground until the following breeding season. Returns of reared grey partridges shot on some estates have been as low as 10%. But in this respect red-legs have proved far more satisfactory and percentages shot in a season have been more nearly comparable with those generally anticipated from reared pheasants, i.e. between 30 and 40% This is largely because reared red-legs emulate the behaviour of their wild brethren and flush singly or in small numbers on a shooting day instead of in a complete covey or pack as do grey partridges, thus giving the guns better opportunities of taking toll of them.

After completing six weeks in a pen or brooder unit, young partridges should be divided into coveys of 15–20 birds apiece, each group being placed in a standard movable pen, complete with a shelter at one end, for their final hardening-off, preparatory to release. It has been found with red-legs that larger coveys of up to 50 birds each are just as satisfactory after release if this is more convenient.

It is a mistake to release partridges until after the corn has been cut on account of the disturbance caused by farm machinery. But the earliest recommended age for release is at eight weeks old, so this should be no problem. Some people like to keep their birds penned till ten weeks old, but it is inadvisable to delay any longer as they are then liable to start fighting amongst themselves.

Partridge should be released from a pen sited on the edge of some holding crop, such as kale, roots, or a special game mixture, with a stubble, meadow or fallow adjacent to it. The partridges should be moved into the pen at the chosen site, and allowed to become acclimatized for a few days before release actually begins.

Wherever there are partridges there will always be an odd barren pair or so in a normal season which will usually eagerly adopt a covey of reared birds. A keeper should have a good idea of the whereabouts of such pairs on his shoot and be able to site a pen where its inmates will readily be discovered by each of them. Some people recommend that such adoptions should be carried out any time after the reared chicks are three weeks old; this will of course mean moving the original rearing pen to the chosen site, and then when the barren pair have been seen in its vicinity for several days it should be safe to remove the bantam foster-mother and release the chicks into the custody of their own kind. In so far as this reduces a keeper's work in connection with partridges it has obvious advantages. But the number of chicks which can be so disposed of in a normal year will be limited, and where this amounts to only a minority of those being reared, the additional complications it creates may make it more trouble than it is worth.

Various methods have been tried to encourage coveys of reared birds to base themselves in a specific area on release. One is to release half the birds at first from the pen and place food for them outside it; then after three or four days, in which the released birds will have found their way around, to release the other half, a supply of food for the whole covey being continued for as long as they come for it. Another way which is reported to have been found very successful is to release the whole covey except for two birds which are retained in the pen right through to the end of the shooting season. These two act as 'callers' or 'anchor men' to whom the remainder of the covey always return. This does, however, involve extra work in daily feeding and watering of the penned birds, which, depending on their number and how they are spread over a shoot, might or might not be an acceptable additional commitment to the daily feeding of pheasants and also possibly wild duck.

Yet another way to try and hold reared partridges in a given place and prevent them packing with others of their kind is to place the bantam foster-mother in a coop on the edge of the holding cover into which they are released, and leave her there for two or three weeks until her erstwhile charges have settled down and appear to have taken up residence.

As will be realized there is still a lot to be learnt about the release of partridges, and plenty of scope for experimenting by those who feel they have ideas worth testing. But in my own opinion, and it is no more, the crux of the problem with reared partridges is as much an ecological one as it is with wild partridge populations, and that, basically, reared partridges will not thrive in unsuitable habitat any more than will wild ones. Until, therefore, farming patterns change again in favour of the partridge, if they ever do, releasing reared birds and obtaining satisfactory recovery rates from them will depend on a substantial element of good luck as well as good, intelligent management.

Crowding

There is also one further point worth serious thought in this connection; are we being too greedy in the numbers we are trying to obtain? Some shoots are literally packed with reared pheasants so that three figure bags can be achieved when the covert shooting starts. It is my feeling that where this happens, and there are many places where it does, the partridges are literally crowded out. In fact the head of game shot in a season, not the quality of the sport shown, has become the criterion by which a shoot is judged. I believe this is wrong and highlights the danger of game rearing coming to be regarded as a substitute for good management, which it can never be. Reared birds should be used as a supplement to, not a substitute for, wild game populations. If shoots generally paid more attention to the basic principles of management as set out in Chapter 7, and less to the production of reared birds, I believe we should have both better sport and more partridges.

CHAPTER THIRTEEN

PARTRIDGES: SHOOTING

Winter Wastage

THE winter wastage of partridges has been mentioned in passing in previous chapters. It is an important consideration in management and conservation but even more so in the regulating of the shooting of wild partridge populations. In a typical winter it will amount to anything from 35 to 50% of the September total of birds on a shoot, and in exceptionally severe winters can be much higher. The exact causes of these overwinter casualties are not fully understood. Disease, starvation and predation certainly play a part, but after the coveys break up in January/February some birds seem just to vanish. It is thought that a proportion may migrate locally to pair off with birds from other coveys. But although research has shown that birds of the same covey never seem to interbreed, how far a partridge will normally travel to seek a mate is not yet known.

To illustrate the importance of the winter wastage factor in shoot management, let us consider the example of a rough shoot which at the September count has twenty-five coveys on its ground, averaging ten birds each, and taking into account a quota of barren pairs. This makes a total of 250 birds in all. If it has been found that winter wastage averages out over good and bad years together at 40%, it means we ought to allow for a loss of 100 birds. As explained in the last chapter, approximately one third of the nests in the breeding season can be expected to fail due to predation and other causes; so taking into account surviving barren pairs, our twenty-five coveys probably stemmed from around thirty-five breeding pairs in the previous April. We ought, therefore, to allow a further 70 birds for next spring's breeding stock. So out of our 250 partridges in September, we have a shootable surplus of no more than 80, if we want to maintain the stock of partridges on the shoot at its current level. This is, of course, taking a very simple case and other factors may enter into the calculation, such as the number of birds reared from eggs which were picked up, and so on. But an estimate on these lines made at the beginning of a season should give a fair guide as to how many can properly be shot. It also shows the importance of making reasonably accurate spring and autumn counts of partridges on a shoot.

The Shooting Season

Before we come to the various ways in which partridge shooting is conducted, a word about the season. This opens on 1 September and ends on 1 February. In recent years it has been suggested that in the interests of conservation it ought to be shortened, some shooting men proposing putting back the opening date to 1 October, others bringing forward the closing date to 31 December, and yet others a compromise between the two. It seems to me there is a good case for readjusting the season, and valid arguments for chopping a bit off each end. However, although in some years the beginning of September is too early to start shooting, there are many years in which the young birds are well forward and the majority quite properly shootable by that date. So in my view the opening date ought to be left as it is, and whether to shoot or not remain at an individual's discretion. But there is a very wide measure of agreement that partridges ought not to be shot in January, and I believe that bringing forward the closing date of the season to 31 December would be fully justified. But with anti-field-sport bodies seeking to erode, and ultimately destroy altogether, our sporting heritage in Britain, it is much wiser for the time being to leave this also to the discretion of shooting men, than to seek a change in the law.

Methods of Shooting Partridges

Dogging, walking up and driving are the three traditional ways of shooting partridges. The first was a very popular sport in the early part of this century, but the Great War virtually put an end to it. Nowadays shooting partridges over pointers or setters is very rarely seen in Britain. On the Continent where dual-purpose dogs such as the German Shorthaired Pointer are much more popular, shooting over dogs is still widely practised, and in certain parts of Belgium, Holland and West Germany most enjoyable sport can be had in this way by small parties of two or three guns.

Walking Up

Before the decline of the partridge really set in in the early 1960s, walking up partridges in September and October was something looked forward to by many shooting men. The success of a day's shooting depends on local knowledge and a real understanding of the partridges' ways as well as on good organization.

Partridges are birds of more independent character than pheasants. They will much less readily allow themselves to be driven in a given direction over waiting guns, and prefer to follow flight lines of their own choice. Generally speaking they will more readily follow the contours of a slope than cross them and fly to the other side of a valley or glen. When disturbed while feeding on stubbles or pasture, they will usually make for some cover crop, such as roots, kale or potatoes. On a shoot the plan is therefore usually to start by walking the coveys off the outside stubbles and grass fields in order to turn them into a selected cover crop. Those that are visitors from over the march will normally fly back across it, so when walking the boundary fields a flank gun should be placed well forward to intercept the coveys that do so.

When walking up it is most important that everyone in the line should keep in line, and that flank guns ordered to go ahead should maintain station. All fields, and roots, kale and other cover crops particularly, must be walked right out to the hedge or fence. Flank guns especially must not turn inwards short of the corner of a field, or a covey which has run on ahead is quite likely to be missed. The less noise, and above all talking, with which operations are conducted the better. Unruly dogs at which their owners are continually shouting are a curse. Partridges have keen hearing and birds which have already been driven into roots, and possibly also been shot at in the process, are naturally very much on the alert for signs of pending trouble. Unless a shooting party approaches and lines out as quietly as possible along the headland of such a field, every bird in it will take alarm, and in the words of the American Army 'get to hell out of it', thus probably spoiling the climax of an hour or two hours' work.

Cover crops must be walked slowly and methodically. In thick cover, such as mustard or lupins, if the line sets off at a 'gallop', it is very easy for a member of the party to walk straight into a covey skulking near the edge of the field. This will explode in all directions round him, and in the ensuing surprise and confusion somebody may be tempted into taking a dangerous shot. Guns should be spaced no more than forty yards apart, closer if circumstances dictate or numbers permit. If a bird is shot and falls some distance ahead of the line, a halt should be made for the person concerned to reload and the whole line should then go forward to where the fall was marked, when it should stop for the retrieve to be made. The shooter must always try and mark his birds as accurately as possible but if he is to attempt a right and left he may not be able to spare more than a glance for the first bird down. Those not actually shooting can often assist by taking a cross-bearing on the fall, especially in the case of birds which carry on for some distance before they drop and which may well be runners. Having reached the fall, unless the retrieve is made at once, there is always a tendency for other people and other dogs to come along and 'help'. It is much better to wait and let one dog have a fair try before offering assistance. If a dog does take a little time to find, then it is advisable for the person at the mark to place something distinctive on the ground or crop itself such as a white hankerchief or his hat, so that the spot can be readily found again if it becomes necessary to finish the beat and return to make a second attempt at the retrieve.

In marking the fall, it helps to take a line to a prominent object in the far hedge or beyond, such as a conspicuous tree, the chimney of a cottage, or a telegraph pole. Where there are known to be several coveys in a field the less disturbance and delay with which retrieves can be made the better. Some people like to use these early days to round off the training of a young dog; there is no objection to this at all if it is done with due consideration for the rest of the shooting party. But even on the most modest rough shoot a formal shooting day should not be turned into a glorified advanced training session in which everyone has to wait while a particular dog is given first chance at each retrieve. I have seen this happen, and once myself received a 'rocket' from a relative for walking over to pick up a bird which I had shot and had fallen a few yards away in the open, but which apparently he considered should have been left for his young dog to retrieve, even though it had to be brought up from the other end of the line to do it.

Sometimes a field will be too wide to be covered by a shooting party in one beat, and two or more will be needed to deal with

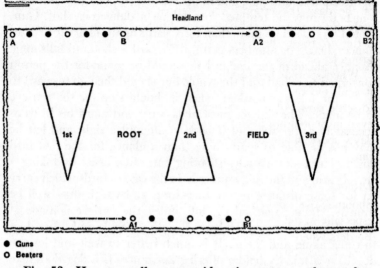

Fig. 53   How to walk-up partridges in roots or other such
cover

it. When this occurs I recommend the procedure shown in Figure
53 which depicts a party of four guns and three beaters lined
out for the first beat between points A and B. The beater at B
should mark the limit of the beat by pulling a turnip and hanging
it on the hedge where it can be clearly seen. The beat is then
taken to the far side of the field where the party turns left and
walks down the headland to positions between A1 and B1. The
beater at B1 again marks the limit of the beat as before and the
return sortie is made. Then the party turns right and moves into
position between A2 and B2, when the final beat is made. The
beater starting from B and B1 on reaching the end of the first and
second beats must make a mark on the ground to indicate positions A1 and A2 to his opposite number from the other flank. I
like this formation because it is simple, and the beat is taken right
out each time. Some people prefer to swing the line round, pivot-
ing on the inside man, but this is more difficult to control and
ensure that the ground in the corners and at the end of each
beat is properly covered.

Coveys must not be pursued too ruthlessly. Those which have
been chased off the stubbles into a cover crop and then pushed out

of that have shown fair sport and should be left alone for the rest of the day. In certain circumstances flushing a covey deliberately for a third time may be justifiable, but in principle it is better to resist the temptation and switch operations to fresh ground.

When sport is brisk and it is a nice sunny autumn afternoon, it is all too easy to go on shooting too long. Partridges like time to settle down of an evening before they jug for the night, and even in September 5 pm is quite late enough to call a halt to the day's sport, while in October this should be advanced to 4.00 pm.

Driving

Shooting well-shown driven partridges can be grand sport, especially in the Downlands of Southern England and parts of the Borders where the birds often come high as well as fast over the guns. Unless birds of the year are very well grown and plentiful, the middle of September onwards is usually considered time enough to start driving.

Reared birds are probably easier to drive in a required direction than wild ones, but to be successful a driven partridge shoot needs to be just as carefully planned and take into account the same factors as a day's walking up. On really open ground beats can be longer, say 1500 yards, than on more enclosed land, and they should also cover a wider frontage, if possible defined by natural features such as a wood, road or river, as this will help to deter birds from running out to a flank when they see the beaters approaching as they will be able to do from a considerable distance. Again, it generally pays to drive birds along the contours rather than across them, though it may often be possible to drive them off the end of a spur in order to show high birds. It is normal practice to drive the birds from an area, A, over the guns so that they pitch in an area, B, which is then driven subsequently towards area A. But driven birds usually fly for longer distances than those walked up, and it is a mistake to try and put the same birds over the guns more than twice in a day.

When a covey is flushed the keeper will usually warn the guns of its approach by blowing a whistle. Driven partridges are often said to require 'quick shooting', but there is more to it than that. As soon as a gun waiting in the line behind a hedge is alerted by the keeper's whistle, he should come to the 'ready' position described in Chapter 4 and look into the 'blue' just above the hedge top. This will enable him to pick up the birds as soon as they come into view. He should not look at the top of the hedge itself. As soon as he sights the covey he must pick the bird he intends to shoot and have eyes for no other until he has completed his shot. Switching targets at the last moment is a common cause of missing and sometimes of failure to get off a shot at all.

Partridges are small birds and with their rapid wing beats give an impression of speed which is deceptive. They are not in fact as fast in flight as a grouse or a pheasant. Thus when the shooter sees a covey coming straight towards him like a pack of animated cricket balls, his first reaction is to whirl up his gun and blaze off both barrels as quickly as he can. This often results in two misses in front, which the shooter will invariably think were misses behind. So next time he will try and give his target a good 'lead' and miss even further in front.

In recent years I have seen a lot of driven partridges shot and am convinced that their sucessful shooting calls first and foremost for very precise gun handling and that, although gun mounting should be smartly executed, this is really a secondary consideration. In fact the shooter wants to adopt a rather coldly calculating attitude to each shot, because simply to 'flourish his bat at the ball' is not good enough. He must concentrate on the bird he intends to shoot and shoot at it. If he fails, let him try and shoot the legs off the next one; this is almost a sovereign cure where over-energetic gun mounting is causing missing in front.

With high partridges, missing behind is the more likely cause, as they then lose the impression of speed they give when skimming a hedge. They should be treated in exactly the same way as high pheasants (see page 222). As the bird approaches the point where you intend to kill it, mount the gun from the ready position to the shoulder in one brisk, polished movement and pull the trigger as the eye dictates when the butt beds home at the shoulder.

Numbering

On some ducal shoots it is alleged that the guns are placed at each drive strictly in order of social precedence, so much so that one commoner at such a shoot, having spent the whole day as a flank or walking gun and hardly firing a shot, is supposed to have remarked to his host at parting, 'Thank you so much for a splendid day watching you shoot; I hope you'll allow me to return the compliment sometime.' However, on most shoots nowadays the guns are not arbitrarily placed by the host at each drive, but draw numbers for their position and move up a stipulated number of places at each succeeding drive, usually either one or two, Unfortunately some people seem quite remarkably stupid and are unable to grasp how this very simple system works, and it is not uncommon to find a distraught figure rushing up and down the line of guns unable to recall his original number, that of his last stand, let alone that which he is supposed to go to now. Such people seem quite unable to help themselves either by noting who they should be standing next to or by equipping themselves with a pencil and paper so that they can write down the information they need to know, having obtained it from whoever is running the day's shooting at the meet.

Numbering may be from right to left or vice versa. The former is the more usual, but a visiting gun who does not know the custom of the shoot should ask. The same applies if he is not certain how many guns are to count, and how many places he is to move up at each stand. If a gun does have genuine difficulty remembering the sequence, then he can jot it down on a card, and strike off each number as he arrives at his peg. At some shoots each gun as soon as he has drawn his number is handed a card with all the necessary information for each drive on it. This is certainly a thoughtful gesture on the part of a host, but its good intent is quite often defeated if the person it is chiefly designed to assist then loses his card !

Of course there are days when a particular gun seems right out of luck, and even when he is in what should have been the best position at a drive, the birds keep conspicuously out of his way. What must be almost a unique case of such misfortune once overtook a friend of mine, who attended a shoot where over 90 head was shot by eight guns of which he was one, but he never dirtied his barrels all day, a fact which, being a good sportsman, he took pains to hide from his host. So when I hear syndicate members grumbling sometimes because they have drawn such-and-such a number and that means they won't get a decent shot all day, I am not a very sympathetic audience, and especially if I also know that the grumbler in question would be hard put to it to do justice to a better number even if he got it.

Stubble Burning

Finally, there is a factor which anyone who looks forward to partridge shooting of any kind cannot afford to ignore, though primarily a farming, not a shooting matter, namely stubble burning. Runaway fires on stubbles terrify gamebirds, and partridges in their panic will fly miles rather than hundreds of yards to escape. The effect on reared pheasants released in adjacent woodlands can be equally dramatic, and cause them to scatter far and wide.

No one aware of the farmers' problem in disposing of unwanted straw can seriously question the need for burning. If it is done sensibly in accordance with the code issued by the National Farmers' Union (N.F.U.) the harm caused to game is negligible. Ample proof of this is provided by some of the best managed shoots in the South of England where some of the stubbles are regularly burnt after harvest, but the ground still teems with partridges and pheasants. Anyone, therefore, who wants to enjoy his partridge shooting in however modest a way must try and arrange that stubbles are burnt under proper supervision.

Some of the main clauses of the N.F.U. code are :

a Never start fires in the evening and allow them to burn out overnight.

b Burn in one direction only; fires lit all round the perimeter of a field will trap wildlife in the centre.

c Burn upwind whenever possible.

d Avoid burning in a strong wind.

e A firebreak should be made alongside hedges, shelter belts and woodlands before burning starts. This can be done by ploughing a strip at least 10 furrows wide. A strip of kale sown for game will also serve as a firebreak.

f Ensure adequate personnel and implements are on site to prevent fires getting out of control; watch out for a change of direction or freshening of the wind.

g Game can be cleared off a field before burning starts either by getting the keeper to dog it or by making a few fast runs across it with a tractor or Land Rover.

h Make certain the person in charge knows the telephone number of the local fire brigade in case the fire gets out of hand.

If a really good liaison exists between a shoot owner/shooting tenant and the farmers concerned a lot of the troubles which may arise over stubble burning can be avoided.

CHAPTER FOURTEEN

PHEASANTS: NATURAL HISTORY

Introduction

IN recent years the attention of shooting men has become so riveted on reared pheasants that the existence of wild populations is in danger of being ignored altogether. Yet even in modern farming conditions, if other factors, such as terrain and climate, are reasonably favourable, good management can enable the latter to thrive and multiply so that shootable surpluses are created which fully justify the effort involved. This possibility may be a matter of more concern to the good private or well-run rough shoot than the wealthy syndicate where numbers in the bag at the end of a shooting day are the primary concern, but it certainly calls for a better understanding of wild pheasants, their needs and habits.

The ordinary British pheasant is but one member of a big family, of which the peacock is probably the largest and most colourful. Although distinctions are often overlooked, there are in fact several variants of what might be called the 'common pheasant' in this country. They all interbreed freely in the wild so that it is hard to think of any of them as a real sub-species despite obvious differences in plumage. The so-called 'English Blackneck' has no white collar and a generally rather dark bronze plumage. The 'Chinese Ring-neck' on the other hand has a definite white collar, cream coloured wing coverts and is of an altogether lighter hue, hens of this strain being also markedly paler. Then there is the 'Mongolian' which, except for his 'clerical' collar, is very similar in plumage to the English blackneck. The 'Melanistic Mutant' with his handsome, almost Black Watch tartan livery, is unmistakable, as is the hen with her rich coppery apparel. The 'Japanese Green Pheasant' is a rather smaller bird, lacking the dark splendour of the melanistic's colouring; its physical hardiness in extremes of wet and cold lends it a special attraction as breeding stock in certain parts of this country. This

180

is an aspect which unquestionably deserves further investigation.

In the British Isles the pheasant is generally a polygamous creature, and in the breeding season it is quite usual to see one cock keeping company with four or five hens. However, this is a state to which management contributes by deliberately reducing the number of cocks on a shoot towards the end of a shooting season. There is evidence from countries abroad and from the Game Conservancy's wild pheasant research programme that in truly wild populations the pheasant is in fact a monogamous bird.

The plumage of cock and hen pheasant is so well known as to need no description here. A cock pheasant normally weighs 3–3½ lb, and hens about 1 lb less. The length of a cock pheasant from tip of beak to end of tail is between 30 and 34 in, of which as much as 20 in may comprise the tail; the equivalent length of a hen pheasant is 21–25 in, the tail being only some 8–10 in long. The wing span of a cock pheasant is approximately 28 in, and that of the hen about 3 in less.

It is widely believed that the age of a cock pheasant can be determined by the length of his spurs. This is often indicative, but not infallible. Young cocks of the year in October and November can be distinguished by their short, blunt spur. But later in the season a bird equipped like a Texas Ranger may not be as old as his length of spur suggests. The only infallible way of ageing cock and hen pheasants is to use the bursa test, as described in the Game Conservancy's booklet *Sex and Age in Gamebirds*.

On the ground pheasants walk or run and, when disturbed, usually prefer to run rather than fly for cover unless pressed in pursuit. However, once on the wing they will fly fast and strongly, a succession of rapid wing beats being used to gain height, which when achieved is followed by gliding on set wings with intermittent spells of vigorous wing beats to maintain height and pace.

Breeding

Almost any sort of cover will serve as a nesting site—hedges, banks, bramble thickets and other low cover in woodlands, reed beds and patches of scrub being popular choices. More exotic sites may include shrubberies in country gardens, ivy-covered walls and old squirrel drays. The nest itself is usually a hollow scraped in the ground and lined with grass or dead leaves. Laying may start at any time in April, and a clutch can comprise from 7 to 20 eggs, but generally consists of around 10 or 12. Hen pheasants are reported to have been found incubating eggs as late as October, and I have myself found one doing so in September. But it must be assumed that such late nests are second or third attempts to raise a family, the hen having been scared into deserting earlier nests. Pheasants are single-brooded. Incubation takes 23–25 days.

Hen pheasants are often denounced as bad mothers, but considering that a hen incubates her eggs, hatches off and rears her brood all on her own without any assistance from the cock, she does not really make such a bad job of motherhood and its attendant problems as is popularly believed. The wild pheasant hatch normally extends over a considerably longer period than that of the partridge, with early broods appearing in May and late ones in July. Thus, when bad weather in June decimates the partridges, pheasants may not fare so badly. Given good weather in the breeding season, the survival rate of young wild pheasants to sixteen weeks of age should be about 40%, i.e. in September after the harvest one should see a majority of hens with four or five poults apiece in attendance. In a poor year the equivalent number will be two or three, whilst in a downright bad year, such as 1972, it will be one or none at all.

But there is a factor which has to be taken increasingly into account; this is the effect of reared bird survivors from the previous season. Some people question whether these hens breed at all in their first season in the wild. There appear to be strong grounds for thinking that if they do, they don't make a very good job of it. In April/May it is not unusual to find solitary pheasant eggs on farm tracks and elsewhere which have just been laid and not removed from any nest.

Acclimatization

Reared pheasants have always possessed the characteristic wariness which distinguishes a truly wild animal from a domestic one. Keepers used to reckon that despite this it took reared birds from two to three years to become acclimatized and qualify properly as wild birds. I believe this is a fair appraisal. It means that with the large numbers of reared birds with which most shoots deluge their ground, the true pattern of wild bird behaviour is becoming increasingly difficult to assess accurately, and many apparent eccentricities are in reality attributable to reared birds in their acclimatization phase.

Though generally considered a lowland bird, pheasants will be found on ground at altitudes of up to 1000 feet. They are acknowledged wanderers, but with reared birds this tendency may well be aggravated by overcrowding.

Feeding

Their food is two-thirds vegetable and one-third animal; the former embraces a wide range of grain, weed seeds, nuts including acorns, berries and roots such as potatoes, artichokes and turnips; the latter includes earthworms, slugs, wireworms and leather-jackets. Although pheasants in large numbers can do quite extensive superficial damage to potato fields, they are on the whole beneficial to agriculture.

Roosting

With reared birds no effort is spared to encourage them to roost in trees where by night they will be relatively safe from predators; but wild birds seem just as happy roosting on the ground and I have found overnight roosts of pheasants on rough ground bordering grouse moors, in snipe bogs and many other places.

The most surprising thing about pheasants in this country is not how many are reared, but how little is really known about them in the wild. In making good this deficiency in our knowledge, the Game Conservancy's research programme into wild pheasant populations could be of great value.

CHAPTER FIFTEEN

PHEASANTS: CONSERVATION AND MANAGEMENT

Habitat

THE importance of providing suitable habitat for game has been discussed in Chapter 7. Now that re-stocking relies more than ever before on reared pheasants, this factor needs more, not less, weight given to it, if shoots are to obtain good value for the money spent on these birds. Any sizeable woodland is not automatically good pheasant cover, nor do tall trees necessarily ensure the showing of high birds.

If one closely scrutinizes the economics of so-called 'commercial' forestry in Britain, it becomes apparent that this is a misnomer, and that even on a grand scale it is seldom genuinely financially rewarding. Without the government grants, tax concessions and alleviation of death duties which attach to it, few would consider forestry a sound business project. However, in recent years a growing interest has developed in the alternative, generally referred to as 'amenity' forestry, and the benefits it less directly bestows. The rising value of sporting rights has done much to lend impetus to this. Stands of purely commercial timber are seldom of much value for their sporting rights, and conversely, amenity woodlands on their own rarely have any great commercial worth. But it is perfectly possible to plant up or reorganize woodlands so that they are reasonably commercial, within the real meaning of that term today, and also attractive to game. With intelligent, competent planning commercial cropping can in due course improve the attractions for game. It is fashionable to bewail the felling of trees, but unless woods are properly looked after they will degenerate into impenetrable jungles which have neither commercial nor amenity value; in fact good husbandry in forestry is just as necessary as in farming or gardening.

As already pointed out, only 5% of an afforested area

needs to be devoted exclusively to the interests of game. But before going into the details of what this entails, and what enlightened management can contribute additionally, it is well to be clear as to the characteristics a good pheasant covert ought to possess. These are threefold; it should provide :

   a Shelter from the elements.
   b Top quality holding cover.
   c Means of allowing high birds to be shown on shooting days.

Shelter

As pheasants spend most of their day on the ground and, it is hoped, their nights off the ground roosting in trees, shelter must be provided at both levels. To give the necessary protection at ground level some form of perimeter windbreak around a wood is required. In Scotland and the north of England a stone wall may often serve this purpose, but further south a bank, hedge or combination of both is more commonly found. A hedge must be stockproof, and have plenty of 'bottom' to it, which means it must also be well maintained.

The trouble with many hedges surrounding woods and shelter belts is that they have been planted too close to the trees. The result is that as the latter have grown the hedge has become increasingly overshadowed and stunted in growth, so that it has had to be reinforced with barbed-wire. Another problem stemming from the proximity of the trees is that the hedge cannot be maintained by tractor-mounted machinery and so neglect also hastens its decline into uselessness. To make a hedge readily accessible for maintenance by machinery and allow it scope for proper growth a clear space of 4–5 yards should be left between it and the first row of trees, dependent on the probable height and spread of the latter when they reach maturity.

The commonest and most satisfactory species used for farm hedges in this country is quickthorn. Such hedges need to be cut and laid at about eight years old so that they are stockproof. They then need trimming about once every three years thereafter and to assist brushing at the bottom should be cut A-shaped and kept to a height of about 4 ft.

Lonicera nitida also makes an excellent hedge and has the advantage of being evergreen. But it may take fifteen years to become stockproof. However, from the point of view of game it could probably be used more often than it is in cases where farm stock is not a problem.

There are other tree species which can be successfully used for hedges, such as beech, but all either take longer to establish or are more difficult to manage than quickthorn or *Lonicera nitida*.

The clear 4–5 yards space between the hedge and outside row of trees should be allowed to develop into a pattern of bramble patches and rough grass which is periodically cut back with a 'Swipe' or similar implement to prevent it becoming too dense. If treated in this way it will provide valuable low cover for nesting, etc.

In parklands, the perimeter cover of a wood is often of laurel or some other evergreen shrub such as rhododendron, usually fronted with a wire fence where they border on a pasture. Rhododendrons feature around the parks of many stately homes, but however much a delight to the eye in springtime, they are not good game cover, and in most instances have been allowed to become impenetrable barriers, 10–15 ft high, to beaters and dogs alike. Laurel on the other hand, if properly managed so that it does not grow too tall and straggly, makes admirable windproof cover; but it is slow-growing and where it has got out of hand it may be advisable to tidy up a section at a time over a period of years rather than a large area all in one fell swoop.

Roosting pheasants like a sheltered 'room with a view'! This is why clumps of larch screened by belts of spruce are popular roosts. At a lower level hardwoods in the shelter of holly trees or other evergreens are also frequently used. This clearly shows how the most favourable roosting conditions are likely to be found in mixed woodlands, rather than those of a single tree species.

Holding Cover

The term 'holding cover' is sometimes used in a vague way to describe cover that is not specifically for nesting, flushing or some other indentifiable purpose. But in my view 'holding cover' means exactly what it implies, namely that it is cover which by virtue of its various qualities is sufficiently attractive to keep pheasants in residence by providing for all their everyday needs, such as concealment, nesting and so on.

The basis of good holding cover should be a patchwork of low cover distributed over the whole floor of a wood, such as bramble and various other shrubs which, although they may lose their leaves, do not die back in winter. Open spaces, through a proportion of which the sun can penetrate, are essential. However, pheasants, except in the breeding season are solitary creatures, and even though reared birds after release seem content to go round in groups, this is but a passing phase. A pheasant does not like being too much cheek by jowl with others of its kind and, to provide the seclusion instinctively sought, the patches of low cover in a wood should be reasonably dense.

In the breeding season this low cover inside a wood will also serve for nesting. In some cases, especially with stands of beech or a single species of conifer the floor of the wood may be bare except for a fringe of brambles and other shrubs round the perimeter. This limits the choice of a nesting site to the area most exposed to the beady eyes of winged predators. Where this situation occurs it should be remedied in the long term by planting up low cover if this is feasible and in the short term by distributing small heaps of spruce or fir brashings inside the wood. Corners of fields can also be wired off and planted up with quickthorn to provide additional nesting cover.

Flushing Cover

In many mature woodlands the birds, when flushed, have to corkscrew their way up through tall timber before they can head for the guns. This consumes a lot of energy and birds having done this and risen above the trees are only too glad to 'freewheel' in a downward glide over the line. A pheasant, like an aircraft, should take off in a straight, steady climb so that when it crosses the guns it has achieved maximum speed and height. The siting of flushing cover is therefore important, as is its texture and shape.

It should be situated about 50 yards back from the tree frontage. It wants to be not more than 6–10 ft in height and can well be less. It must not be allowed to become too dense or birds will exhaust themselves trying to fight their way out of it. It should be triangular in shape with the apex pointing towards the guns. It should have beaters' paths cut through it so that it is divided into sections about 12 ft wide, which can be thoroughly beaten out. In a large wood it may be advisable to have a flushing area half way along as well as at the end.

Many varieties of shrub can be used to provide low cover. For those who want to plant up cover on a 'no cost' basis, ordinary bramble can serve very well; but though readily available on most shoots it is awkward to handle and transport. Also in good growing conditions it will in a matter of a few years turn into a formidable entanglement from which pheasants will not readily flush and even stout springer spaniels will have difficulty in penetrating. In my opinion the most manageable low cover is that provided by *Lonicera nitida* which will grow almost anywhere, is not attacked by hares or rabbits and when necessary can be fairly easily kept under control by a man with a slasher. But snowberry and certain of the cotoneasters can also give very satisfactory cover of this kind. A complete list of suitable shrubs is contained in the Game Conservancy booklet *Forestry and Pheasants*.

Cover of intermediate height is also important, particularly in offering additional shelter from the wind within a wood. Hazel and chestnut coppice, elder and holly are excellent in this respect. Rather overgrown laurel is useful, but serves better if maintained as low cover. Yew appears quite frequently in British woodlands but can be poisonous to pheasants, and other species are to be preferred. A belt of this middle-height cover directly in front of

Lonicera nitida   Hazel coppice   Spruce   Hedge

Fig. 54   Cover to give a graded take off from a flushing area

A well designed flushing area like this allows the birds to get quickly clear of entangling cover, so that they can climb freely towards the tall trees at the edge of the wood, and then fly on strongly at their best pace over the guns.

a flushing point will help to give a graded climb to the tall trees beyond (see Figure 54).

Rides

The provision of adequate rides in woodland is important to the forester so that he can extract his crop and to the shooter so that he can properly manage his pheasants and shooting. A main ride should be at least 20 yards wide and well cambered for drainage purposes. Where circumstances allow, it should run north and south, rather than east and west, so that it catches the maximum amount of sunlight, especially in winter. As explained earlier, entrances/exits should be angled so that the wind cannot blow straight down it from one end to the other. Rides in which guns are to stand also need to be of this width, or when hardwoods grow up their branches will obscure the field of fire overhead. Also if a gun is to do justice to well-shown birds he needs a reasonable field of view.

Subsidiary rides should be at least 5 yards wide, and it is much better if they can be 10 yards, as they will then be more satisfactory as a firebreak. But all rides to serve this last purpose adequately in summer must be periodically mown. I have already described how a feed ride should be established, and again unless a ride is at least 10 yards wide it will almost certainly become overshadowed by branches when trees grow up and so be unsuitable for this purpose. It is therefore very important to give full consideration to the system of rides needed in the initial planning of a woodland, and the bigger it is the more this is so.

Cover Planning

Foresters always love to fell a wood wholesale and have done with it before replanting. But from the point of view of shoot management this can be disastrous. However, to fell a wood in sections at intervals of years, each of which is then re-planted, can be perfectly acceptable, as will be the cutting back of every alternate hazel or chestnut stool when coppicing. But now that there are so few commercial outlets for hazel and chestnut coppice, this will probably have to be a job either done by the keeper or for which the shoot has to pay the forester. Chestnut coppice, unless it is tended, will grow into trees by any other name, and if it is allowed to get to this stage is of very little value as game cover.

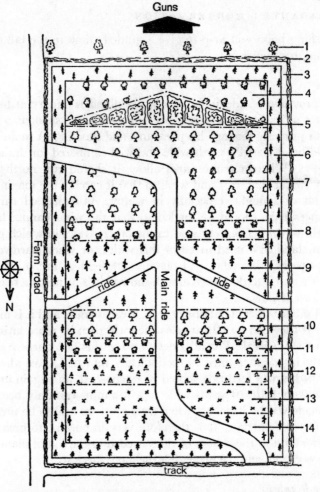

Fig. 55 A hypothetical well-laid-out pheasant cover

The aim should be to create a woodland with a varied pattern of high and low cover, and having ample perimeter shelter at both levels. In the diagram this is achieved by the means shown, but various alternatives can be used to suit different circumstances.

1 Outer fringe of beech trees	8 Belt of chestnut or hazel coppice
2 Stockproof perimeter hedge	9 Larch
3 15ft gap between hedge and trees	10 Mixed hardwoods
4 Hazel coppice	11 Chestnut or hazel coppice
5 Flushing area—*Lonicera nitida*	12 New plantation
6 Outer belt of spruce or firs	13 Felled area awaiting replanting
7 Main area of mixed hardwoods	14 Larch

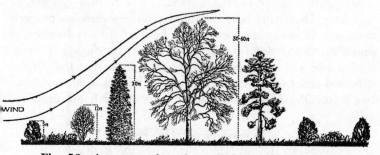
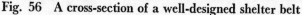

Fig. 56   A cross-section of a well-designed shelter belt

A well planned shelter belt should have the shortest shrubs and trees on the outside and the tallest in the centre, so that when the wind hits it, it is eased over the top with the minimum turbulence.

In fact in woods where coppicing is likely to pose a problem, a better alternative may be to plant up elder, which pheasants always seem to find attractive, and which furthermore thrives on poor and damp soils.

The shape of many mature woodlands has been governed by the contours of the ground and such features as roads and rivers. Few big woods, except for the conifer plantations of the Forestry Commission, are laid out in an exact geometrical pattern. But the hypothetical wood in Figure 55 illustrates the sort of basic layout which a shoot owner/manager should try in principle to create, with its varied pattern of cover. By no means all woods have a perimeter belt of spruce or fir to give shelter to the interior of the wood nor is it always feasible to provide this in one operation, but it should certainly be possible to phase in something of this kind over a period of years. Also in some cases shelter may be furnished by a dip in the ground which will make a tree screen unnecessary.

A point seldom mentioned, but an important one when planning a new covert, is the selection of the end at which it is intended the guns should stand. If circumstances allow, it is desirable to drive it from north to south, so that on those rare, bright sunny winter days, when the birds seem to fly at their best and a good bag is in prospect, the guns do not have to shoot into the eye of the sun.

So much then for the main coverts; a great deal can also be contributed by shelter belts and small spinneys if these are properly managed. If one of the former is to fulfil its primary function of providing shelter for farm stock it should be shaped in cross-section like a not too sharply pitched roof, so that the wind is deflected and eased over the top with a minimum of turbulence (see Figure 56). This means that the cover of which it is comprised

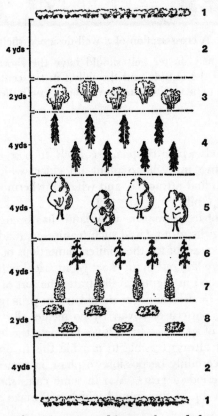

Fig. 57a   A suggested layout for a shelter belt

1 Quickthorn Perimeter Hedge, 2 Open Space in which rough grass and brambles can be allowed to grow for nesting cover, 3 Hazel or Chestnut Coppice, 4 Two Rows of Spruce, 5 Mixed Hardwoods, e.g. Sycamore, Beech, etc., 6 Larch, 7 Lawson's Cypress, 8 Laurel. This list is not exhaustive, and other alternatives may serve better in certain conditions.

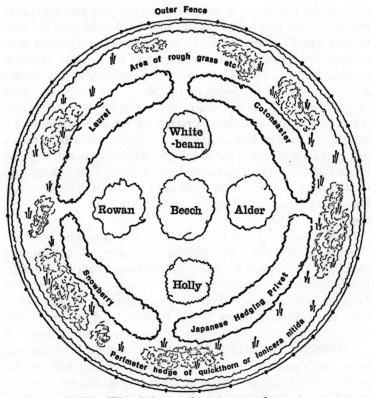

Fig. 57b   A layout for a game spinney

Don't try and crowd too much into a game spinney, a certain amount of open space is just as important as in a larger covert. In time shrubs will spread of their own accord, and will be assisted in this if they are periodically trimmed in height. Comprehensive lists of suitable shrubs and trees are contained in the Game Conservancy booklet, *Forestry and Pheasants*.

must be lowest on the outside and highest in the centre. A suggested layout for a shelter belt is shown in Figure 57a.

Some old parklands contain numbers of small round spinneys, maybe no more than 30–40 yards in diameter, and are often surrounded by a stone wall. They usually have an outer fringe of shrubs, such as rhododendron or laurel, and a few trees in the centre. As a youngster I used to shoot over one such place in Yorkshire, aided by my host's elderly springer spaniel. A hunt

G

through the half-dozen or so spinneys in the park and the shelter belt at the end was just about the limit for the old dog. We used to beat out the whole lot at our leisure in not much more than an hour and a half, and that was our sport for the day. Although no birds had been reared for a number of years, there were always a few pheasants to be found on the 'shoot' and out of the three or four we usually flushed one or two would be shootable. There was a memorable occasion on which we returned home with a record bag for the beat, two cock pheasants and a hen; to my dying day I shall recall the old dog standing in the hall wagging his tail and gazing at his master with a look of pure delight on his face as if to say, 'Wish we could have more days like that'. Such little incidents lend a special enchantment to one's sport.

Small spinneys of that kind can make very attractive cover for game, especially pheasants. Existing ones, however forlorn they may look, can usually be successfully taken in hand. They must first be fenced to keep out stock, and allow a perimeter hedge of *Lonicera nitida* or quickthorn to grow. However, before this is done any necessary felling should be completed to remove old, mature timber, especially horse chestnut, elm or beech, though it will probably be advisable to leave one or two of the better, smaller trees. The cleared area should then be planted up with shrubs, such as laurel, one of the cotoneasters, snowberry, etc., and up to five or six hardwoods which will not grow too tall, such as rowan, alder, holly, or hornbeam. If small areas of ground, useless to farmer and forester alike, are planted up in the same way, a valuable network of small coverts can be created, which can transform an indifferent shoot into a good one. The Game Conservancy's *Game and Wildlife Plant Pack* is ideal both for making good, and new planting. A typical game spinney layout is shown in Figure 57b.

Pheasant Rearing

Now we must turn to pheasant rearing. Before describing the various methods used, there is one aspect which is worth more consideration than it usually receives. It has become so traditional for 'good' shoots to rear their own birds that in some cases the practice seems to have become almost self-perpetuating, and to prohibit examination of alternative methods of restocking now available, which might prove more satisfactory and better value for money. Pheasant rearing involves a lot of work, starting with the catching up of birds in January/February. These are penned in an open-topped aviary after their wings have been brailed to prevent them flying out. Alternatively they can be kept in movable pens covered with 'Ulstron' netting, in which case they need not be brailed. The eggs laid have then to be collected, set and hatched in April/May/June. The rearing and release of the resultant chicks follows and continue until some time in September, after which the poults have to be fed and minded in covert. The process occupies a keeper fully from the beginning of May onwards, and for a good deal of his time in February/March/April. It must be open to question whether all this time devoted exclusively to pheasant rearing is fully justified or whether a shoot would be better served if a keeper had more time to deal with other matters, such as management of habitat, predator control, etc. On a big estate employing several keepers, where the pheasant-rearing programme can be taken care of by, say, two of them, leaving the remainder free to attend to other jobs, the question is not of such consequence, as in the case of the single-handed keeper, who can only do one or the other.

Some shoots nowadays buy in eggs from a game farm, which they then hatch. This absolves a keeper from the daily chore of attending to penned birds and gives him more time for other tasks. But it seems to me that a still better compromise lies in the purchase of day-old chicks from a game farm. This frees a keeper entirely from all the problems of the rearing field until some time early in May. In 1973 the price of day-olds, allowing for the normal discount for quantity, was about £32 per 100. So for a shoot accustomed to setting some 3000 eggs, the purchase of 2500 day-olds at a cost of £800 should mean that, given 80% rearing success, 2000 poults can go to covert. This is a little higher figure than might normally have been anticipated from the 3000 eggs. Though the annual outlay of £800 may seem superficially a high price to pay, it must be remembered that the shoot is thereby spared the considerable capital cost of incubators and suitable accommodation for them, also the expense of establishing and maintaining an aviary for penned birds. Another aspect is that the keeper may be free to tackle a job on the shoot for which a contractor would otherwise have to be paid. But assessing the

balance of financial advantage in a particular case is a problem
to which every shoot must find its own answer.

The Rearing Season

Where a shoot intends to obtain eggs from its own resources, the
keeper should start catching up in January. Birds should be
penned in the proportion of five hens to one cock; all should be
examined to make sure they are free of any signs of disease, injury
or other blemish. To enable the hens to come into lay in tip-top
physical condition, the penned birds must be well and correctly
fed. Where a proprietary food is used for this purpose, breeder's
pellets should be fed, *not* layer's, a mistake sometimes made.
Laying normally starts in early April and eggs should be collected
morning and afternoon.

Egg Care

The site for the aviary should be on sheltered, clean, well-drained
pasture, with, if possible, a southern aspect so that it enjoys plenty
of sunshine. On no account should a field be chosen on which
domestic poultry of any kind have been kept. Low cover in the
form of cut boughs of evergreens should be provided to simulate
nesting cover; brashings serve this purpose excellently.

By keeping the birds penned into June it is possible to obtain
an average of 30 eggs per hen, but some people prefer to settle
for 20 and then to release them in the middle of May, so that
each hen can produce a brood of her own in the wild. Since to
obtain a given number of eggs the latter policy requires half as
many birds again to be penned this idea does not seem to me to
have any special merit.

Eggs for hatching in incubators should be rigorously screened
so that they are all, as far as possible, of uniform size, shape and
colour; any eggs at all abnormal in any of these respects should
be rejected. They should not be set for longer than seven days
before incubation starts. This means that incubator capacity
becomes the critical factor in deciding how many birds need to
be penned. About two-thirds of the total hens penned will lay
every day; thus 150 hens should have an output of approximately
100 eggs per day, so an incubator with a unit capacity of 500
eggs will be able to have one unit filled every five days, while
an exact seven-day rotation would require the penning of approxi-

mately 110 hens. However, cold weather and other factors can adversely affect the rate of laying, so it is always wise to pen rather more birds than the minimum necessary. Where eggs are to be hatched under broodies screening need not be so exacting and eggs may be left to set for up to a fortnight without appreciable loss of hatchability.

Pheasant eggs are best stored while setting and awaiting incubation in ordinary commercial papier-mâché egg trays, which should be stacked on a shelf by lots in accordance with the day on which they were collected and be housed in a rather damp, cool building, such as an old dairy or cellar. Wooden huts with low pitched roofs, especially if these are of corrugated iron, are not suitable storage places because on a sunny spring day the interior temperature can rise above 70° F., which is sufficient to start the eggs germinating.

Once eggs have been procured, there are two ways of hatching them : either under broodies or in incubators. The former unquestionably demands more attention on the operator's part, while the latter calls for a higher degree of accuracy and technical skill. Intensively reared chickens do not make satisfactory broodies and free range fowls are becoming increasingly hard to find and more costly to buy for use as broodies, quite apart from any risk of fowl pest which may have to be taken into account. So, from an operational viewpoint, it seems to me that the balance of advantage in hatching gamebirds' eggs in large numbers lies overwhelmingly with incubators. Where small numbers are concerned, even though secondhand still-air type incubators with a capacity of 100–200 eggs can be bought quite cheaply, broodies can, I believe, still play a useful part.

Although unforeseen disasters can occur with broodies, as for example when one hen, having successfully hatched off her chicks, suddenly turns cannibal and slays the lot, they are generally less catastrophic than those which may result from a comparatively minor error in operating an incubator. But many elementary mistakes with incubators could be avoided if people would read and follow the maker's instructions; so if a secondhand machine is acquired which has no handbook one should be obtained from the makers. Success with either broodies or incubators is largely a matter of following an established routine correctly. Those applicable are clearly set out in detail in the Game Conservancy booklet no. 11, entitled *Hatching Gamebirds' Eggs*, which will well repay careful study by anyone engaged in rearing pheasants, irrespective of whether he is an old hand or a novice at the job.

Once hatched, there are four methods of rearing pheasants:

a The open field.
b Movable pens with Broodies.
c Brooder units.
d Intensive systems.

The first two involve the use of broody hens, the last two do not.

The Open Field Method

The Open Field Method has been in use the longest but, although still practised by some keepers, it must be considered outmoded in the light of more modern methods. The field selected for rearing should possess the same characteristics as that for an aviary, i.e. it should be a well-drained, sheltered, level pasture with a southern aspect, and a close-cropped sward which has not been contaminated with domestic poultry of any kind. In preparation it should have been chain-harrowed, rolled, and given a light dressing of phosphatic fertilizer earlier in the season to encourage the growth of clovers.

The coops should be placed in rows about 20 yards apart with 15 yards between each coop. They should be put in position several days before the newly-hatched chicks with their foster-mother hen are to be introduced so that the ground under them is dry. A typical coop, complete with its removable front 'door', is shown in Figure 58. Some people advocate a hinged or sliding roof to the coop to give easy access to the chicks, but in my experience adequate access can be obtained by having a removable bar at the front, while a fixed roof makes the coop less liable to damage in transit and storage. About 70 coops, which will cover an area of approximately $4\frac{1}{2}$ acres, are as many as one man can look after.

Eighteen chicks are as many as a broody hen can manage. When they have dried off after hatching and are moved to the rearing field great care must be taken to see that they do not get chilled. Having been placed in the coop, after the broody has settled to her task, they should be shut in and left for several hours. Chicks after hatching do not require feeding for the first twenty-

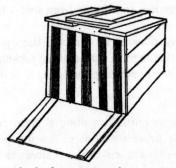

Fig. 58 A typical pheasant-rearing coop with removable 'front door'

four hours of their lives, as they are sustained by the nourishment they have received from the egg yolk. The time for which they are initially left shut in the coop should be judged on this basis.

Chicks reared by this method have to be shut in their coops each night and should be released again first thing each morning. It therefore becomes increasingly important as the chicks grow older that the coops in which they are housed are well-ventilated, otherwise if they are let out from an overheated, stuffy coop into cold, damp morning air they are liable to catch a chill or contract various respiratory diseases. The coops need not be moved for the first three days, but thereafter should be moved on to clean ground daily.

To furnish both shade and cover from winged predators, boughs of evergreen should be placed on the ground a short distance in front of, or alongside, each coop. In fact, an inherent problem with the open field system is the magnetic attraction it has for predators of all kinds. Against these, precautions are necessary both by day and night. Tainting fluids (e.g. Renardine), hurricane lamps, low-set electric fences, fluorescent metal strips and other such devices are all used to keep night prowlers such as foxes at bay.

The birds are normally put to cover after six weeks, as by then there is danger of overcrowding in the coops and the task of shutting them in at night has become wellnigh insuperable.

During their time on the rearing field the chicks should be fed a good proprietary game food and it is advisable to follow the

maker's instructions in progressing from one variety to another
as the chicks grow up.

Despite its many obvious limitations, the open field method
has one distinct advantage in that feather picking, which can be
such a scourge in more intensive methods, is almost unknown.

The Cotswold System

The Cotswold Game Farm has done a great deal of excellent
work in pioneering other methods of rearing pheasants, one of
which has come to be known as the 'Cotswold System'. This is
really a development of the open field method. An 8 ft long run

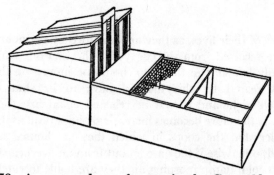

**Fig. 59 A coop and run for use in the Cotswold rearing
system**

is attached to each coop in which the broody is housed, while the
chicks have the use of the run. This is made with solid sides
either of planking or corrugated iron sheeting and is roofed with
1 in wire or 'Ulstron' netting. The last 18 inches of the roofing in front of the coop should be made of transparent plastic
attached to a wooden frame, the whole being hinged to provide
a door through which food and water can be placed in the pen,
and which when closed gives shelter from rain. A 'Cotswold'
coop and run are shown in Figure 59.

The chicks are reared in the coop and run up to six weeks of
age, before being put to cover. The success of the Cotswold
System depends a great deal on correct feeding in accordance
with the routine and foods recommended by the Cotswold Game
Farm, which have been evolved after much painstaking research.

It may be significant that such criticisms as I have heard of the Cotswold System have only occurred in cases where the prescribed diet has not been followed.

This system allows approximately seven times as many birds to be reared on a given acreage of ground as the open field method. If the coops and runs are correctly placed on flat ground there should be no problem with predators and a keeper need not be present throughout the day on the rearing field. Although, in my experience, given good management, the system works admirably, outbreaks of feather picking may occur and if they do the only satisfactory answer is either to debeak all the poults in the pen concerned or else equip them with 'bits', as described shortly.

The Movable Pen System with Broodies

The true Movable Pen System of pheasant rearing is basically merely a variation on the Cotswold theme. A typical movable pen, some 10 ft × 6 ft × 4½ ft high, is shown in Figure 60. The coop for the broody is built on to one end and a sun parlour for dusting, which is highly desirable, can be constructed at the other. The sides are normally boarded up to 2 ft and the remainder enclosed by wire netting. The top of the pen should be roofed with 'Ulstron' netting so that birds flying up against it do not damage themselves.

The broody can be let out to run with the chicks, but is usually confined to the coop. After the first three days the brood is not shut in at night. The pen can well be left *in situ* for the first

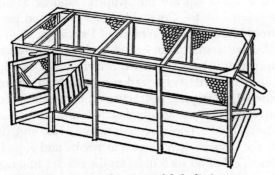

Fig. 60 A movable pen with built-in coop

week, except that the area under the coop may become very dirty; if therefore it is considered desirable the pen should be pulled forward some 3 ft every other day so that the coop is on clean ground. For the next fortnight of the chicks' lives the pen should be moved twice a week on to fresh ground and thereafter up till their release at six weeks of age it will need to be moved at least every other day and in bad weather it may be necessary to do so daily.

The field chosen for the pens should fulfil the conditions already described for the previous two methods. In hot sunny weather it is advisable to place boughs of evergreen either in the pen or on its roof to give shade.

If a diet with a high animal protein content (28%) is fed, as with the Cotswold System, then the risk of outbreaks of feather picking is diminished, though it may not always be eliminated, and if and when an outbreak does occur, the only answer, as before, is prompt debeaking or 'bitting'.

In my own experience of both the Cotswold and movable pen systems, the only real advantage of the latter over the former is that it calls for rather less expert management; on the other side of the coin, movable pens are considerably more costly to buy or make.

Brooder Units and Systems

With the growing difficulties of obtaining satisfactory broodies and the danger of fowl pest it seems to me the future of pheasant rearing, other than on a very small scale indeed, must lie with Brooder Units. Two excellent ones for rearing 100 chicks at a time to 6–7 weeks old are the 'Rupert' outdoor game brooder system marketed by the Cotswold Game Farm and the 'Brooda-matic', from Messrs Walker Wishaw of Lancaster.

The 'Rupert' system is based on a circular galvanized metal igloo into which is built a paraffin heater unit. This igloo should be sited in a 10 yard × 10 yard pen roofed with nylon netting (see Figure 61). Complete instructions for operating the brooder and constructing the pen are obtainable from the Cotswold Game Farm. The method of operating is simple and easy and, if correctly followed, the 'Rupert' gives excellent results and is probably the most economical of all such units on the market in terms of both running costs and capital outlay.

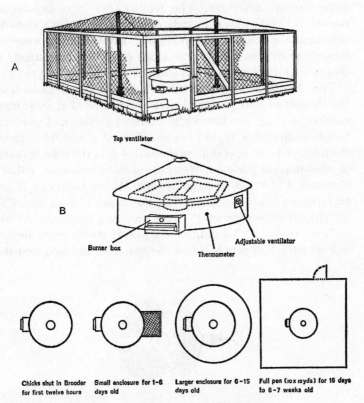

Fig. 61   The Rupert brooder layout

In diagram *a*, the unit is shown in a 10 yard × 10 yard pen, as recommended by the makers. Diagram *b* shows the brooder unit and its heater system. Diagram *c* shows how access to the enclosure should be enlarged as the chicks grow up.

The 'Broodamatic' works off mains electricity and the heater unit offers similar advantages to the 'Electric Hen' mentioned in Chapter 12 in accommodating chicks on it as well as under it. Again the outer shell is igloo-shaped and the whole is constructed of fibre-glass-reinforced plastic. This gives first-class heat insulation, which not only keeps down running costs and minimizes heat loss in the event of a power failure but also prevents overheating of the interior on a hot sunny day. All the electric parts are sealed so that the whole unit can be thoroughly scrubbed and washed before storage after use. The temperature is thermostatically controlled. This is an extremely durable unit which should well withstand the rough and tumble of many seasons of usage and thus allow its rather higher purchase price to be recouped. The complete unit is illustrated in Figure 62.

The 'Fordingbridge System', which the Game Conservancy has developed and perfected over the course of a considerable number of years, is substantially different in design. The brooder house is altogether bigger, being 5 ft square and $4\frac{1}{2}$ ft high at the front with the roof sloping down to 4 ft at the rear. It is made of resin-bonded plywood. Heating can be supplied by either an electrical, Calor gas or paraffin unit. Where electricity is used, an infra-red lamp is advocated as the source of heat, though an 'Electric Hen' is successfully used by many operators. A run is built up of 10 × 5 ft frames, the whole set-up being depicted in Figure 63. Full details of how the system should be operated are

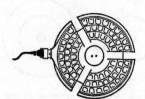

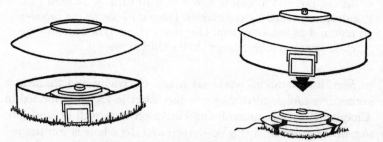

Fig. 62　The Broodamatic unit

This is an extremely well designed and robust brooder. The heater unit, like the electric hen, allows birds to roost on it, as well as seek warmth under it. Its fibreglass reinforced plastic construction makes it exceptionally easy to clean after use.

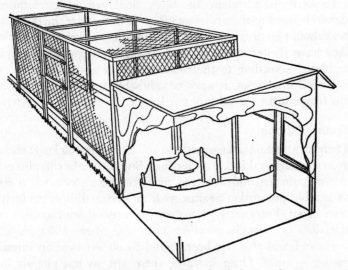

Fig. 63   A 'Fordingbridge' brooder house and run

This type of brooder unit has been used with great success
for a considerable number of years. Electric, calor gas, and
paraffin heaters can all be used in conjunction with it, and its
versatility in this respect is a big point in its favour.

given in the Game Conservancy's booklet *Pheasant Rearing*, and
if these are followed very satisfactory results can be obtained.

Larger Brooder Units

For those who require them, larger brooder units accommodating
200–250 chicks at a time are made by some firms. But management of these bigger units can pose special problems and for the
ordinary shoot the 100-chick size has been found generally easier
to operate and to give the more reliable results. A competent
keeper should be able to look after twenty 'Rupert' or
'Broodamatic' rearing pens without any difficulty. But whatever
size of unit is employed, overcrowding should at all costs be
avoided. It is often tempting to try and insure against losses and,
if fortune smiles, possibly gain a dividend by packing, say, 120
chicks into a unit designed for only 100. But overcrowding can
lead to all sorts of unforeseen calamities and any such temptation
must be sternly resisted.

In all brooder systems the birds' final two weeks in the unit should be used as a 'hardening off' period. So after the third week heat should be progressively reduced until, for their last fortnight, they have shelter only and no heat. This programme should be regulated according to the weather and, if an abnormally cold, wet spell intervenes, it may be advisable to leave heat on at a low temperature for a day or two longer.

Feather Picking

There are certain recognized causes of feather picking, such as overcrowding and incorrect feeding. But outbreaks can also occur in well-managed movable pen and brooder systems when every reasonable precaution against such an eventuality seems to have been taken. Fortunately, however, given good management, this vice does not usually manifest itself until after chicks are three weeks old and this has been found to obtain even in intensive rearing systems. Once it starts, there are, as has already been indicated, only two real cures *debeaking* and '*bitting*'. With birds in movable pens and brooders, it will probably be sufficient to deal with an outbreak if and when it occurs, but in intensive rearing systems discussed below it is advisable to anticipate the trouble.

Debeaking

Debeaking is a simple operation in which the tip of the upper mandible is removed. This can be done either with a sharp pair of surgical nail clippers or with a proper electric debeaker which cauterizes as it cuts. The latter is powered by an ordinary car battery and how it is used is shown in Figure 64. This operation should not be performed on chicks under ten days old. If no more than the final quarter inch of the beak is removed, it will grow again in the matter of a few weeks and the chick be none the worse. Many experienced shoot managers, whose reared birds will have to be debeaked anyway at three weeks of age, prefer to have the operation done at ten days old as they reckon the stress suffered by the chick will be markedly less and everyday veterinary experience supports this belief. Debeaking may be carried out again subsequently as necessary, and some American game farmers apparently do so up to three or four times without ill effects to their birds, but in this country twice is usually found sufficient.

Fig. 64   How to use an electric debeaker

When debeaking, the 'nail', comprising the last $\frac{1}{8}-\frac{1}{4}$ in of the top mandible, should be removed. The instrument is operated off a car battery, and should be used like a pair of surgical nail clippers; it cauterizes as it cuts.

Bitting

A recently developed alternative is a small metal or plastic wire bit (see Plate 21), the bar of which prevents the bird completely closing its beak, and the ends of which are secured in the nostrils with a special pair of pliers to hold the bit in place. These are fitted at three weeks, and must be cut out with metal snips when the poults go to the release pens at the age of seven weeks. If the birds are to be held longer, the bits must be changed for larger ones at this age. It is most important that *all* birds are bitted and subsequently debitted; to minimize the chances of any bird being overlooked it has been found advisable to deal with them in groups of five at a time; then as soon as all five have been checked they can be let go and replaced with another quintet which are duly operated on.

Several keepers I know who have tried out bits for the first time have become most enthusiastic about them, and although it takes slightly longer to 'bit' than to debeak, they all claim that bits produce much the better plumaged birds. From my own observations I believe this is true.

Intensive Systems

The introduction of Intensive Pheasant Rearing based on deep litter poultry systems is comparatively new. Nissen huts which can be simply and conveniently partitioned into sections 10 ft square are very suitable for the purpose. Unused farm buildings, such as unwanted stabling and pigsties, can also be converted, but they must be clear of rats and rat-proof. Each 10 ft square section will house 100 chicks, and an 'electric hen' has been found a most satisfactory way of providing heating. The birds are thus housed for four weeks, heat being progressively reduced during the last week. They are then moved to an unheated brooder unit with access to a grass run for a two-week hardening-off period.

In whatever building is used for intensive rearing, adequate ventilation and light are necessary and in these respects Nissen huts have proved very satisfactory. The eerie gloom in which the interior of intensive domestic poultry units always seems to be shrouded should be avoided. Young pheasants need proper light to see to eat and drink. Good feeding is essential.

Given first-class management and suitable buildings, intensive pheasant rearing can be very successful and allows one man to look after a much greater number of chicks/poults than is other-wise possible.

The plumage of a pheasant in addition to serving as a fur coat has also to do duty as a raincoat. In this latter capacity it is necessary for natural oils to be present to act as the waterproof-ing agent and the presence of these is stimulated by preening. But brooder and intensively reared birds which have never been wet do not preen, so no natural oils are present in their feathers and they therefore have no raincoat. If poults go to the release pen in this condition and on the night following their arrival are drenched by a summer storm accompanied by a sharp drop in temperature, they are particularly vulnerable to chilling, and heavy losses, running into hundreds, can occur in a matter of hours. To help safeguard young pheasants from such a misfortune they should be given a light shower-bath with a hose on a fine day two or three times during their hardening-off period, being shut out of the brooder house during the process and while they are drying off in the sun afterwards.

Having reared our birds, the final stage is to release them into covert so that as few losses as possible are incurred. The traditional method of doing this followed rearing on the open field. On the chosen day at the end of the six-week rearing period, after the birds had been shut in their coops for the night, a sack was gently drawn under each coop, and lightly tacked in place. The coops with their occupants were then transported to covert the following

4 A pheasant catcher made of wire netting and hazel stakes, which is being 'fed' by the keeper.

5 A young conifer plantation. Woodlands of this kind are generally useless cover for game.

26 An old-fashioned feeding ride; if kept well strawed with clean, fresh straw, and regularly fed these will hold birds splendidly, but they should prefer-ably have a minimal overhead canopy of tree branches.

7   A cock pheasant coming well to the guns.

28   An excellent pattern of strip burning on a grouse moor.

29   A line of grouse butts, which well illustrates the need for care in marking safe arcs of fire so that you do not shoot 'down the line'.

morning soon after first light. They were left in place on the ride selected as the release site for an hour or so after arrival to settle down, then the front door of the coop was slid open sufficiently to allow the poults to emerge at will, one at a time. Later the door was removed altogether, and when in a day or two the poults had become reasonably acclimatized to their new surroundings, a start was made in phasing out the broodies and coops. A few of the latter were left for a considerable time to help hold the birds, while a nucleus of broodies would be released to accompany their charges in the woods with the same object in view and also to encourage them to go up to roost in the trees at night. A very similar system is used in transferring birds to covert from movable pens.

The Release Pen

Where there are no broodies, another method had to be devised. The basis of this has become the release pen. There are several aspects to this : the choice of a suitable site, the construction of the pen, the move of the poults to the pen and their subsequent management.

Warmth for wild creatures is contingent on three things—being dry, out of the wind, and in the sun. The site of a release pen should be well-drained, either by virtue of a natural slope, good artificial drainage or a combination of both. It should be sheltered from cold northerly and easterly winds, and preferably have a southern aspect. It should also have open spaces, clear of long grass or other low lush cover, in which birds can enjoy the sunshine; these open spaces play an important role as drying-out areas after rain and should amount to about a third of the total area of the pen.

There should be an abundance of reasonably dense, low cover to give shelter from winds and draughts at ground level. If necessary, natural resources in this respect can be reinforced with artificial windbreaks of straw bales. Shelter from rain should be provided at selected feeding and dusting points. Good low cover is also needed to give the newly released poults shelter from view; it should be appreciated that young pheasants fresh from a brooder are probably just as scared of the strange new world in which they find themselves as would be a clutch of novices, convent born and bred taken straight by bus to Piccadilly Circus and released there !

As the poults will have had the first four or five primary feathers of one wing cut prior to release, the cover in the pen must include plenty of low branching trees, such as elder, easily accessible for roosting. In fact a rather scrubby bit of woodland with a few tall trees sprinkled throughout it can make a splendid site for a release pen provided it fulfils certain other conditions. It should be beside, or part of, one of the main coverts in which the birds are to be held. Late stubble burning should not be likely to occur on any nearby fields. If there is kale or some other 'game' crop in the vicinity so much the better.

The size of a pen should be dependent on the number of birds it is to hold. Each inmate should be allowed an area of about 8 square yards of ground. In terms of perimeter length this means that a pen to hold 100 poults will have to be built with a circular perimeter 100 yards long; however, as the number of birds increases this ratio progressively decreases and 1000 birds will require a pen with a perimeter of only approximately 1000 ft, in order to allow each bird the stipulated area.

It has been found inadvisable in practice to place more than 1000 poults together in one release pen. To cater for a greater number a second pen should be built which, if expedient, can be in the same general area as the first, with a gap of not less than a hundred yards between the two. This arrangement has been found the most convenient from the point of view of management and control of losses in the event of a fox gaining entry to a pen or some other calamity occurring. The aim should always be to have as few release pens as possible, i.e. one for every thousand birds or part of a thousand. It is a mistake, other than in very exceptional circumstances, to distribute poults in penny packets in release pens dotted all around a shoot. Pheasants will spread out of their own accord; the problem is to keep them within the bounds of a shoot.

The pen itself should consist of a 2 in mesh wire netting wall at least 7 ft high fastened to 4 in diameter ash or larch poles at 9 ft spacing, and set about 18 in into the ground depending on the type of soil. A wall of this height will require two 4 or 5 ft wide rolls of wire netting. The bottom of the lower roll should either be firmly pegged down or a 9 in flap turned outwards and buried; on hard, stony ground the former ought to suffice but on softer ground the latter is recommended. The bottom of the upper roll of wire netting must be securely fastened at short intervals to the top of the lower roll, to prevent foxes, feral cats and other creatures forcing an entry, which if the netting is slackly mounted and ill-secured along the junction between the rolls they will easily be able to do. Any surplus netting over the height of 7 ft should be turned outwards to form an anti-fox fringe. The gateway should be soundly constructed, so that the actual gate is a good fit, and be secured by a bolt at top and bottom and a padlock and hasp in the middle. Any trees or branches overhanging the fence should be cleared or cut back.

There are two schools of thought about providing anti-fox grids at ground level in the fence to allow poults pursued by dogs or predators to run back inside. Some shoot owners maintain that a fox which can find a few potentially easy victims outside a pen is unlikely to bother with the more difficult task of trying to force

Fig. 65 An anti-fox grid built into the wire netting fence of a release pen

The grid should be built of stout wire, each square being $3\frac{1}{2} \times 3\frac{1}{2}$ in. The wire netting baffles, to guide in panic stricken birds fleeing from a pursuer, are essential. Note the wire netting funnel on the inside.

an entry to get at the birds inside it. They do not therefore bother with this refinement. However, for those who think differently a funnel entrance with a $3\frac{1}{2}$ in anti-fox grid made of stout wire over its mouth and wire mesh baffles to guide the fleeing birds into it is easily constructed and one is depicted in Figure 65.

When the time comes actually to transfer the 6–7 week old poults from brooder to release pen they should be given as little cause for alarm as possible. A factor in assisting acclimatization on arrival will be to transfer the feeders and drinkers with which they have become familiar in the brooders to the pen. A wicker laundry basket or wooden crate makes a suitable conveyance for the poults, the latter being the easier to clean after use.

The Release

The release point selected in the pen should be well screened and give immediate access to low cover. The lid of the crate or basket should be propped open sufficiently to allow the birds to emerge easily. The back of the bottom of the basket should also be propped up to assist their exit. The poults should be left to move out into cover in their own time; they may well take ten or more minutes. They should on no account be hurried. Each crate-load of birds should be released at a different point in the pen, so that they are evenly spread throughout the whole area of low cover. Irrespective of the number of birds being released, times of arrival should be staggered so as to help them to settle in tranquilly. Thus in a thousand-bird pen the poults should be released into it in batches of 250 at 48 hour intervals. With smaller numbers, the batches can be reduced to three; and with two hundred or less, to two.

If the release goes smoothly and the site for the pen has been well chosen, the poults should start going up to roost on their first night without any trouble.

If the birds in a release pen are to be hand-fed on a strawed ride, this must be done regularly every day at the same time, the keeper announcing his arrival by whistling the birds up in the traditional manner. If daily hand feeding is impracticable, adequate hopper feeding must be arranged instead. A supply of drinking water is essential for reared birds in covert.

About a fortnight to three weeks afterwards, poults will start to fly out of the pen, numbers increasing as more come into moult, shed the stumps of their cut primary feathers, and grow new ones. To retain the birds in the coverts where they are wanted, these should be kept free from disturbance and adequate feeding arrangements must be made. Finally I can only stress once again —the more pheasants it is desired to hold in a given woodland, the better its holding cover must be. Pheasants are inveterate wanderers and, unless their needs in respect of cover are really well catered for, no amount of walking-in will stop them from seeking more congenial conditions elsewhere. We are in danger of forgetting that good habitat means more wild birds with better chances of breeding success, and therefore less need for reared birds, resulting in a substantial saving in the running costs of our shoots and in all probability better shooting as well.

Wing-tagging poults before they go to the release pen provides a means of checking on their future movements, on the ratios of reared to wild birds shot, and other information. It is strongly advocated by the Game Conservancy. Unless a shoot owner/ manager and his keeper are of a genuinely inquiring turn of mind, have definite information which they are prepared to take the trouble to collect, and intend to persevere with the scheme for a sufficient number of years to make it worthwhile, it is merely a form of lip service to science and a complete waste of time. But where it is properly organized, and intended to serve a useful purpose in promoting better shooting, wing-tagging is to be encouraged.

CHAPTER SIXTEEN

PHEASANTS: SHOOTING

Walking Up

THERE are those who consider that shooting walked-up
pheasants is no sport at all. In my view this does less than
justice to the many good rough shoots which show excellent
sport with pheasants. Walked-up birds may not make as big claims
on marksmanship as well-shown driven birds, but they often offer
a great deal in the way of dog work and fieldcraft to enable a
gun to get a shot at all, which more than compensates for any
less exacting demands on simple shooting prowess. Also there are
times when birds come just as high and fast as the best at any
covert shoot. My gamebook records a number of such occasions
which have provided really exciting shooting.

A pheasant blundering up at one's feet in a field of roots may
look as big as a turkey and the easiest target in the world. Yet
it is not only indifferent shots who have been seen to miss handsomely with both barrels, and be left gazing in utter disbelief as,
with a contemptuous wiggle of its tail, another cock pheasant has
sped on its way unscathed. A keen shot of my acquaintance used
to denounce the walking-up of pheasants in colourful terms; but
I discovered that in practice he was rarely able to hit such birds.
They say everyone has his own particular hell, and I feel sure
this man's was the prospect of being a permanent walking gun
in a covert shooter's paradise!

To obtain good sport from walked-up pheasants the same care
and forethought are necessary in management and organization
as with partridges. This is often not well appreciated. Some people
seem to think pheasants will always be where they are wanted,
when they are wanted, and will fly how they are wanted, irrespective of such considerations as weather, the clearance of crops and
so on. They move off from the meet talking at the tops of their
voices, and as they line out on arrival at the first beat, dogs are
whistled up and shouted at while guns to flank or head the cover

keep up a merry chatter as they move into position. This is
followed by general dismay and bewilderment when twenty
minutes later they have drawn a blank!

Even in woodland the human voice will carry at least a hundred
yards, and over a field of roots or kale considerably further. The
mere sound of it serves as a warning to every pheasant to move
off elsewhere and this they will do. On the other hand, if pheasants
are surprised at close quarters in cover, they will usually seek to
escape detection by lying low and letting the danger pass.

In making plans to walk up pheasants, three basic factors
should therefore be taken into account :

a Having regard to the weather, crops and other circumstances,
the places where the birds are most likely to be found.

b How these places can best be approached and arrangements
completed without prematurely alarming the birds.

c How the cover can be beaten out thoroughly, so that birds
are not walked over, and provide the best sport.

Until the chill winds and frosts of winter drive pheasants to
the shelter and warmth of the woods they will prefer to roam
the fields by day and roost wherever the fancy takes them at night.
Thus it is on the stubbles, in the roots, hedgerows and other open
cover that those who seek wild pheasants in October and early
November are likely to find them. Walking up pheasants on these
autumn days should be planned on a somewhat similar basis to
that on which partridges are tackled, that is the birds should be
worked from the outside fields and hedgerows into some more
centrally-placed cover. Pheasants always tend to fly back to their
home wood, so when shooting the march, a gun should be well
forward on that flank to deal with any 'visitors' going home. Also
unless a rough shoot is richly endowed with woodlands it is a
mistake to beat out a main covert too late in the afternoon as this
will disperse the birds to the boundaries at a time when they ought
to be returning to roost.

When guns line out for a beat they should do so with as little
commotion as they can and keep their dogs at heel. A gun or guns
to head a beat should take up position as quietly and unobtrusively
as possible.

Dogs can be invaluable in helping to beat out cover, but they
must be under proper control and not work too far ahead of the

guns. I do not propose to attempt to argue which breed is the best for the rough shooter; I have seen Springer Spaniels, German Shorthaired Pointers, Labradors, Cocker Spaniels and Golden Retrievers which have all been admirable workers and would face the most punishing cover; equally I have seen others of each breed which would have been far better never let out of their owner's car. My own choice of dog for rough shooting would be one of the first two named breeds, but both require firm, competent handling if they are to deliver the goods, and not everyone is willing or able to keep their dog sufficiently in hand to enable it to work accordingly.

Beats must be tailored in size to suit the number of guns and beaters. They must not be too wide, and the denser the cover, the closer the spacing between individuals in the line will need to be if it is to be beaten out thoroughly. In more open cover, such as root fields, a common fault is to go too fast, which means birds are walked over and flush behind the beat. However easy the going, the line must make good its ground methodically and this can only be done if a nice steady pace is set. In really dense cover, every patch of brambles, etc., will need investigation; a few taps with a stick on the top of a thicket may only encourage a pheasant to lie lower; the end of a stick should be inserted at the bottom of any such cover and be rattled around briskly.

By December and January much of the cover from which pheasants could be hunted up earlier in the season will have died back and they will be found mainly in the better furnished woodlands, shelter belts and copses. Shooting should not go on too late in the day, or birds may be hindered from going up to roost; the right time to stop is about 3.30 pm. Also the same ground should not be shot over too frequently; in these last two months of the season once a fortnight is quite often enough. Too much disturbance of any kind will merely drive pheasants to seek quieter quarters elsewhere.

Taking Walking-up Shots

I have already indicated how easy it is to miss a straightforward shot at a walked-up pheasant. There are usually two reasons for this; firstly, the commotion the bird makes as it flushes flusters the shooter; his instinctive reaction is to shoot quickly in case it escapes; as a result he shoots too soon. Secondly, on a nice dry day, a pheasant in good fettle makes a quick getaway, at the start of which it usually climbs steeply, so that the over-eager gun almost invariably shoots under it.

The right way to take these shots is to pause, adopt the correct stance with the feet, simultaneously bringing the gun to the 'ready' position. Then fix your eyes on the bird. It will probably follow a course something like that depicted in Figure 66, i.e. it will quickly gain height and then follow a level path. When it is about 30 yards away is the time to mount the gun and shoot, being careful to bring the stock up to the cheek and not to bob the head down to meet it which will cause the shot to go low; this will leave plenty of time before the bird is out of range for a face-saving second barrel if required. It is not a difficult shot but it does need to be properly judged; if it isn't and the gun is just whirled up and fired a first barrel miss under bird A, as depicted by line A in Figure 66, is likely to be followed by a miss above and behind bird B, as shown by line B, due to over-correction, and failure to realize how the line of flight has flattened out.

This, then, is the classic shot at walked-up pheasants, with which so many a youngster is confronted the first time he takes the field in their pursuit. There are, of course, many others with which he

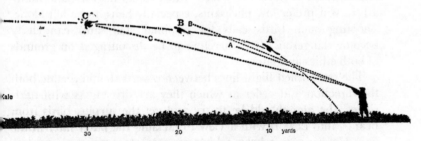

Fig. 66 Shooting walked-up pheasants

When a pheasant is flushed from low cover it usually climbs rapidly as with bird A, and the tendency is to shoot under it, as with shot A. It will then flatten out, as bird B has done, and probably be missed behind, as has happened with shot B. Both these shots have been taken too close; let such birds level out in flight, and shoot them at around the 30 yard mark, as in the case of bird C and shot C; this will allow plenty of time for a second barrel, if needed.

will have to learn to deal, but none quite so galling to miss or so special to this sort of shooting.

Covert Shooting

The management of driven pheasants, generally known as covert shooting, calls for much more elaborate arrangements. Ability to show high, fast-flying birds depends chiefly on two factors, namely competent covert management, which has been dealt with in the previous chapter, and taking advantage of natural topographical features so that birds can be flushed from high ground in order to fly over guns stationed in low ground. Actual presentation of the birds to the guns is a matter of good beat organization and it is then up to the guns to prove themselves sufficiently capable shots to make a good bag.

In planning a day's covert shooting there are a number of factors to be borne in mind. The first is to be clear as to your aim; this should be to produce a sufficient number of well shown birds to give the guns an excellent day's sport. I cannot emphasize too strongly that quality plays just as big a part in this as quantity. The guns for their part should appreciate that, although a host and his keeper will like to see a good bag made, it is a sporting occasion, not a hired assassins' benefit! A gun is not expected to shoot every bird which comes his way, and many a host will prefer low pheasants, especially hens, to be left alone. Shooting such birds calls for minimal skill, and can easily become dangerous. It is therefore to be discouraged on grounds of both ethics and safety.

The established flight lines between coverts should dictate both the direction and order in which they are driven. As with partridges, the aim should be to try and get the surplus birds from beat A into beat B with a view to tackling the latter later in the day. However, two beats which are very close together, say two sections of a wood separated only by a ride, may pose a special problem due to the effects of the disturbance caused in the second part, when the first is being shot; but a situation of this kind can usually be satisfactorily resolved with a little judicious experimenting. But how the various problems posed by individual beats can be solved can probably best be illustrated by an example.

A typical covert shoot situation, based on ground I know, is shown in Figure 67 (not to scale). The 'High Wood' is the main

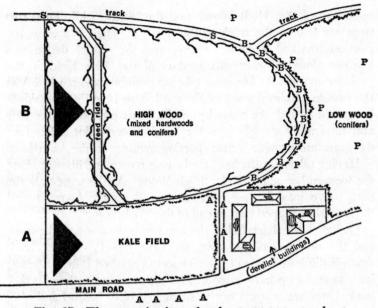

Fig. 67 The organization of a beat at a covert shoot
(A full description is given in the text.)

feature. It is about 50 acres in extent and rises sharply from the
track at the eastern end to form a plateau, which shelves gently
down to the 'Kale Field' on the southern side, and thence to the
main road. To the north of this wood the ground falls away
steeply beyond the track to a river. To the east of the 'High
Wood' is the 'Low Wood', which is quite an extensive spruce
plantation, with trees now about 15 ft high. The 'High Wood'
is good pheasant cover, several hundred birds being released in
it each year. Those which flush in the region of the top contour
give the guns at B some really testing shots.

The 'Kale Field' is about 10 acres in size, the top half being
kale, and the bottom half roots. A strip of kale is also sown in
some years right down the western boundary of 'High Wood'.
There are some good woodlands for pheasants away to the east
of 'Low Wood' and there is a big covert about 400 yards south
of the main road, echeloned back a little to the west in relation
to 'High Wood'.

The beat is conducted in three phases. First a sweep is made
across the 500 yards of fields and rough ground up to the western

boundary of the 'High Wood' and the 'Kale Field'. Then two stops are left on the track to the north of 'High Wood' in the positions marked S on the figure, and the rest of the beaters line out along the western boundary of the 'Kale Field' in the positions marked A. The guns take up positions also marked A at the eastern end, and south of the road. This is really a blanking-in operation and the majority of the birds put out of the kale and turnips fly straight into the 'High Wood'. But a few face the guns and provide a nice sporting overture to the main beat.

Having taken out the kale, the beaters return and line out along the western boundary of the 'High Wood'. At the same time the guns move into the positions marked B on the figure, round the horseshoe-shaped eastern end of the 'High Wood'.

Owing to the sharp fall of the ground to the north of the track and the thickness of the cover in 'Low Wood', marking birds down is difficult. Some of the pickers up, marked P in the figure, have to stand up fairly close behind the guns, and others further back. Guns are warned not to shoot low birds behind and also, because of the hillside in front, to be careful when taking shots at any but high birds after the beaters appear on the crest.

The two stops at S join the beat, and move down with it. A walking gun comes down the southern flank in the 'Kale Field', a little ahead of the beaters, and stop short of the first gun, B.

This beat produces some really first class birds, heading high and fast for the covers beyond 'Low Wood'.

Beat Organization

Beaters, irrespective of whether they are blanking in or tackling a main covert, must proceed slowly and methodically. They should not talk or shout, except to pass on any necessary instructions from the keeper in charge, who is the only person who has a speaking part in the proceedings. They must keep in line and evenly spaced. Having been lined out by the keeper, they must not then congregate together in twos and threes for a chat whilst awaiting the signal to start the beat. A keeper should exercise needful control with a minimum of shouting.

Some estates allow dogs to work with the beaters, others do not. In Scotland, dogs are more often seen in this role than in England, but this may be because Scottish keepers seem to me as a rule better dog handlers than their English counterparts. Any dogs so employed must be kept steady and under firm control.

Sometimes to prevent birds escaping to an open flank, sewelling —bits of coloured cloth tied at intervals along a long cord—is set up on hazel or ash sticks pushed into the ground so that the cord is about 2 ft high, and a stop is employed to keep gently tugging one end, so that the coloured cloth strips keep dancing about and the birds are scared to run past them. An instance in which such a device might well be used is along the track to the north of 'High Wood' in Figure 67 by the more easterly of the two stops marked S. Sewelling can also be used to help to make pheasants flush where there is a lack of suitable cover.

When a flushing point is reached, a considerable number of birds may be milling around in the area. If several of them take wing simultaneously at intervals down the line, the example may prove infectious and far too many flush at once for the guns to be able to deal with them. In such a situation the keeper in charge should halt the beat and, while the rest keep up a gentle tapping with their sticks, should himself go forward quietly and flush a few birds here and there, so that a bouquet of about half-a-dozen pheasants at a time is sent over the guns. When the number in the flushing area is sufficiently reduced in this way, he can order the beat to resume and the covert be taken out to the end.

Shooting Driven Pheasants

Turning now to the actual shooting of driven pheasants, the first thing every gun should do on arrival at his peg is to establish where it is, and is not, *safe to shoot*. His host, or whoever sees him to his place, should ensure that he is told everything he needs to know in order to shoot safely. But this does not absolve a gun from the responsibility of satisfying himself that he is fully informed in this most important respect.

Some people allege that if driven pheasants are shot properly they should be killed well in front and not fall behind the shooter. In my opinion this is absolute nonsense.

The majority of driven pheasants shot in Britain are probably no more than 60 ft high and so qualify as merely middling high. Such a bird is shown at E in Figure 68; when it arrives over a mark on the ground 35 yards in front of the shooter, it will be just within his maximum effective range of 40 yards. If he lets

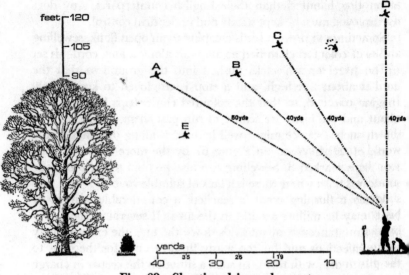

Fig. 68   Shooting driven pheasants

When shooting genuinely high pheasants, it is most important to allow the birds to come well in before the shot is taken, or they will be out of range. Even the 60 ft high bird, E, will offer a 30 yard shot, which is a very fair range, when it is over the 22 yard mark on the ground.

it come in closer, to over a mark on the ground 25–20 yards in front of him, it will still give him a shot at 30 yards range, which many would consider a reasonably long shot.

Really high birds *must* be allowed to come well in before they are shot at, or they will be out of range. Also to assist in killing them cleanly the shooter must fix his eyes firmly on the head. In my estimate any bird at 90 ft or over counts as genuinely high. In Figure 68, the bird at A is flying at 90 ft but is 40 yards out from the shooter and so is at an actual range of 50 yards. It will not be until it is over the 26-yard mark on the ground in front of him that it will be within 40 yards range, as depicted by bird B. Similarly the higher bird at C in the figure will need to be over the 19-yard mark on the ground before it is within 40 yards shooting range, while the ultimate 'Gabriel', marked D, will need to be right over the shooter's head to be within this range.

In tackling these high birds it is therefore quite wrong to

attempt to shoot too soon, and equally the 'ready' position should
not be adopted prematurely. It will be much more profitable to
relax and watch for a moment a fellow gun dealing with a bird,
and so gain an idea of their speed.

The pace at which high birds are travelling is very deceptive
until they have come well in and the eye can properly assess it.
It is invariably much faster than it appears at a distance. I have
mentioned in Chapter 4 that premature gun-mounting is one of
the main causes of high pheasants being missed behind, and I
would stress it again. If the shooter starts to mount his gun too
soon he will do so in a leisurely fashion which appears commen-
surate with the speed at which his target is approaching. He will
suddenly realize he has misjudged the speed and that, instead of
his gun muzzles overtaking the target, the reverse is happening;
by then it will be too late to remedy the situation! To provide
the impulsion to give the requisite 'overthrow' for these high shots,
the gun must be moved really sharply from the 'ready' position
into the shoulder and the trigger pulled without hesitation on first
aim; the slightest check in the rhythm is fatal. High pheasants
call for exceptionally accurate shooting, but this must not be
thought of in terms of 'aiming', as in rifle shooting, but in those
of the finesse with which the gun is mounted and fired. Really
well-rehearsed, polished gun mounting is the key to success.

But even the finest shots are fallible and there will always be
some birds which are not quite hit fair and square, and in consequence carry on to fall some way behind the line. It is
an important aspect of organization to ensure that there are
adequate pickers-up in attendance at a shoot. But however alert
they are and however excellent their dogs, it may not be possible
in the time available, or for other reasons, to find all such birds
which fall well behind the line at the end of a drive. It used to
be the accepted thing that there was a pick-up the day following
a big shoot to make sure that any cripples which had previously
escaped detection were retrieved. Nowadays this routine is not
always as strictly adhered to as it used to be, and still ought to be.

Being able to show and shoot genuinely high pheasants calls for
expert management and marksmanship. These two attributes do
not always go together. But anyone who can make just claim to
both has indeed earned a distinguished place for himself among
the shooting men of his day.

CHAPTER SEVENTEEN

GROUSE : NATURAL HISTORY

Introduction

THE Red Grouse, *Lagopus scoticus*, is indigenous and unique to the British Isles. Some claim that Ireland has a distinct sub-species. But as stories abound in that country of importations from Scotland and Yorkshire in the last century and the early years of the present one, the authenticity of this seems questionable.

The colouring of the plumage of grouse in Britain varies extensively. The real 'red' form is found mostly in the Western Highlands and Islands, also in Cumberland and Wales. In the east of Scotland, Durham and Yorkshire a darker bird of a handsome Titian bronze colour predominates, while in the north of Scotland, parts of Perthshire, Dumfriesshire and Yorkshire birds with white ticking on the tips of the feathers of the breast and belly are common. There is considerable overlapping of these various forms but, generally speaking, hens tend to be slightly lighter plumaged than cocks, and both are paler plumaged in summer than winter. Unlike partridges and pheasants, the legs of grouse are feathered. The cocks are easily distinguished from the hens by the striking scarlet wattle over the eye. They are essentially birds of moor and hill, being normally found at altitudes of from 500 to 2500 ft. However, there are places where they exist at sea level, and others where they may be discovered at heights of up to 3500 ft. As may be surmised, to survive in such circumstances the grouse is a hardy creature.

The cock is slightly bigger than the hen. Body weight varies with the time of year, but a healthy, well-grown cock in August should weigh about 24 oz and a hen in similar condition 21 oz. The length of an adult male from tip of beak to end of tail is about 15 in, the hen being around 1 in less. Wing span is approximately 18–20 in.

As will be further explained in the next chapter, grouse are territorial birds. In November they start to pair. Although early snowfalls may make it seem that the birds revert to packing, it is probable that these seeming packs are merely paired birds congregating together in such available areas as are clear of snow, in order to feed.

Breeding and Growth

The hens start preparing their nest in March. This is a hollow scraped in sheltered ground, sparsely lined with grass, moss or heather. A young hen in good fettle will lay about ten eggs. Clutches numbering 12–17 eggs have been recorded but are rare, and an older hen will normally lay a smaller clutch of six or so. Incubation is by the hen only and lasts for 20–24 days. Provided rain or snow does not obliterate a nest, fertility can usually be reckoned at 100%. Unless bad weather intervenes, the hatch spans a comparatively short period comprising the latter part of May and the early part of June, the peak being in the last week of May.

Grouse chicks feather up very quickly, and by three weeks of age possess all their basic flight feathers and are well on the wing. To enable them to do this a nutritious diet is essential. Although insects contribute a significant part of their food, this is on a smaller scale than in the case of young partridges. Probably of more importance is the quality of the available heather. Although the cock grouse continues in attendance on the hen and her brood, it is primarily in a protective capacity and brooding in the early days is entirely by the hen. The chicks reach maturity in about twelve weeks.

The principal food of grouse is the ling heather, but they will also, at appropriate times of the year and according to availability, eat a variety of berries, such as blaeberry, crowberry, bog cranberry and cloudberry, the flowers and seeds of various grasses and rushes, and the gleanings of oat stubbles.

The Covey

The family group, or covey, usually remains together as a unit until some time in September when it breaks up, and what is known as 'packing' starts. The reason for this is that the cocks begin disputing for territories. These are assumed by the strongest and most aggressive males, and in October/November there is a complete reshuffle of all the previous year's territories on a moor,

H

and those for the coming year are taken up. The hens selected by the cocks with territories pair off with them, and the remaining birds on a moor, which do not breed, pack together in groups of males and females respectively, and constitute the surplus population of the moor. If this surplus is not accounted for by shooting, it simply dies away from starvation and other causes. By the following spring any surplus has been totally eliminated, apart from a few grouse fortunate enough to fill any gaps which occur through misadventure in the ranks of the territorial birds.

Distribution

The red grouse is widely distributed throughout the moorlands of Scotland, those on the eastern side of the country being the most prolific. This is partly because the heather grows better there in the drier climate, and also because the moors are more naturally fertile as in many instances they are situated over a limestone sub-stratum. Grouse are found as far north as the Orkneys, but not in the Shetland Islands. In England, some Yorkshire moors sustain the highest grouse populations in Britain, and there are also excellent moors elsewhere in the other northern counties. Grouse are reasonably abundant on some Welsh moors. They have been successfully introduced on Exmoor, but other attempts to introduce them to moorlands in southern England have failed in the course of a few years.

It is not always properly understood that land which is suitable for grouse is of little worth for anything else except the limited grazing of cattle and sheep. The presence of grouse is in no way prejudicial to the latter and operations to encourage high grouse populations in fact enhance the grazing value of the land. The failure to grasp this essential truth has led to the decline of certain grouse moors in the Western Highlands and, among other acts of folly, has been a decisive factor in ruining the grouse moors of Southern Ireland, on some of which good bags were made regularly in the years prior to 1922.

CHAPTER EIGHTEEN

GROUSE MOOR MANAGEMENT

Introduction

F ROM a practical shooting man's viewpoint quite the most informative textbook on the subject is still the report entitled *The Grouse in Health and in Disease*, published in 1911 by the Committee of Inquiry which was set up in 1904 under the chairmanship of Lord Lovat. Although the Grouse Unit of the Nature Conservancy, which started work in 1956 and is still in being at the time of writing, has contributed quite extensively to our scientific knowledge of grouse and their behaviour, it has not added anything of particular significance to the precepts of good management proposed in 1911. It may be argued that in some respects these recommended doing the right things for what now appear to have been the wrong reasons; but for those concerned with practical management rather than the accumulation of scientific data this is largely academic.

There are four main aspects to good grouse moor management :

a Management of the heather.
b Drainage.
c Predator control.
d Organization of shooting.

The management of grouse is a very different proposition from that of partridges and pheasants. Creating high grouse populations depends solely on good management of habitat and shortcomings in this, or havoc caused by the weather, cannot be repaired by stocking up with a few hundred more reared birds. Also, although various attempts have been made at winter feeding, grouse do not readily respond to communal feeding except in times of dire need, as for example during and after heavy snow. So it is impracticable to give medication and antibiotics in food or water in order to try and control outbreaks of disease, as can often be done in the case of pheasants.

227

But before discussing these aspects of management there is one factor which casts such a long shadow over everything else to do with grouse that it must be disposed of first. It is what is known as 'grouse disease'. This is generally considered synonymous with strongylosis, but recent scientific evidence casts doubt on whether this is always so. However, it is probably so near the truth that any divergence from it is of little practical consequence in actual moor management.

Grouse Disease

Strongylosis is endemic in grouse and periodically attains epidemic proportions. It is caused by the round-worm, *Trychostrongylus pergracilis*, which is a whitish-coloured, hair-like worm approximately half an inch in length. These parasites reside in the caecum, or blind gut, of a grouse, and burrow into the caecal wall causing a haemorrhage. Few birds are entirely free of strongyli and the number present in any one grouse can vary from tens to thousands, infestations of up to 13,000 having been found on autopsy. Sometimes apparently healthy birds, well up to weight and in seemingly good condition, are found to contain several thousand. But generally speaking the heavier an infestation, the weaker a bird will be and the more likely to be 'diseased'. The point at which infestation ends and disease begins is an imponderable and depends on the physical condition of each bird. As long as it has sufficient stamina to prevent the strongyli gaining the upper hand it will remain technically free of disease. But once body weight drops below a critical point, which is in effect one of no return, physical deterioration becomes rapid and death soon intervenes. So an adequate food supply on a moor which will sustain the grouse in good bodily condition is a potent factor in keeping the onset of disease at bay.

The female strongyle worm lays its eggs in the caecum and these in due course pass out of the bird's body in its droppings. Given suitably humid, mild atmospheric conditions the eggs will then develop and hatch within forty-eight hours. But in really dry weather they will remain dormant and eventually die. In cold weather the eggs can survive in a dormant state for several weeks and then germinate. The critical factor is moisture and lack of this is fatal.

When the eggs hatch, the tiny larvae either burrow into the

droppings or the moist earth, where the first stage in their development occurs. The metamorphosis which they undergo takes several
days. When they emerge in their new form, they climb the wet
stems of heather and install themselves in the crevices of the leaves
on the shoots, where they undergo a further transformation, or
moult, which involves the growth of a sheath. When this is done
the nematode is infective to grouse, and no further development
can occur outside the 'host' body. Moisture is once more necessary
to enable the larvae to climb the heather stem, but after it has
settled down amongst the leaves, it can survive for a long period
in dry conditions.

If at this stage a grouse eats the heather in which the nematode
resides, it passes by way of the gizzard into the caecum where it
undergoes a third and fourth moult to attain adulthood and
become reprductive, thus starting the whole cycle over again. But
the nematode may succumb in its host's gizzard. To grind up the
tough fibres of the heather, grouse prefer the sharp, hard frag-
ments of quartz when they seek for grit, and despite its protective
sheath of cuticle a nematode may not survive the passage through
the gizzard of a bird well equipped in this respect.

This brief outline of the life cycle of the strongyle worm should
make clear the advantages of well-drained grouse ground and good
supplies of quartz grit, in addition to the question of food supply,
in helping to counteract strongylosis. Equally, it highlights the
inherent disadvantage of moors in regions of high rainfall, such as
the west of Scotland and Wales.

Grouse Territories

Another consideration in moor management is the size of grouse
territories. On really first-class grouse ground there may in the
spring be a pair to every 5–10 acres and on good ground one to
each 10–15 acres, while on poor ground the density may be only
a pair to every 100 or more acres. It is almost no exaggeration to
say that heather is everything to a grouse in providing for its basic
needs of food and shelter. It has been found that young heather
has a far higher nutritional value than old and is always preferred by the birds themselves where available. But older, taller
heather is required for nesting cover, the shade it provides for
young broods, and the concealment it affords from winged predators, especially when grouse are in moult in July and early August.

Each territory should therefore have areas of heather in varying stages of growth.

Heather

The life cycle of heather is one of about 50 years, during which it goes through four distinct phases. These are :

(1) *Foundation*. In this roots are established and early growth occurs. It normally lasts from 3–6 years. By the end of it there will be an open sward of individual plants, each about 6 in high.

(2) *Building*. Growth continues and the sward becomes denser until the ground appears completely carpeted with heather. This lasts for about 10 years, and by the end of it the plants will be up to 3 ft high.

(3) *Maturity*. This phase also lasts for around 10 years. It is typified by the outward spread of the branches of the plants and the whole sward beginning to develop a ragged appearance. As shoots begin to die back and drop off, debris starts to accumulate on the ground.

(4) *Degeneracy*. This occupies approximately the last 25 years of the plant's life cycle. It is marked by a growing accumulation of debris on the ground and the appearance of pronounced gaps in the sward as well as by its increasing raggedness.

The progress of this cycle can be accelerated or retarded by a variety of factors. Thus the drainage or fencing-off of areas may hasten maturity. On the other hand heavy grazing by sheep or deer may perpetuate the building stage, an effect which biting northerly and easterly winds on exposed slopes can also have.

From the point of view of food, heather is at its most nourishing in the early foundation years; it then declines rapidly year by year in this respect, until at around 10 years old its nutritive value stabilizes. So from this aspect heather over this age serves no good purpose. Another point of relevance is that a grouse stands only about 12 in tall, and so in heather higher than this, the fresh green shoots will be out of the bird's reach.

The growth of heather on a grouse moor is regulated by burning, known in Scotland as 'muirburn'. The times of year when burning is permitted are laid down by law. In Scotland burning may take place from 1 October to 15 April, and in a wet season an extension is obtainable up to 30 April; on deer forests situated over 1500 ft above sea level a further extension can be obtained up to 15 May. In England and Wales the period during which heather may be burnt is from 1 November to 31 March. In Southern Ireland no limitation on heather burning is enforced. Large tracts of moorland are burnt by those with grazing rights throughout the breeding season and summer. The fires sometimes burn out of control for days on end. This has probably contributed more than any other single factor to the decline of grouse populations and their present day scarcity in that country.

The aim of muirburn should be to obtain a clean, quick burn which removes all the trash but leaves the butt of the mainstem, or stool, and does not kill the roots, so that regeneration will take place from shoots springing from the stool. If this is done properly, a carpet of new, young heather should have appeared within two or three years of burning. If the roots are killed because the fire has been too intense, regeneration will have to be from seed, which takes immeasurably longer.

Regeneration from the stool occurs most readily from heather in the building stage. With very mature and degenerate heather the debris on the ground literally adds fuel to the flames and increases the likelihood of too hot a fire and so of killing the roots of the heather. It may also result in the underlying peat catching fire. This is very difficult to extinguish. Heather of this kind is accordingly more difficult to burn successfully and, when it is, regeneration from the stool takes longer.

It has been found from observation of the behaviour of grouse that when broods, and even adult birds, are feeding in young, short heather they are reluctant to move out more than about 15 yards from the protection afforded by taller growth, so that they can quickly take cover should a winged predator or other danger threaten. It is therefore useless to burn large squares of heather as the central area will not be used by the birds. Burning should normally be in a pattern of narrow strips, 30–40 yards wide.

Ideally, the rate of growth of heather should dictate the rotation on which it is burnt and on good grouse ground if this was the only criterion it would be one of about ten years. However, other factors, such as the weather, availability of manpower and materials, etc, have to be taken into account as well. It has been found that in the period during which burning is permitted the weather is only suitable on an average of twenty days. One team of men can burn a maximum of 20 acres in a day. It has therefore come to be recognized that the shortest practicable rotation on which heather can be burnt is one of about 16 years.

Muirburn

Muirburn is the most important operation in grouse moor management. Not only should it therefore be carried out as efficiently as possible, but at every possible opportunity. The respective merits of autumn and spring burning are sometimes hotly debated. But any such argument is really beside the point; a properly managed grouse moor should be burnt in due season whenever the weather allows. If burning is only undertaken between the New Year and 15 April it will normally be impossible to burn the requisite acreage, and the penalties of underburning a moor are far graver and more sure to follow than those supposedly likely to accrue from autumn burning.

All muirburn should be done to a soundly conceived plan. Every beat will have a proportion of its territory, such as hill tops and exposed slopes where the heather is so sparse and the depth of soil over the rock so slight that it is best not to burn at all. There may also be patches of waterlogged ground, which either have not been or cannot be drained, usually known as 'flow' ground, and on which the heather is so poor and stunted that they can be left out of the ordinary rotation and only burned, if at all, in exceptionally dry years. As with pheasant cover, priority should always be given to the best grouse ground; if there is bad weather in the burning season it will be quite difficult enough to burn the correct acreage of this without bothering with ground that will never give a comparable reward for the time and effort expended on it.

Ideally burning should take place in fine weather with a light breeze, when the heather is dry but the ground damp. This will give the quick, clean burn already described, avoid the danger of the fire becoming too hot, and so of setting the peat alight, and also of burning so quickly that it gets out of control. All fires should be burnt towards a firebreak. This may be a natural feature such as a road, ravine or stream, or ground previously burnt. Where there are no firebreaks, or insufficient on a moor, they will first have to be created by burning, so that there is an adequate pattern of them to contain any danger from 'runaways' in subsequent strip burning.

It has been found convenient in practice to burn in strips of 500–700 yards in length, which if they are 30–40 yards wide means that each 'fire' covers about 4 acres of ground. In favourable weather conditions, one team of men should be able to burn four or five such strips in a day. This team should consist of at least three men, and four is preferable, the beat keeper being in charge. The fire can be lit either by a torch of heather or newspaper, a paraffin burner, or flame gun. The first named, although it may sound a trifle old-fashioned, is usually perfectly satisfactory. Once the fire is under way, one man should move up along each flank to prevent it spreading sideways, while the other two should hold back so that they can obliterate any patches left burning at the rear of the advancing fire. For this purpose they are all best equipped with proper modern aluminium firebeaters with flexible heads. These are practically indestructible, unlike home-made besoms with a wooden shaft which if used particularly vigorously in a moment of crisis may break. It is advisable to have in reserve in the Land Rover several five-gallon knapsack fire extinguishers.

Weather can change quickly and unexpectedly on a moor. A wind may spring up suddenly and catch unaware those whose attention has been devoted to the fire. If this occurs one man from the team will need to go quickly to fetch the fire extinguishers. But with a three-man team the two left on their own while he is doing so may find the fire too much for them and be unable to prevent the start of a runaway. Another reason why a four-man team is preferable is that it is essential to be certain a fire is really out before the team leaves to start another one; with four men, one can be left behind to make good the final surveillance, while the other three men set off to start the next fire; to do this with only two men is to invite trouble. A four-man team is therefore not only an insurance against a fire getting out of control but also enables burning to be speeded up, which in an operation where time is of the essence, is the most crucial consideration of all.

Draining

In former times drains had to be cut by hand, and making them was simply a question of availability of manpower. Nowadays

H*

caterpillar tractors equipped with a suitable plough can do the job better and more economically. However, the origin of a burn or stream on a moor is often a spring, surrounded by an area of bright green grass which generates valuable insect life; because of the lack of proper drainage this may create a boggy area around it. In order to eliminate the bog but retain the advantages of the moist area immediately around the spring, it may be desirable to start the drain a matter of some yards from the source of the spring.

Flow ground is often a plateau between rising ground on either side, which a herringbone pattern of drains leading into either an existing stream or a main drain could convert into useful grouse ground. But where such ground is in a saucer-shaped depression it may be impracticable to drain. However, of the moors where drainage is genuinely impracticable, there are many where it could lead to a major improvement in grouse holding capacity if a well-planned scheme was put into effect. Nowhere is this more obvious than in the case of many moors in Southern Ireland.

Predators

The two predominant predators on a grouse moor are foxes and carrion, or hooded crows. Thanks to legislation which has now banned the use of the gin trap in Scotland, tackling both these creatures has become a major task for keepers, to whom the only effective legal method left is shooting with gun or rifle which is very time-consuming. Certain scientific gentlemen have asserted that predation has very little effect on grouse populations. However, those who have to deal with grouse moor management in practice claim the contrary and there is every reason to believe that they should know what they are talking about. In the spring when grouse are nesting, both foxes and carrion crows will quarter a moor relentlessly in pursuit of prey. By this time the surplus grouse of the preceding year have all died, so for every hen taken on the nest, or clutch of eggs destroyed, there is no replacement. It is easy to argue, as scientists do, that this destruction only represents a proportion of the birds that would anyway not be shot in the following season. But this is a law of diminishing returns, because, as will be explained in the next chapter, the fewer grouse there are to shoot on a moor, the smaller the *proportion* that in fact is shot. Predator control is therefore an important aspect of moor management, and it is essential that it is recognized as such.

Carrion crows usually roost in the woods on the fringes of a moor. They can be shot there as they flight in of a winter's evening, often in numbers running into hundreds, though once they realize their roost is under fire they will circle round well out of shot until darkness allows them to drop in undetected. The best way to deal with them is to mark their nests and shoot out these in the spring, at the same time dealing with such of the parent birds as one can. But, as already indicated, it is a lengthy process unless the keeper can get assistance.

The best time to tackle foxes is also in the breeding season, when the vixen has her cubs in a cairn, or elsewhere underground. This will require terriers and probably a rifle rather than a shotgun; it may also mean waiting out all night.

Wild cats, black-backed gulls, golden eagles and peregrine falcons are other predators. The first are of no concern except on moors north of the Great Glen, though their numbers and range appear to be increasing. Both species of black-backed gulls can, however, be real pests and should be dealt with accordingly. The golden eagle and peregrine are protected by law and, though they can take quite a heavy toll of grouse, their numbers are so comparatively small that predation by them is not normally a serious problem.

Heather Hazards

But, however good the management of a moor in all these basic respects the ultimate arbiter of fate is the weather. Heather suffers from what is generally known as 'frosting', i.e. frostbite, as in the case of a human being. Scientists may say that this is really a form of dehydration, and not strictly frosting, but as far as moor management is concerned this is merely playing with words; the outcome is that a part or all of the foliage of the heather, depending on the severity of the attack, is killed. The result is that it does not provide food for grouse in the following year, and a food shortage with consequent starvation occurs. This is liable to aggravate strongylosis and transform it from an endemic condition into a chronic disease.

Heather is also subject to attack from the heather beetle, which causes damage superficially similar in appearance to that of frosting. The heather beetle thrives in moist conditions and damage is most frequent on ill-drained ground and in wet seasons. It is most prevalent in mature heather. This pest is therefore best controlled by following the tenets of good management in properly burning and draining the ground.

The presence of sheep and cattle in reasonable numbers on a grouse moor is generally beneficial, though they can do extensive damage to young heather and in certain circumstances it may be necessary to take steps to prevent this. The existence of rabbits and blue hares is a very different matter; the former in particular can easily become pests, and where myxomatosis does not exert the needful control, trapping and snaring in the spring will have to be rigorously pursued.

Some owners and keepers maintain that strongylosis follows a seven-year cycle and there is evidence that the 'disease' seems to occur with about this sort of frequency. However, it is the weather and other such factors that exert the decisive influence in this matter. In the slightly unlikely eventuality of several successive years of good weather at burning time, in the breeding season, and in the summer, strongylosis might well be confined to local outbreaks instead of spreading in a wholesale epidemic.

On some moors bracken is a scourge. Where it gains a hold it suppresses and kills the heather. Until recently the only way to get rid of it was by cutting, which usually meant scything. But now a spray has been developed which is most effective and, if sprayed from the air, it is, despite the expense, a really efficient method of control.

New Ideas in Management

In recent years various new ideas in moor management have been tried out. Modern machinery, such as the 'Swipe' and different types of forage harvester, has been used to cut heather where burning has been held up owing to bad weather. Such machinery has only a limited application, confined to reasonably level stretches of ground, unencumbered by rocky outcrops. Although this achieves the object of cutting overgrown heather, it lacks the cleansing effect of burning, i.e. it does not destroy strongylosis nematodes or heather beetle larvae, also it leaves a great quantity of trash on the ground, which ought to be cleared. Attempts have been made to do this by baling, and then using the bales for winter feeding when the ground is snow-covered; these have not been very successful.

Trials have also been made in the use of fertilizers to stimulate the growth of heather. In certain cases this has resulted in a dramatic improvement in the heather, and in the grouse-holding capacity of the area concerned; but it is costly and the areas involved need to be fenced off to keep out sheep and cattle. This is a practice still very much in the experimental stage, the effect of which little is known. It is better not attempted by those concerned with ordinary moor management.

For many years it was considered impracticable to rear grouse. But in recent times advances in animal nutrition have enabled this to be done successfully. However, reared grouse develop two characteristics which make it virtually impossible to use such birds for restocking; they grow incredibly tame and take almost a season to become as wild birds. Unless they have access to heather from their earliest days, their gizzards become too soft to deal with such harsh fare when they are released on a moor and they die of starvation.

Conclusion

It will be seen from all the above that, although our knowledge of grouse and their habits is increasing, turning that knowledge to good account so that we can produce more consistent and bigger grouse populations is a very different matter, and the 'Midas' touch in this respect still eludes both the scientist and the practical grouse moor manager.

Meantime, although a well-managed moor will suffer from 'grouse disease' periodically along with those not so well-managed, it should reap its reward in the effects being less devastating, and recovery from them quicker; it will also in the long term be able to show far superior sport. But there remains the all-important question of how the shooting of a grouse moor should be organized, to which we must now turn.

CHAPTER NINETEEN

GROUSE SHOOTING

Introduction

WELL-SHOWN grouse provide the most exciting sport of all. There are several reasons for this. On a fine day the grandeur of the scenery and bracing air on a grouse moor combine to induce a feeling of special well-being in all concerned. The birds offer a rousing challenge to the guns. To send good birds over the butts calls for the exercise of greater skill and knowledge in the organization of a day's shooting than is the case with either partridges or pheasants.

Grouse, like both other birds, can be shot over dogs or by walking-up, as well as by driving. However, the breeding stock which a moor can carry is dictated by circumstances, such as the weather and state of the heather, over which management, even at its best, has only limited control. It is therefore entirely fruitless to try and increase that breeding stock by shooting lightly. On a properly developed, well-managed moor neither dogging nor walking-up will ever be able to account for anything approaching the actual shootable surplus of birds, which if not shot will die anyway of other causes, and increase the risk of disease on a moor. The only possible exceptions in principle to this are moors in some parts of the west and north-west of Scotland which are inherently poor grouse ground. So, enjoyable though dogging and walking-up can be, neither should normally be considered anything other than a pleasant 'fringe benefit' when the serious shooting of a moor is planned. As there are so few significant differences between dogging and walking-up grouse and pursuing the same forms of sport with partridges I do not propose to devote any more space to them in this chapter.

The first problem to be dealt with on some moors is that of accessibility. Some of the best grouse shots unfortunately suffer from the infirmities of age or injury which limit their mobility. It is useless having a first class beat on a moor which can only be

reached after a walk too long and rough for the 'veterans' of a
shooting party to accomplish in comfort. Every line of butts
should be reasonably accessible from a Land Rover. To achieve
this may require the building of additional, all-weather, motorable
tracks across a moor. This will obviate the need for ponies and
ponymen, which, although they lend a pleasing traditional touch,
are hard to justify nowadays on economic grounds, other than
in exceptional circumstances. However, a pony can get where no
Land Rover can, so on certain high moors, and in places where
there is also stalking, and possibly ptarmigan to be considered,
some ponies may still earn their keep.

Butt Construction

The construction of butts often leaves much to be desired. Nothing
is more irritating to the shooter, or potentially more dangerous,
than a badly designed and built butt. The floor of sunken butts
is sometimes allowed to become like a snipe bog into which the
waiting shooter slowly but remorselessly sinks; if he then attempts
to turn quickly to take a shot behind, he may find he is unable
to move his feet and has to save himself from falling over. Equally
unsatisfactory are duckboards or planks which have become
coated in slime, and to a man in studded brogues can resemble
a skating rink. A plastic cartridge case on the wooden floor of a
butt can prove no less a hazard than the proverbial banana skin.
Butts must be properly maintained and well constructed.

Grouse butts seem to come in all shapes and sizes; some are
built of stone, others of peat or old railway sleepers. Some are
round, others square, some H-shaped, and yet others consist of
just a front wall. Some are built on the ground, some partially
sunk, some fully sunk. The need for the last is normally rare and,
as they almost invariably have to be drained so as not to become
waterlogged, are best avoided unless absolutely necessary.

One of the aims of butts is to provide concealment for the
shooter, his attendants, dogs and trappings. In this connection
the experience of a friend of mine, a keen shot, who as a result
of an injury has only limited use of his legs, is of interest. He has
to shoot from a seat. He has found that by keeping still and not
moving until the grouse have come well within range he can sit
in front of the butt. It is only if he moves prematurely that birds
will swerve aside. I believe this has a wider application than is

generally recognized. Keepers love exhorting guns to keep down in a butt to avoid turning incoming grouse; it would be much more to the point if they were told to keep still and to ensure that their loader, girl friend or whoever else is in the butt did the same. So, although the simple concealment offered by a butt is important, even more so is the degree to which it masks movement. If this was more fully appreciated, I believe lines of butts could sometimes be more advantageously sited than they actually are.

The best concealment is clearly offered by round or square butts, and for this reason they are to be preferred, but with one major proviso. Round butts have no clearly defined front, and even if markers are placed in the top of the wall to indicate the limits of the safe arc of fire it is all too easy for a shooter who finds himself in the thick of things to lose his sense of direction and shoot straight down the line. Square butts are therefore the most satisfactory of all, and permit double drives.

The dimensions to which butts are built vary quite extensively. Taking the case of a typical square butt, the entrance should be in the middle of one side. The walls should be 4 ft 6 in high and sloped slightly inwards towards the top. The interior dimensions at ground level should be 6 ft × 6 ft. The thickness of the walls should be about 2 ft at the base, tapering to 1 ft 6 in at the top. Irrespective of whether stone or peat is the principal material used in their construction, the walls should always be topped with two or three layers of peat in order to prevent damage to gun barrels. As regards flooring, if the ground is well drained it may be unnecessary to make any special provision; but where it is necessary to do so, as usually in the case of semi-sunk butts, a floor of properly levelled and packed hardcore, through which water will drain, is preferable to duckboards or planking as it provides a better foothold and is more durable.

Where there are sheep on a moor, it is advisable to fence them out of the butts in the close season or they will use them for shelter, and can do a surprising amount of damage. A well-made grouse butt is shown in Figure 69.

Grouse Driving

Other considerations besides concealment affect the siting of butts. In order to appreciate the significance of these, it is necessary to

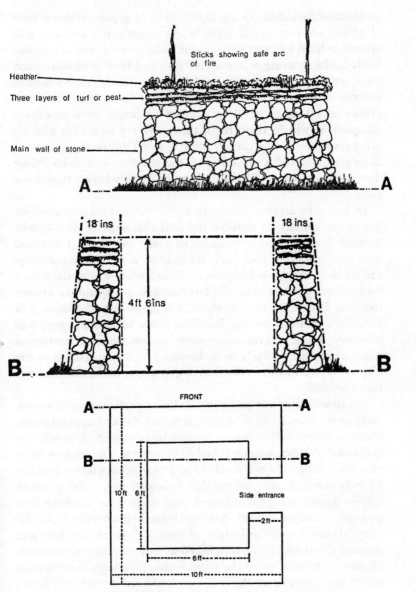

Sticks showing safe arc of fire

Heather

Three layers of turf or peat

Main wall of stone

A — — — — — — — — — — — — — — A

18 ins   18 ins

4 ft 6 ins

B — — —   — — — B

FRONT

A — — —   — — — A

B — — —   — — — B

10 ft   6 ft

Side entrance

2 ft

6 ft

10 ft

Fig. 69 A design for a square grouse butt

Butts of this kind can be built of stone or turves; if the former
is used the walls should be topped with three layers of turf to
prevent damage to gun barrels.

understand something of the flight habits of grouse. When coveys of grouse are put on the wing by the beaters, the majority will appear to head for, and settle in, the same general area of a moor. Early in the shooting season such flights will be of little more than a minute's duration, though from then onwards this time will soon become extended to nearer two minutes. If on a still day a grouse cruises along at a speed of around 45 mph, as is normally accepted, it will in these flight times cover $\frac{3}{4}$ of a mile and $1\frac{1}{2}$ miles respectively. It is usually possible to get grouse to go forward if they are flushed a second time, but if attempted a third time they almost always 'refuse' and swing back whence they have come.

In order to account for as many of the shootable surplus of grouse on a moor as possible the majority must be shot before packing limits the opportunities to make big bags. Therefore, even in a so-called 'bad' year, the rule on a well-managed moor should be to shoot hard and early. If, in such a season, the young birds of the year are generally late-hatched it is a mistake to wait too long before starting to shoot. Cheepers in mid-August will contribute nothing to the breeding stock of a moor and will probably die of starvation or some disease within a matter of weeks. They are unlikely to make much of a contribution to the bag and it is a waste of time delaying shooting unduly in the hope that they will.

We should base our plans on the flying performance of grouse early in the season. So we can reckon that the average maximum distance grouse will allow themselves to be driven on a still day is about two miles, accomplished in two stages. In order to intercept them a line of butts needs to be placed somewhere about the $1\frac{3}{4}$ mile mark. It also means that drives of over 3000 yards in length should not be attempted, and some may consider that generally speaking ones of 2500 yards are long enough. With this latter distance, provided there is only a light breeze blowing, upwind drives can be accomplished as easily as those downwind. However, on days when the wind is strong enough materially to affect the distances grouse will fly, it will mean they will travel further downwind and decidedly less far upwind. So the organization of the various drives will need to be modified.

If we take the case where the wind speed is half that of the grouse's speed, the distance the coveys will travel upwind will be halved, while that which they travel downwind will be half as much again. Thus, in the upwind drives, unless the beats are shortened only the birds flushed in the second half will reach the butts, let alone help to fill a subsequent beat, and in the downwind beats, although the birds will cross the line of butts all right, they may go on too far to fill a subsequent beat. This makes clear the need for shorter upwind drives in such conditions. Although it may sound something of a contradiction the same should apply to the downwind drives so that the birds are only taken one stage instead of two, and fill, instead of overflying, the next or subsequent beat.

To meet the need to adjust the lengths of drives in strong winds, the best course is often to interpose a new line of butts, but this must depend on consideration of all the factors involved in the overall organization of the shooting.

In high winds grouse favour sheltered ground and can most readily be driven to other sheltered ground. To try and drive them towards exposed slopes is to court failure. Except in extremes of weather grouse tend to follow a well-defined flight pattern, to which the coveys conform year after year. Generally speaking these established flight lines travel along the contours rather than across them. But however they go they will well repay study. It is this and the other factors already mentioned which should dictate where butts are sited every bit as much as the provision of concealment. I have at times shot from lines of butts which seemed to have been positioned with concealment as the sole criterion and the coveys have never come well to them. They have always left me with the impression that either the drive was just too long, the line of butts wrongly angled or some other fundamental factor had been misjudged. As with everything, the ideal in siting a line of butts is rarely attainable; in my view the least important and first consideration to be sacrificed should be concealment, but with this I know many experienced moor owners and keepers will disagree profoundly. However, I firmly believe it to be right, though of course concealment cannot be ignored altogether, and to take it to that extreme would be stupid.

There is one more consideration concerning the building and siting of butts; when grouse driving first became fashionable towards the end of the last century, butts, or shelters as they were then called, were often built 60 to 80 yards apart. It has come to be recognized that this is much too far, because coveys passing centrally between any two butts will not be properly within range until they are almost level with the line, which will encourage dangerous shooting. In order to observe the safety angles depicted in Figure 39 (page 98) the maximum permissible distance between butts is 56 yards. But it is generally recognized nowadays that the proper spacing is 40–45 yards. However, there are places on some moors where it is necessary to make an exception and site a butt, usually one of the flank ones, in splendid isolation from its fellows. I know of one such instance on a moor where I used to shoot and lucky indeed was the occupant of that butt as he usually enjoyed exceptionally good sport. With grouse a flank gun can often look forward to as good, if not better, sport than his fellows in the centre of the line, instead of being rather left out in the cold as is generally the case in covert shooting.

A typical day's grouse driving consists of five or six separate drives, the last of which is a repeat of the first, the overall plan being designed to get as many birds as possible back into the first beat for the last drive of the day. How this can best be put into effect on a moor depends largely on the shape of the ground and the principal features on it. Where practicable the plan should be based on a series of drives each comprising one side of a quadrilateral or pentagon, depending on how many there are. But where a moor is long and narrow or comprises only one main feature, which has length but little depth, it may only be possible to drive to and fro or the birds will be driven off the ground altogether. Where 'to and fro' driving is practised it may well be necessary to employ two teams of beaters in order to cut down the delay between drives. This is an added expense and another reason for not adopting this system unless no other is practicable.

Beaters and Beating

The duties of a beater are seldom given much thought. As far as many people are concerned, including some shooting men, they might be summarized as being simply to line out where he is told and then, when ordered by the keeper, to advance towards the sound of the guns, pursuant upon Napoleon's famous precept that no General who did so could go far wrong! But a great deal more is expected of a good beater and particularly so on a grouse moor.

Sometimes a line of beaters will move straight towards a line of guns, but there will often be occasions when it will have to move obliquely. A case in point is that of a cross-wind, when their line of advance may have to be into the eye of the wind and towards a party of flankers sited almost at right angles to the line of butts.

Moorland keepers seem to have a touching faith in the virtues of a crescent-shaped line of beaters and, if left to their own devices, will seldom rely on a straight line. The reason behind this appears to be that the beaters on the wings will be able to flank birds in. But in my experience this usually proves no more than a pious hope. Flanking is an art in itself, to which we will come in a moment; its success depends on achieving surprise at just the right moment. A flank beater who is in full view of a covey as soon as it becomes airborne up to three hundred yards away lacks this essential virtue from the start and the odds are therefore that he will fail in his purpose, as he usually does. It is my belief that greater use could profitably be made of straight lines of beaters, because it is the approach of what appears to be a continuous line which is a major factor in sending the coveys forward in the right direction. The broken nature of the ground on most Scottish moors means that, in order to achieve this effect, parts of the line may at times have to hold back while others press forward so that the whole line tops a ridge as one man. If this is not achieved and one or two men appear at one end of a ridge before the rest they can have exactly the same effect as flankers and turn coveys, possibly out of the drive. An alert beater should be able to spot where things are liable to go awry in this way and use his own initiative to adjust his pace accordingly.

Before a beat starts there are three points which should be appreciated by both guns and beaters. The first is that the sound of the human voice carries a long way on a grouse moor and if the guns engage in idle chatter coveys within earshot of the butts may hear them, run back down the beat and take wing at a critical moment when they are likely to attract others to follow them out of the beat. If this happens when birds are on the move in considerable numbers it may well mean the majority never face the guns at all and the beat is ruined. The second concerns a covey which decides to settle just out of range in front of the butts, usually early on in a drive. If allowed to remain it may distract other coveys into doing likewise and also when it later

takes flight it may lead others after it out of the beat. The answer
is to shoot at any such covey the moment it is seen to be about
to land, which will ensure it clears off before it can exert a
seriously misleading influence. The third is mainly of concern
to beaters. Grouse very quickly become used to the movement of
human beings on a moor, such as shepherds tending their flocks,
hikers and others. They will often therefore prefer to sit tight
when beaters approach, rather than take flight. So the more
beaters in a line the better, and they must work methodically
and not go too fast. However, on a well-populated grouse moor,
the flushing of one covey may start a chain reaction causing others
to follow suit, thus making their task easier. Conversely, in a bad
year when grouse are thinner on the ground, this is less likely to
occur and the task of the beaters is made that much harder. It
will also mean that in a bad year a smaller proportion of the
total number of birds on a moor will probably be flushed than in
a good one. Thus in the former the need for really efficient beating
is even more important than in the latter. Unlike covert shooting,
if beaters on a moor wish to make a certain amount of noise to
encourage grouse on their way, there is no reason why they
shouldn't. But thick heather needs to be beaten out just as
thoroughly as thick woodland cover. Every beater and flanker
should be equipped with a stout stick, about 4 ft 6 in long, to
which a white flag is securely fastened. This flag should be about
$2 \times 1\frac{1}{2}$ ft in size. Each person should be responsible for his or
her own, and seeing that it is kept clean, which will entail it being
regularly washed.

So the task of beaters on a grouse moor is not as simple as it
might at first sight appear. Coveys can easily be walked over by
someone whose heart is not in the job and, because of the longer
fields of view, an ill-timed appearance on a crest by one who has
not got his wits about him can easily turn birds out of a beat.
The need for an alert and conscientious team of beaters, well
briefed by the keeper in charge, is even more essential than in
covert shooting.

Flankers

The task of flankers is to turn birds which are about to fly out
of a beat back into it, so that they pass over the guns. A corollary
to this, which is not always equally well understood, is that birds

which are going forward satisfactorily of their own accord should be left alone, because if they are 'flanked' they may be diverted out of the beat. So flanking calls for both experience and good judgement. It is not a task which should be entrusted to the very young or very old. Flankers should be selected from the cream of the beaters and must be able to be relied on to take prompt and appropriate action on their own initiative.

The actual siting of flankers in relation to a line of butts is dictated by ground and weather. How exactly they should be placed in any given conjunction of circumstances should be decided on the spot. There is always a tendency to tuck flankers away on reverse slopes so that they are well concealed until the critical moment arrives for them to reveal themselves. This is fundamentally wrong because in order to do his job properly a flanker must be able to see everything that is going on. It is, for example, a misplaced effort to try and flank in a solitary bird if such an action is likely to turn a following covey out of the beat. So, although a flanker must remain out of sight until the right moment arrives for him to show himself, he ought to be on a forward slope where he can see exactly what is happening. This may mean he will have to lie low in scant cover, from which in due course he will have to spring to his feet; he will probably have to do this, not once, but several times during a drive. A competent flanker must therefore posses physical agility in addition to his other qualities.

If flankers are accompanied by dogs, as they sometimes are, these too must stay hidden with their masters. In this respect one always thinks of light-coloured Labradors and Springer Spaniels with a lot of white in their coats as being most likely to show up. However, a jet black dog is no less out of harmony with its surroundings in regard to colour, and black Labradors or flat-coated retrievers show up surprisingly vividly from the air and require to be just as carefully concealed as lighter-coated dogs.

Shooting Grouse

Although a blackcock will comfortably outstrip them in flight, grouse are generally, and deservedly, considered to be fast-flying birds. Shooting them is often bungled because people fail to appreciate this and start to mount their guns too late; as a result the incoming covey is on top of them before they are ready, all is confusion and two misses behind are recorded. A contributory factor in this is the difficulty of judging distances on a moor, which is aggravated when butts are placed on a reverse slope with only a short field of view to the front. But to a discerning eye even a moor has its distinctive features and it should be possible while waiting for birds to come forward to pick out an oddly shaped patch of heather, a prominent rock or a scar in the peat at an estimated 40 yards range over which one should shoot at one's first bird. Unlike pheasant shooting, the temptation is to start gun mounting too late instead of too soon and, unless the shooter provides himself with some means of judging distance, he will invariably be caught napping.

Grouse usually fly low over the heather. While waiting for the coveys to come forward many shooters gaze intently into the far distance. In consequence, when birds actually fly into view at close quarters they have difficulty in re-focusing in time and so further handicap themselves.

As a target the incoming grouse resembles a cricket ball; so the shooter's eye need only be fastened on it, not a particular part of it as in the case of a high pheasant. Then, if the gun is correctly mounted and the trigger pulled on first aim a kill should result every time. However, these fast, low incoming grouse do require very fine judgement and this is particularly so with slightly angled shots which, contrary to popular belief, are very easily missed in front.

As explained in Chapter 4, the shooter should keep his weight well forward in order to deal successfully with grouse. But this should not be exaggerated to the point where poise is sacrificed or the shooter will prejudice his ability to turn quickly for a shot behind.

Shooting grouse requires every bit as good co-ordination of hands and eyes as that of the tallest pheasants and I believe also a higher degree of mental alertness and physical awareness, which for me endow it with the extra special quality that makes it the supreme sport in Britain.

'Old Cock Grouse'

In conclusion there is one final aspect of grouse shooting to be disposed of. The shooting of old cock grouse at the back end of the season, in November and December, used to be strongly advocated as being beneficial to the breeding stock. As it is only the most dominant and aggressive cocks which are able to win territories for themselves on a moor I very much doubt if the premise on which this assertion is based is correct. Further, I do not know how it is possible to distinguish old from young cock grouse at this time of year until after they have been shot, nor have I ever been able to find a keeper, or other advocate of the system, able to explain how this is done. I believe therefore it is a practice which has no real place in good grouse moor management, and one which should be discontinued where it still survives as being more likely to do harm than good.

CHAPTER TWENTY

DUCK ON AN INLAND SHOOT

Introduction

THE wildfowler who pursues his sport on the estuaries and saltings often rather looks down his nose at those who rear and shoot duck on inland waters. The former is certainly the more challenging and exciting, but the latter can provide a shoot with a useful asset from which a lot of genuine good sport can be had. However, it does call for competent and imaginative management. If these qualities are lacking, reared duck can easily produce a sporting fiasco. To this extent therefore the wildfowler's reservations are justified.

The crux of the problem is that wild duck, i.e. mallard, are easy to rear and, unlike pheasants, will become exceptionally tame, have no urge to stray and, being natural gluttons, will eat so much that they grow too heavy to fly. But, people ask, does this ever really happen? One occasion when it did comes specially to mind.

As a picker-up I was asked to go forward when the guns were all in position to flush the duck off a lake as the keeper and beaters were otherwise employed. The lake was about an acre in size and surrounded by thick cover terminating in a broken fringe of reeds around the water's edge. There must have been over a hundred duck on the lake as my dog and myself made as dramatic an entrance as we could. Three genuine wild duck on the far side promptly took flight. A moorhen ten yards away executed a crash dive any submarine commander would have been proud of. But the bulk of the duck with one accord headed straight for us as fast as their paddles could carry them uttering ecstatic little quacks as they came. Thereupon, slightly disconcerted, I launched my dog. They took him for a lap of the lake still quacking excitedly among themselves despite a few well-aimed clods thrown into their midst as they passed me. Even one of the guns discharging two barrels across their bows failed to disturb the cheerful tenor of their progress. Realizing it was a clear case of no flying today I called my dog out. As he stood on the bank and shook himself, he looked at me as if to say, 'If that's your idea of a joke, count me out on the next one!'

If wildfowl are to become a serious addition to the attractions of a shoot there is a great deal more to it than just rearing a few mallard.

Natural History

Wild mallard are widely distributed throughout the British Isles. A resident pair is just as likely to be found on a fairly secluded farm pond as on the quiet reaches of a Hampshire trout stream or the dark waters of a Highland tarn. Other species, such as teal, gadwall and pintail also nest and breed here but prefer the greater seclusion of waters well removed from human habitation and disturbance. The numbers of all our resident species are augmented in winter by migrant visitors, but those of the mallard are by far the most predominant at all seasons. The mallard is therefore the duck on which inland shoots mainly rely for their sport. However, by creating habitat and conditions favourable to this species, others will also be attracted, which, if circumstances encourage them to stay and breed, can in the course of a few years become a substantial bonus and lend an added interest.

The plumage of the mallard duck and drake respectively is so well known as to need no description. The birds measure about 23 in from tip of bill to end of tail and have a wingspan of some 26 in. The weight of an adult is about $2\frac{3}{4}$ lb.

Pairing can start as early as November, but the birds usually stay together in flocks until January, when the pairs start to go their separate ways in search of nesting sites. Reasonably thick cover is normally selected for this on ground within easy reach of water. But sometimes trees or stone walls are chosen, particularly if they are thickly covered in ivy. The nest is made from grasses and leaves, and lined with down. The first eggs are laid in early March, though in mild winters a start may be made in February. A complete clutch is around 12 eggs; incubation is by the female alone and takes from 24–28 days, generally the latter. After hatching, as soon as the young are dried they are led straight to water by the duck and thereafter tended by her alone, though some instances of the drake being in attendance have been recorded.

Unfortunately clutches laid in February/March in nests by the banks of rivers or streams are often lost due to flooding and it is recommended that eggs found in such sites be removed for hatching in incubators or under broodies and the nest itself destroyed. When an early nest is lost, irrespective of by what agency, a second is then made and another, smaller clutch of 8–10 eggs laid. Taking losses of first nests into account, it has been found that the main hatching period occurs in the first half of May.

In their early days the young ducklings are extremely vulnerable to predation by rats, mink, pike, moorhen, carrion crows and other pests which exact a heavy toll. The rate of survival to maturity of broods averages under 50%, i.e. about 5–4. A comprehensive plan for trapping, and other action against predators, should therefore be an integral part of any scheme to encourage wildfowl to take up residence on flight ponds or other waters on a shoot.

Habitat Improvements

As with gamebirds the most important single factor in building up high wildfowl populations is the creation of congenial habitat, and in doing this the same basic principles, suitably adapted, apply. Thus duck do not like bleak, windswept expanses of water any more than pheasants relish bare-floored, draughty woodlands. To provide shelter the shore-line of a loch, or even a small pond, should be deeply indented with a number of bays which offer protection from the wind, from whatever direction it may blow. Where these are lacking it should be possible to create them either by digging out the bank with earth-moving machinery or by the construction of artificial breakwaters. Except where the banks are sufficiently high to make it unnecessary, this shelter should be reinforced by hedges and shelter belts planted at least 20 yards back from the shore line. These will also give valuable cover from view, for ducks like privacy.

Ducks, and especially ducklings, need gently shelving beaches so that they can wade ashore. Shallows, where the water is under 2 ft in depth, are necessary to allow the growth of reeds and other water plants, which provide a valuable source of food as well as cover at surface level. Where shallows do not exist they will have to be created, possibly at the same time as machinery is being used to dig inlets, and burr reed and other aquatic shrubs can then be planted up.

An island or islands in a loch not only give additional shelter but also provide useful nesting cover secure from the attentions of ground vermin. Lakes which have evolved on abandoned industrial sites, such as disused quarries and gravel pits, are usually typical of just how uninviting a vast, open stretch of water must seem to wildfowl as a biting nor'easter sweeps across the surface. Artificial islands can, however, be made out of rafts, as described fully in the Game Conservancy's booklet *Wildfowl Management on Inland Waters*. It seems to me that much greater use could be made of these to improve the attractions of many ponds and lochs; they are neither difficult nor expensive to make, but they must be securely anchored and allowance made for any seasonal variation in water level.

The development of an area for wildfowl may involve the actual making of a flight pond or series of ponds. There are various ways in which this can be done. The one which usually comes first to mind is to build a dam across a stream at a suitable point so that the ground behind it is flooded. However, this is probably the most tricky, and liable to run into difficulties, unless an expert is employed to supervise the construction, which means added expense. In case this is thought unduly alarmist, I can recall two instances of a dam made to an owner's own specification, and in each, due to seepage, it had to be rebuilt professionally at considerable cost. But provided due care is taken and the cost is acceptable excellent flight ponds can be created by this means.

Often the ideal site for a flight pond is in a piece of flat, marshy ground where damming is impracticable. In this kind of situation it may be possible to excavate one with a drag line, if the ground is not too unstable to carry the machinery. A first-class design for such a pond is contained in the Game Conservancy booklet already referred to. This can be adapted to suit local conditions where necessary. If, however, the state of the ground does not allow the employment of machinery, blasting charges may be used instead. It has been found that circular pools some 5 yards across and about 7 ft deep in the centre can be created in this way. The only subsequent work necessary is to cut back the upright rim, which is about 6 in deep, with a spade so that duck can wade out.

Individually, large expanses of water are not needed to attract wildfowl in sizeable numbers. A complex of small pools, such as can be made with blasting charges, will serve just as well, provided the whole area in question is basically attractive to duck.

Nesting Boxes

It is the Dutch who have largely pioneered the use of nesting baskets and boxes for wild duck and the Game Conservancy which has in recent years carried out trials with them in this country. It has been found that the duck take a season or two to become accustomed to them but, once they do, those which are put out are fully utilized. Examples of different types of basket and box are shown in Figure 70. Their outstanding advantage is the complete concealment they give from the keen eyes of avian predators, particularly carrion and hooded crows. The banks of rivers are a favourite hunting ground of crows, and the eggs of many a nest, inadequately concealed in natural cover in the early spring, are taken by them.

Fig. 70   A Dutch nesting basket and one kind of home-made nesting box for duck

The Dutch nesting basket is probably the most satisfactory form of artificial nesting site for wild duck, and once the birds have become accustomed to them they will make full use of them. The Dutch frequently site them on sticks as shown, but in this country, owing to the variations in water level we are liable to experience in both lochs and rivers, it has been found advisable to site them on artificial islands. If set on sticks, they must be the correct height; if too high, the duck will not be able to climb in; if too low, they are liable to be flooded, as depicted in Figure 71.

The Dutch often place their nesting baskets on crossed posts driven into the bed of the pond or stream, as depicted in Figure 71. This is fine if the water level remains constant. But on most British waterways, where there is an inherent risk of flooding causing a sharp rise in the level, if the basket has been correctly positioned it will mean that any nest it contains will be drowned. It has been found more satisfactory in this country to site both nesting baskets and boxes on rafts or artificial islands, so that variations in the water level do not affect them. They can also equally well be sited on real islands, or even in cover round the banks of a loch. But in the latter case they are more vulnerable to mammalian predators.

Fig. 71   A nesting basket overtaken by floods

Feeding

As has been indicated at the beginning of this chapter, wild duck have keen appetites which they are just as willing to indulge in the wild as when hand-reared. They also have catholic tastes. They enjoy the seeds and shoots of many land and aquatic plants, also acorns, blackberries, potatoes and all kinds of cereals, particularly barley and maize. Animal foods include various insects, fresh-water snails and other small crustacea, worms, frogs, tadpoles, small fish and eels. In former times all sorts of ghoulish morsels, such as rabbits' paunches, to which they were supposed to be particularly partial, were deposited in flight ponds to lure them in. But nowadays it has come to be recognized that such foods as barley, maize, brewers' grains and potatoes serve just as well and are much pleasanter and easier to handle.

It has been found that about a stone (14 lb) of barley a day will suffice for a hundred duck. Overfeeding will cause late flighting of a morning. The food, whatever it is, should be distributed in the shallows with a small amount on land just above high-water mark. The recommended time to feed is in the evening as the light begins to fade, i.e. about half an hour before flight time. Opinions vary quite considerably as to the times of year the feeding of flight ponds, etc., ought to begin and end. The Game Conservancy suggests making a start in June, so as to get resident duck into the habit of flighting in, and to continue until the end of the following March to encourage migrants to return the following season. This seems a sound policy and I have myself found it to work well in practice.

As with pheasants, there is no doubt that a well-thought-out 'winter' feeding plan pays off, though with duck it has to begin rather earlier in the year. In my experience it is even more effective in drawing in birds from elsewhere. If a flight pond is unable to be tended daily, it is well worth considering setting up a Parsons automatic feeder, as described on page 116.

Where the shallows of waterways are muddy and the banks soft, duck dibbling in the former and foraging on the latter can cause serious soil erosion. Canada geese, which are now becoming quite abundant in some parts of the south of England and like mallard are not so shy of human presence and disturbance as others of their kind, can similarly play havoc, especially with young grasses on newly sown ground which is being rehabilitated in the immediate vicinity of reservoirs and gravel pits.

Rearing Programme

The whole process of rearing, releasing and subsequently managing wild duck is so similar in its basic principles to that of pheasants that I do not propose to describe it in detail here. It is very fully and clearly explained in the Game Conservancy booklet already mentioned above. Before embarking on a duck rearing programme, I believe much more careful consideration ought to be given to exactly what it is intended to achieve. In too many cases wild duck appear to be reared merely to provide easy targets for indifferent marksmen. This is wrong. In my view the aim should be to provide a nucleus on which a substantial resident wild population can be built, which in its turn will form the core of a prolific winter migrant population.

To appreciate what can be achieved in this way by good management and carefully regulated shooting on favourably situated waters a visit to certain Scottish lochs can be most revealing. Two of those I know present an enthralling picture of a winter's evening, as the different species of wild duck prepare to flight out to feed and the grey geese, pinkfoot and greylag start to flight in to roost. The air is filled with wild music as the duck summon their fellows to make ready to depart and the incoming squadrons of geese announce their approach and receive a welcome from those already on the water. Each loch is four or five score acres in size; the duck can be numbered in hundreds, and the geese in thousands. They are a stirring sight. Both lochs are well sheltered, one by woodlands which in most places come down to the water's edge, and the other by its surrounding hills. They are also little disturbed at any time of year apart from a few anglers in summer, and neither is shot very much more than half a dozen times in a season, though big bags are made when they are.

Shooting Management

Keeping disturbance at all times to a minimum and taking every precaution against over-shooting are essential to the maintenance of high wildfowl populations. This is particularly true of shooting at morning and evening flight; if this is overdone, nothing will drive the birds away from an area more surely, and once this has occurred it is very difficult to attract them back. There are many places in Southern Ireland where wildfowl, and geese in particular, have been driven away for good by over-shooting.

If the size of an area and other conditions permit, it is a sound plan to set aside one pond, or piece of marsh, as a wildfowl sanctuary on which shooting never takes place. This will provide the birds with a sure haven of peace and quiet such as they need if they are to stay; it will also serve as a breeding reservoir. A typical example of this is on a shoot which has a woodland pond, about 1½ acres in extent, which is really part of the grounds of the big house. Duck breed there, and reared duck are released on it, but it is never shot. However, duck flight between it and the river on the estate where excellent sport is had, while two small ponds in coverts elsewhere on the shoot almost invariably have duck on them.

Duck on an inland shoot are much more problematical than pheasants. If the wind is wrong it can make shooting impossible. If in hard weather waters freeze over the majority will disappear, though if patches of water can be kept open by breaking the ice, and straw is spread on the ice over which grain is distributed, a

I

useful nucleus will probably be encouraged to remain. In really prolonged hard weather a halt should be called to shooting and, if measures such as those just described are stepped up, it will be surprising the number and variety of wildfowl which arrive to take advantage of them.

Duck Shooting

Duck may be included as part of the normal covert shooting programme or be shot at evening flight either as an 'extra' or an altogether separate item in the shooting calendar. If they constitute only a minor enterprise the former is usually the more suitable, but if, as in the case of the two Scottish lochs mentioned above, they warrant special arrangements the latter will provide the better sport. Flighting is usually conducted from hides either situated by the loch or river side, or some way back from the water on known flight lines. The local topography and cover will dictate which is the more suitable. Both duck and geese are fast-flying, heavily plumaged birds which, except in conditions of strong winds and heavy rain, prefer to flight in high in the air and descend steeply to their chosen landing place at their destination. I have already dealt in Chapter 3 with the technicalities applicable to guns and cartridges in their shooting. The most important rule for the shooter to observe is that he does not fire at birds which are really out of range. This is a matter which should also be borne in mind when hides are being sited as, unless good judgement is exercised based on adequate experience, they can easily be placed where the majority of birds on still evenings, and there are bound to be some, will be not merely high but out of shot. One of the secrets of successful wildfowl shooting is to let the birds come well in before firing and flighting duck and geese on inland waters is no exception.

As regards actual shooting technique, as in the case of pheasants the shooter must fasten his eyes steadfastly on the head of his target. If he doesn't his eye will automatically pick the centre and a tailed or missed bird will be the result. This is important with duck, but even more so with geese, which must be hit well forward if they are to be killed cleanly. Fortunately, poor light usually forbids premature gun mounting but, as with all high birds, the gun should be moved smartly and incisively into the shoulder when the moment comes to take the shot. Some fowlers

like to infer that there is a special mystique in dealing with high
duck and geese, but this I do not believe. If the shooter observes
the same drill as for high pheasants, mounts his gun correctly,
obeys the dictates of his eye and fires on first aim, then he should
be no less successful.

For this kind of shooting, as much as true wildfowling, a dog
which is a good retriever in water is almost indispensable in order
to be able to make reasonably sure of recovering wounded birds.
Although there can be valid exceptions, I do not like to see guns
setting out unaccompanied by such a companion.

CHAPTER TWENTY-ONE

WOODCOCK

THE woodcock is held in unique esteem and affection by shooting men. To make good a right and left on the comparatively rare occasions when an opportunity offers is a coveted distinction. It is a shy, unsociable bird and, perhaps because of this, our knowledge of its life and habits is far from complete. Modern research to repair this deficiency owes much to the interest taken by Messrs Bols, the famous Dutch liqueur firm, who some years ago formed the 'Bols Woodcock Club'. Through this club a great deal of assistance and encouragement have been given on an international scale to further the investigation of this fascinating bird.

Natural History

Woodcock are resident in many counties of England, Scotland and Wales, and all those of Ireland. In Britain these resident populations, which are relatively static, are annually augmented towards the end of October by large numbers of migrants from northern continental countries, which make their first landfall on the East coast and in particular in East Anglia. From thence some move on, via the southern counties, to Cornwall and the Scilly Isles. In parts of these two latter places large bags of 'cock can be made in a good season. Considerable numbers also arrive in Southern Ireland at about the same time. The return migration occurs in February and March.

The handsome brown and black dappled plumage of the woodcock is well known. The average overall length of the bird is about $13\frac{1}{2}$ in, of which 3 in comprise the bill. The wingspan is some 18 in. Variations in weight are considerable and birds ranging in size from 8 to 15 oz are common. Some giants are occasionally recorded, such as one weighing 27 oz shot in 1801 and another of 24 oz killed at a later date.

The breeding season begins in March and the nesting site is

usually in woodland, often at the foot of a tree; in northern counties birch trees are frequently favoured for this purpose. The nest itself is a hollow scraped in the ground and lined with dead leaves. A clutch usually consists of 4 eggs but 3 or 5 are quite common. Incubation is by the female and lasts for about 21 days. The fledglings are subsequently looked after by her alone.

Whether or not the female 'airlifts' her young has been hotly debated for years. Recently Messrs Bols initiated a study to sift all the evidence on this point and determine if it was true or false. In the subsequent report the evidence of eye witnesses who have actually seen woodcock carrying their young was considered so overwhelming as to place the issue beyond any reasonable doubt. So the sceptics who have always maintained that it was physically 'impossible' appear at last to have been confounded. It seems there are two methods by which the young can be carried. The more usual is that in which the chick is held between the thighs of the parent bird, the beak sometimes being used to help keep the 'passenger' in position and the bird appearing markedly tail-down and laboured in its flight. The other is that where the chick is carried pick-a-back which, although the rarer of the two, seems no less adequately authenticated. Using the first method the whole brood can if necessary be ferried one at a time across an obstacle. It is claimed that two or more at a time have been seen carried pick-a-back. It appears that the young are transported in one way or the other as much as a matter of convenience in surmounting an obstacle as to escape any threat of danger to them. The eye-witness accounts in the report make fascinating reading and I recommend them to anyone interested in the subject.

Woodcock feed chiefly on earthworms, though insects and their larvae, small freshwater crustacea and some vegetable matter are also consumed. They usually lie up by day in dry woodlands on high ground. Mixed conifer and hardwood plantations with ample low cover comprising laurel, rhododendrons and other evergreens are specially favoured. Young conifer stands containing plenty of brambles and bracken are also well frequented in some places. Thick scrubland is likewise popular and in cold weather resort is often made to sheltered hillsides thickly covered in bracken. At dusk the birds flight to their feeding grounds on marshes and soft ground beside burns and springs. The return flight to the high ground is made about first light. But when feeding is curtailed by dark nights, or frozen ground, they will continue feeding by day in open ditches, beside ponds and even on ploughed fields.

Woodcock normally rest up by day on the ground, but there are recorded instances of them roosting in trees, and on one occasion a bird flushed by my dog appeared to have been doing this, judging by the behaviour of the dog and the rustling made by the bird as it broke cover. In flying to and from their feeding grounds they follow a regular flight path.

Shooting

Shooting woodcock is always an exciting experience whether it is incidental to a day's pheasant shooting, at a properly organized 'cock shoot, or flighting them of an evening. The important thing is that it should not become too exciting.

Because, when flushed, a woodcock often appears to weave its way unhurriedly through the trees in a rather butterfly-like manner, it is not always appreciated that it can exhibit a very smart turn of speed indeed when it so decides. Also 'cock, when flushed in the daytime, are reluctant to face open country, and having flown clear of a wood are liable to turn quickly back into it again. When they come forward at a covert shoot they generally appear through the trees and not above them and, instead of either climbing or pursuing a level course as they come into view, are quite likely to be swooping down towards the guns. It is the combination of these factors which makes the bird such an elusive quarry, requiring the shooter to make up his mind on the instant whether to fire or not, and it is this in turn which sometimes leads to dangerous shooting. In my view, therefore, woodcock at a covert shoot are best left alone unless they come forward well up in the air and can be shot against a clear background of sky.

Shooting driven 'cock is an entirely different proposition from driven pheasants. The cream of such shooting in the British Isles is probably now to be found in Cornwall and the Scilly Isles. Good days can still sometimes be had in parts of Southern Ireland. But all game conservation and management in that country have been so neglected for so long, during which time habitat has either become drastically changed or just quietly deteriorated, that the good sport formerly enjoyed with woodcock is now rare.

When driving woodcock the guns should stand almost up to the covert's edge, dependent on the height of the trees. As driven 'cock fly very unpredictably, the beats want to be kept short; 250 yards is quite long enough and shorter beats often serve better. The beating must be thorough and in really thick cover the ideal answer would be a well-trained team of Clumber spaniels, which were originally bred specially for this sport. But nowadays cockers or small springers are more readily available and, provided they are steady, can probably manage quite as adequately.

The third method of shooting woodcock is to intercept them on their evening flight line as they quit the covert, where they have rested up in the daytime, for their feeding grounds. This requires good local knowledge because the flight line must be known exactly and may only cover a frontage of a hundred or so yards. Each gun must know precisely where the others are standing and no one must move from his stand until the flight is declared over by whoever is in charge. The guns should be placed fairly well back from the covert's edge, virtually as for pheasant shooting. The 'cock normally start to flight a little later than duck. They appear over the treetops and then usually swoop downwards, flying fast and straight. If possible they should be shot just as they come into view against the sky over the tops of the trees. In the failing light the moment they dive below treetop level they will be lost to sight, and the only way to deal with them then is to turn and take a shot behind. This is essentially a sport for safe shots and, unless they are also competent marksmen, they will be lucky to touch a feather. The whole flight is normally over in about half an hour, but on a good evening the sport can be fast and furious, and it is always exciting.

As regards shooting technique, in my experience successful woodcock shooting is a slightly specialized knack, but it is not difficult to master. The key points are that the shooter must be on the alert, and the moment he is warned a bird has been flushed he should come to the 'ready' position described on page 80. Then, as soon as the bird is sighted and he decides it is in range and safe to shoot, he should mount his gun briskly and shoot straight at it. It is fatal to be put off by the bird's weaving flight which will only induce indecision and consequent dithering with the finger on the trigger instead of pulling it on first aim. Alertness and well-attuned reflexes are aids to both safety and good shooting. One of the reasons why woodcock cause dangerous shooting is because a gun gets caught unawares, becomes flustered, finds the bird has changed direction and chases it with his gun muzzles regardless of where they may be pointing.

A 1 oz load of No. 7 shot serves admirably for 'cock. But at a covert shoot a standard load of No. 6's will prove just as deadly if it is correctly placed.

Woodcock flushed from a Scottish hillside and streaking down over the guns in the glen below offer sport second to none and only matched by grouse and pheasants at their best.

CHAPTER TWENTY-TWO

SNIPE

SNIPE are always considered a formidable challenge to the shooter. They are a very small target. Their flight is swift and erratic. They can sadly dent the reputations of accomplished game shots who go in pursuit of them for the first time. To shoot snipe consistently well demands more than just ordinary skill as a marksman. Whether this extra quality is a matter of experience, mastery of a special shooting technique or a combination of both is arguable. However, there can be no disputing that a sound knowledge of snipe and how to tackle them is an aid to enjoying good sport. So, before reaching for gun and cartridge, let us look at these aspects.

Natural History

There are three varieties of snipe in the British Isles, the Great Snipe, the Common Snipe and the Jack Snipe. The first named is only an occasional passage-migrant. It is bigger and about 3 oz heavier than the Common Snipe. There is also a difference in the number of tail feathers. But at what might be termed 'sportsman's range' these differences are not noticeable. However, it is by law a fully protected bird in Britain. The Jack Snipe is also a migrant which usually appears in substantial numbers. It is not protected by law but is so tiny, averaging a mere 2 oz in weight, that it is not worth serious consideration, though it may sometimes be shot at in error or out of frustration.

The Common Snipe is our quarry. It is about $10\frac{1}{2}$ in in length, of which the bill is $2\frac{1}{2}$ in. The average weight is 4 oz. It has handsomely dappled buff plumage with black barring, and a distinctive white belly, which is the most eye-catching feature as it jumps from cover in front of a shooter. There is a resident breeding population distributed throughout suitable habitat in Britain, and notably in such areas as the Norfolk Broads, the western counties of Wales, the West of Scotland and the Western Isles.

It is found throughout Ireland. From the evidence of ringed birds these populations appear to be largely sedentary apart from local dispersal. About the period of the full moon in October they are joined by large numbers of migrants.

Snipe live and breed in wetlands, such as marshes, water meadows and boggy areas of moorland. The breeding season is from the beginning of April onwards. The nest is sited in a tussock of grass or reeds and lined with grasses. A clutch consists of an average of 4 eggs. Incubation is by the female only and takes about 20 days, but when the fledglings leave the nest they are tended by both parent birds.

Snipe feed mainly on various species of worm, but some insect larvae and vegetable matter are also eaten. They feed at night and rest up by day.

Habitat Management

To obtain the best value from snipe ground it should be managed in a somewhat similar manner to a grouse moor, so that there is a variegated pattern of cover in different stages of growth throughout the whole area. Although snipe will happily stand in water to feed, they like to rest dryshod and to do both their feeding and resting in shelter from the wind. So, just as a grouse moor should have short heather for feeding and tall heather for cover, a well-managed snipe marsh or bog should have patches almost bare of reeds for feeding, surrounded by areas of tall reeds to give shelter. This can be achieved in a number of ways.

In large areas of bog, burning is the most satisfactory method and the best time to do this is in dry weather in the autumn. It should be done in strips not more than 50×20 yards in size. Reeds, despite their sappy fibre and damp environment, can burn surprisingly fiercely once a fire takes hold, so there should be a team of at least three men to control the fire and other precautions similar to those already described for heather burning should be observed. The fire is generally more difficult to start, but this can be overcome by the discreet use of paraffin. Many snipe bogs are quite small and, if burning is carried out in these, the size of the strips should be proportionately smaller, so that a patchwork of high and low cover is established.

Parts of some bogs, well-favoured by snipe in winter, dry out in summer and provide rough grazing for cattle. If it is possible for the beasts to be tethered so that they graze out a series of circular patches interwoven with taller cover an ideal effect for snipe will be achieved. As another alternative to burning, reeds can be scythed by hand, but this is a laborious method and, if it is to be properly completed, the trash which has been cut should then be removed.

Burning or cutting should be planned on a rotation, but owing to the wide variations in the speed of re-growth which depends so much on local conditions, it is hard to give any general advice as to what this ought to be; however, five to six years may serve as a useful guide line.

To improve habitat the Game Conservancy advocates the use of small blasting charges to make little pools each a few feet in diameter. As far as this is likely to create an area of reasonably dry ground in their immediate vicinity it may be advantageous. But having myself shot over a good deal of typical snipe ground in Scotland, Wales, Ireland and England it seems to me more a way of providing additional hazards for the shooter than increased attractions for the snipe.

In prolonged hard weather, such as we had in the winter of 1962–3, snipe suffer severely and countless thousands die of starvation. Unfortunately almost nothing can be done to alleviate their condition in these circumstances. Various sporting and animal welfare organizations always issue pleas to put an end to shooting, which most sportsmen worth their salt will have done already of their own accord, and if harsh reality is faced is little more than a symbolic gesture anyway, however right it is that it should be made.

Snipe Shooting

Snipe can be either driven or walked up. When organized on a grand scale with a party of ten or more guns, it is usual for a majority of the guns to stand, while the minority drive the birds to them. Good bags of 40–100 birds may be made in this way. But in my view by far the more enjoyable sport is obtained by a small party of two or three, where the accent is on the walking rather than the standing. Such a party, composed of experienced guns who are competent shots and know their ground, can in the course of a season account for a lot of snipe. But it is a sport for fit men.

Good local knowledge is essential to those who walk the bogs, in knowing where the snipe lie and where the dangerous places and other snags are. By far the worst hazards are bog-holes, which are indistinguishable on the surface from any harmless puddle, into which the shooter steps and plummets to his waist in icy water. The wise snipe shooter always carries a change of nether garments in his car. Even if one has walked a bog for years without mishap, there may still be a bog-hole lying in wait, often for an unsuspecting guest who has just been told there is nothing to worry about!

According to the weather, snipe do move around a good deal, and a bog which is full of birds one day can be almost empty a week later. Some people therefore say shoot snipe as hard and often as you like while you can. But if snipe are disturbed too much, they quickly become so wild that walking them up is a waste of time. So if one wishes to shoot them in this way small snipe bogs should not be shot more than once a week, and one must take one's chance with their comings and goings.

Some experienced shots vigorously assert that snipe should always be walked downwind. This is because they have to jump into the wind and then turn to go with it, which allows the shooter a valuable extra moment in time in which to take his shot. Others say, no less forcefully, that snipe should be walked upwind, because then they do not hear the shooter's approach so soon, which allows him to come to closer quarters, thus again giving him more time to take his shot. In my experience the latter school of thought has the greater merit, but it is more often the lie of the land, i.e. the shape of a bog and the likely whereabouts in it of the snipe, that dictates how it has to be walked. Also, if it is one of those days when snipe are lying well, whatever direction the wind is coming from is not going to affect the issue materially, unless it is blowing really strongly. Equally, if they are jumpy, whichever way they are walked will not make them any less so. But in a high wind I have always found walking upwind the better ploy where other circumstances have allowed.

Before a storm, snipe are usually very much on the alert. However, the day following a storm which has blown itself out overnight, so that the birds have been able to eat their fill in peace during the last hours of darkness, can well mean that they will lie like stones, and if the bogs are walked slowly and thoroughly terrific sport can then be had.

Another argument among experts is over the moment at which it is best to take the shot. Some say wait until the snipe has stopped zig-zagging and then shoot as it straightens out. Others say the moment it jumps is the time to fire. This latter is I believe the right answer; unless snipe are sitting exceptionally tight it is very rare indeed that it is necessary to give them any liberty before taking the shot, as sometimes has to be done with walked-up pheasants. In fact successful snipe-shooting seems to me in the final analysis to depend on slick, incisive, polished gun mounting more than in the pursuit of any other quarry. In particular the shooter's head must be kept still, and not bobbed down to meet the stock.

Good quality patterns of adequate density are essential to kill snipe cleanly and where they alone are the quarry I would un-hesitatingly recommend the use of No. 8 shot. Where teal or golden plover may intervene in any numbers No. 7's will probably serve better, but good results at snipe cannot be expected with any larger shot size used in conjunction with a game gun with normal open borings.

Clothing

Some people splash around happily in gumboots and, if the water comes over the top, empty them out and carry on shooting. But I do not enjoy shooting with cold, wet feet and recommend good quality thigh boots with studded composition soles. They should have a strap with a loop on it which goes over the shooter's belt to hold up the tops and prevent the boots pulling off in a quag-mire. Modern boots of this kind are now so light and well made that the reservations about such footwear which applied in former times are no longer relevant.

Walking a snipe bog can be warm work even on a cold day. Modern wind-proof, insulated shooting jackets have made the wearing of bulky woollen sweaters unnecessary. Any jacket of this type which is light, supple and waterproof should suffice; a hare pocket in which shot snipe can be carried for the time being will save having to carry a gamebag. To avoid getting a wet bottom, a pair of waterproof shorts made from some robust material which does not tear easily on barbed wire is a worthwhile addition.

Marking Fallen Birds

However carefully snipe are marked when they are shot, they
have an uncanny capacity for vanishing, even if they fall dead.
If they are runners they can put a surprising distance between
themselves and the fall by the time the shooter arrives to start
looking for them. Some people, even quite experienced sportsmen, are apt to scoff at the idea of a wounded snipe being able
to get far away; but I have seen a dog pick up the scent, plunge
through a hedge, and set off at a gallop across a meadow, to the
astonishment and fury of its owner. But the dog had the better
of it because it returned with the snipe, which it retrieved over a
hundred yards out in the field, and the distance had been covered
by the wounded bird in no more than two or three minutes. A
good retriever is therefore an undoubted asset to the snipe shooter,
provided it is also steady. Unnecessary noise in controlling a dog
will alert every snipe within earshot and ruin the chances of
surprise on which success so much depends. So unruly dogs are
best left at home. Another point worth bearing in mind is that
snipe bogs can be punishing going for a dog, and one with both
size and stamina is desirable.

Snipe can provide superb sport. To enjoy it to the full one needs
to be both physically fit and properly equipped. But once one
develops the taste for it, a day in pursuit of the 'long bills' will
always be a source of special pleasure. When you can shoot ten
in succession with a cartridge apiece you will indeed have begun
to master the art of snipe shooting.

CHAPTER TWENTY-THREE

BLACKGAME

Natural History

IF the pheasant is our most colourful gamebird, then the Black-cock is certainly our most distinguished. The red wattle over the eye, the lustrous blue-black sheen of the body and wings, the lyre-shaped tail, and the white rump all combine to lend it an air of aristocratic splendour. It is also blessed with the stature to display these attributes to advantage. The average weight of blackcock is $3\frac{1}{2}$ lb; their length from tip of beak to end of tail 20–22 in; their wingspan about 24 in.

The female of the species is known as the Greyhen and is a smaller, plainer bird, with reddish-brown plumage barred with black. At close quarters its forked tail clearly differentiates it from a grouse, but otherwise it is easily confused with the latter except that it is bigger, its markings more pronounced, and in flight its wing beats appear more measured and sustained. An average weight is about $2\frac{1}{4}$ lb and length 17 in.

In law the species is designated as 'blackgame' and is one of only eight specifically named as game in the Game Act of 1831 (see Chapter 33). Naturalists seem, however, to prefer to call it the 'black grouse', as do many keepers in Scotland. But as the former is the more distinctive and the title of this chapter I propose to continue with it.

Blackgame are birds of marginal ground, where forest, moor and cultivated land are to be found in close proximity to each other. They perch freely in trees, but generally roost on the ground. They may be found feeding in the woods, on the moor or on the stubbles. They were at one time widely distributed throughout the afforested areas of Britain, but are now confined to parts of Devon and Somerset, notably Exmoor, the north midland and border counties of England, many parts of Wales and generally in Scotland. There are none in Ireland. As mentioned in the Introduction, they were severely persecuted by state-sponsored forestry interests in Scotland and the Borders between the two world wars and as a result became very scarce for a while. But their numbers are now increasing again. Outside Scotland their fine sporting qualities seem very little appreciated. It is perhaps symptomatic of this that the Game Conservancy has never shown any interest in them whatsoever.

Blackgame are territorial birds but, unlike red grouse, the blackcock is polygamous. Displaying may start as early as January and is normally in full swing in March. However, it is April before the greyhens visit the 'leks', as the gatherings of males for display purposes are known.

The site chosen by the greyhen for the nest may be in a woodland or out on the moor. It is usually a hollow scraped in the ground and scantily lined with bents in a well-sheltered place, but sometimes an old nest in a tree is used instead. Egg-laying generally starts in May, but occasionally towards the end of April. The size of the clutch varies quite considerably from 6 to 10 eggs. Incubation is by the female only and takes 24–25 days. She then looks after the fledglings also on her own.

The family party or covey seems to break up fairly soon after the young are able to fend for themselves. Thereafter the birds go about in packs, often of cocks and hens respectively, though sometimes of both sexes. But these packs are comparatively small, usually totalling no more than 10–25, though larger numbers have been recorded.

The food of blackgame is mainly vegetable. In winter it includes the buds and shoots of conifers, particularly larch and Scots pine, also the buds of birch. It is their predilection for the former which has given the birds a bad name with foresters, but in my belief their depredations in this respect have been exaggerated to provide an excuse for treating them as pests. Bilberry, bog myrtle, and catkins also feature in their diet, as in due season do the fruits of rowan, hawthorn, wild strawberry, cranberry, crowberry, etc., as well as the leaves of heather, grasses and sedges. They enjoy the gleanings of stubbles, and in spring and autumn consume a limited variety of insects.

Shooting

Blackgame used to be shot regularly in considerable numbers in the lowland counties of Scotland, such as Dumfriesshire and

0   A vivid illustration of how the column of shot can be seen by a shooting coach, and of how in certain weather conditions the camera, and the unpractised eye, can pick it up, in this case on a grouse moor.

31   A dramatic view of a rising grouse, as a walking gun may see him.

32   A wild duck being retrieved from a rehabilitated gravel pit; the island, inlet, and shelving banks which have been 'built-in' are noteworthy.

3　A close-up of a blackcock in full plumage in flight.

4　A wildfowler shooting from a hide over decoys.

35   Ptarmigan flushed from the high tops heading out over the glen.

36   A rare camera 'shot' of a snipe as the shooter sees it when it jumps.

Wigtownshire, though the record bag for the British Isles of 252 was made in a day's driving at Cannock Chase in Staffordshire as far back as 1860. Nowadays they are most frequently an 'extra' in a day's grouse shooting. It is worth remembering that the season does not open for them until 20 August, and many young black-cock of the year do not attain their full plumage until the end of September.

It has become customary not to shoot greyhens, though where blackgame populations are numerous there is no really valid reason for not doing so.

When a blackcock comes forward at a grouse drive, it usually stands out clearly, due to the higher altitude at which it flies and the apparently effortless ease with which it outflies any accom-panying grouse. It has been estimated on reliable authority that on a windless day a blackcock can travel at a top speed of nearly 70 mph, a speed only matched by the teal and golden plover, which places it amongst the fastest quarry pursued by the shooter. Its pace is undoubtedly deceptive, and it will pay the shooter to pause for a good look at a blackcock before he mounts his gun to fire, for, even though it may not be travelling at full speed, he will almost certainly miss behind.

Whether blackcock are driven or walked-up it should be remembered that they will go in the direction they want, and it is a waste of time trying to get them to take a different line. But if guns can be placed to intercept them, excellent sport can be had. For those who enjoy walking the fringes of the moor in October, blackcock will often be found on the oat stubbles. If guns can move into position unobserved, and another member of the party then drives the birds over them, they will provide excellent shooting. On one such occasion I have seen a dozen blackcock in the air at the same time, which of itself is a magni-ficent sight, and I was not unduly sad that on that occasion they eluded our efforts to come to terms with them.

Except when displaying in the spring time, blackcock are extremely wary, and plans to obtain a shot at them need to be well laid and well executed. The few opportunities which I have myself enjoyed and that have been brought to a successful conclusion have all been memorable in some special way which makes certain incidents recorded in one's gamebook a particular pleasure to recall at a later date. In my view blackgame are deserving of far greater attention by conservation-minded sportsmen than they receive and need if their future in Britain is to be assured and their sporting potential realized.

CHAPTER TWENTY-FOUR

CAPERCAILLIE

Natural History

THE Capercaillie is a member of the grouse family and is our largest gamebird, though in law it is not listed as game. Its name derives from the Gaelic words meaning 'cock of the wood', which is an apt description, for when the male 'caper' puts in an appearance in a pheasant covert one and all keep a respectful distance. The cock with the red wattle over his eye, his bearded visage, and subtly shaded plumage of contrasting dark browns, greens and greys, cuts an impressive figure. Their average weight is 9–12 lb, length 35–36 in, and wingspan about 40 in. The colouring and general appearance of the female are not unlike that of a rather large hen pheasant with a short tail; average weight is 4–7 lb, and length 25–26 in.

The indigenous race of capercaillie became extinct in Scotland about 1762. The species was first reintroduced from Sweden around 1872. But these early importations were not very successful, and it was not until birds were brought to Taymouth in Perthshire in 1837 and 1838 that they became firmly re-established in Scotland; hence their omission from the Game Act of 1831. Since 1837, capercaillie have steadily extended their range and are now comparatively numerous in many parts of the Highlands and some areas in the Lowlands. They died out in Ireland at an earlier date than in Scotland and have never been reintroduced.

They live in coniferous woodlands of spruce, larch and Scots pine in hilly districts, and prefer those which contain a good deal of undergrowth. In the autumn local migrations occur to lower lying mixed woodlands, but a return is made to the higher ground in winter. Cultivated land, such as stubbles and turnip fields, is occasionally visited. They spend a lot of their time in trees, in which they perch freely, and roost at night, save in heavy snow, when they sometimes burrow into it in order to roost. Capercaillie are held to be polygamous.

The hen usually scratches a nest among the pine needles on the forest floor at the foot of a tree, though nests have been found on open moorland up to heights of 1500 ft and very occasionally in trees. Egg-laying starts in April and a complete clutch is normally from 5 to 8 eggs, though ones of up to 15 have been recorded. Incubation is by the hen on her own and takes approximately 28 days. After hatching the brood is looked after and reared also by her alone.

In winter, capercaillie feed almost entirely on the buds and shoots of conifers, but in spring and summer a wide variety of other vegetation is added to their menu, such as grasses, clovers, bracken shoots, the berries of juniper, rowan, hawthorn, cranberry, bilberry, raspberry and blackberry, also oats and the flowers of heather; quantities of insects such as beetle larvae and ants are consumed as well.

Shooting

When flushed from the heather on a moor by a party of walking guns, a cock caper lurches into the air presenting a target that can hardly be missed and offers very poor sport indeed. But the same bird flushed by the beaters from the trees on the side of a glen is an entirely different proposition and will descend on the guns like a whirlwind, and unless they know their business he will leave behind him a line of very red faces each looking askance at two empty cartridge cases and nothing to show for them. I can find no authoritative information on the speed at which capercailzie are able to fly, but I have seen them comfortably outdistance pheasants travelling high and fast. If the blackcock is acknowledged to be capable of almost 70 mph, then it seems reasonable to assume the capercaillie is no slower. As driven birds they do therefore in my opinion offer very fine sport indeed. If one comes forward when pheasants are being shot, it should be treated in much the same way as a blackcock *vis-à-vis* grouse, in that the shooter should pause and take a good look at it, so that his eye has a chance to register its greater speed, which because of its more leisurely seeming flight is not immediately obvious. He should then treat it as any other fast flying target, and with his eye fixed firmly on the bird's head, mount his gun briskly to the shoulder and pull the trigger on first aim.

I have seen caper killed stone dead in the air with a standard load of No. 6 shot. If birds are allowed to come well in, and the charge is properly directed, there can be no doubting the effectiveness of this shot size. But my own preference would be for No. 5's, and if capercaillie were the only quarry a 'Maximum' load of No. 4 shot would technically be better still in view of their size.

Because capercaillie are polygamous, it has become customary, as with greyhens, not to shoot the hens. This is probably basically sound policy, but should not be an inflexible rule if it is felt desirable to control numbers locally. Caper can in fact be more damaging to plantations of young trees than the much maligned blackgame and can also drive away pheasants, so control may indeed sometimes be necessary.

However, the caper is in the main a most interesting and spectacular bird, of which our detailed knowledge is comparatively scanty, and as such is I believe rightly regarded as a welcome addition to the gamebird populations on an estate.

CHAPTER TWENTY-FIVE

PTARMIGAN

Natural History

THE Ptarmigan is the remaining member of the grouse family in the British Isles and has fairly been described as a 'Highland Grouse'. It is indeed a bird of the high tops, being found only at altitudes of 2000 ft and above in the hills of Scotland, unless driven temporarily to seek shelter on lower ground by blizzards. Its summer plumage is somewhat similar to that of the red grouse, but has more of a khaki brown background with more pronounced black and white mottling, while the underparts of the body are entirely white. At the autumn moult the whole body and wing plumage changes to white, except for the black tips to the tail feathers, and the leg feathering becomes markedly more dense. The average weight of ptarmigan is about $1\frac{1}{4}$ lb, their length 13–14 in and their wingspan 20 in. The female is generally slightly smaller than the male.

As might be expected of birds living in such rugged surroundings, they love sunning themselves when opportunity offers. The cocks also frequently perch on boulders or prominent rocks, and both sexes exhibit a fondness for dusting. They feed mainly first thing in the morning and again in the evening. In winter they will burrow vigorously through loose snow in order to obtain food.

Pairing occurs later than with grouse and the female does not start preparing a nest till late April or early May. This is a shallow hollow scraped in the ground amongst such vegetation as grass, heather or crowberry, and is sparsely lined with grass. The site chosen is usually in the shelter of a rock. Egg-laying begins towards the end of May and a clutch normally comprises 5–9 eggs. Incubation is by the hen only and takes 24–26 days. The young are brooded by the hen while the cock stands guard. They are able to fly when 10 days old. The family usually remains together as a covey until late in the autumn when the birds all tend to pack.

However, the cocks sometimes abandon their families at an earlier date and join together in packs of their own.

The food of ptarmigan is largely vegetable, consisting mainly of the shoots and leaves of heather, various berries, such as cloudberry, cranberry, bilberry and bearberry, and the seeds of sedges. Insects are occasionally eaten.

Shooting

Walking the tops for ptarmigan is a thrilling sport. It demands a high degree of physical fitness and, unless the shooter is really alert, the birds when they take wing will catch him unawares more often than not. They will sometimes lie well, and at others be quite unapproachable. Because of the magnificent camouflage their plumage provides, when they are lying well it is possible to walk right on top of them without seeing them till they rise. But they will on other occasions run ahead of a walking gun and can then sometimes be spotted as they pause with their heads showing in silhouette above a rock.

Unlike grouse they will usually fly out across the glen to a neighbouring hilltop when flushed, and if the ground slopes abruptly a dead bird can fall many feet below the shooter. A fit, active retriever, which is also really steady, is therefore worth its weight in gold.

There is no sport more enjoyable or challenging than walking up ptarmigan on a fine day in late August or early September. It is astonishing, even when the hills look at their best on such a day, how the birds manage to survive, let alone raise a family, in such rugged and barren surroundings. It is even more surprising that the record bag for ptarmigan, made in Ross-shire in 1866, should stand as high as 122 shot in a day. Most sportsmen will be delighted to return with two or three brace, and will probably have shot well to obtain that.

CHAPTER TWENTY-SIX

HARES AND HARE DRIVES

Introduction

THE hare has been counted a beast of the chase for centuries and is defined as 'game' in the Game Act of 1831. But in Britain hare shooting is generally contemplated with little enthusiasm and is regarded by many as more of a necessity to control a pest than as an enjoyable sporting occasion. This attitude is markedly at variance with that of continental sportsmen who hold the creature in much higher esteem and welcome an invitation to a hare shoot. A beater will as a rule accept a brace of rabbits at the end of a day's shooting with alacrity, but the offer of a hare will be as cursorily declined. If the quantity of hares in the bag outnumbers the guns, it is sometimes difficult even to give them away. Yet on the Continent they are gladly accepted.

This horror of hares displayed by countrymen, notably farm workers, has long puzzled me. If the subject is broached, an awkward silence usually ensues. The only information I have ever been able to obtain as to the reason for this attitude was from a sporting padre who held that it was all wrapped up in ancient superstition and folklore concerning witches and witchcraft. One can but assume therefore that in those far off pre-Common Market days the import duty on spells from Britain was so prohibitive that continental hares escaped the curse placed on their British brethren. One curious outcome of this state of affairs is that it currently pays shoots to sell their hares for export to the Continent instead of for home consumption.

Natural History

The brown, or common hare is widely distributed throughout England, Wales and Scotland. On the high ground in Scotland it is replaced by the blue, or mountain hare, the coat of which in winter turns white so that it blends with the background of snow in which it lives; it is also a slightly smaller animal.

In length the brown hare is about 24 in, and weighs on average 8 lb, though specimens of over 13 lb have been recorded. Its fur is brown, with white belly and black tips to the ears, and in winter is rather more tinged with grey than in summer. Hares feed by night and rest up by day, though a certain amount of daylight feeding also takes place. The resting place, known as a 'form', consists of a shallow depression in the ground, in a tuft of grass or similar low cover, in which it is extremely inconspicuous and difficult to detect. When they move out to feed at dusk they may travel many miles, up to 30 having been recorded, before arriving back at their form towards dawn.

Courtship among hares is a common phenomenon in the spring, but there are usually several litters in a year, and does have been found in young as late as December. There are generally four young in a litter, which are born fully furred and with their eyes open. They have the use of their limbs, and are capable of movement within a short time of birth. Each takes up its own separate form within a short distance of the others and the doe visits them in turn to suckle them. By the time a leveret is a month old it leads an entirely independent existence. But in that month mortality caused by predators, such as carrion crows, foxes and feral cats can be heavy.

Hares live off an almost entirely vegetarian diet and have a voracious appetite. They prefer cultivated land and will eat young cereals, brassicas, forage crops and grasses of all kinds. In allotments and market gardens they display a preference for carrots, turnips, lettuces and other green vegetables. They can also do considerable damage in young forestry plantations; although they are reputed to be particularly destructive to conifers, in my experience they are even more so to hardwoods, particularly hazel and beech. It has been said that six hares will eat the same amount as one sheep. Hares are not, therefore, looked upon with a very friendly eye by either farmers or foresters.

Hare Populations

It has long been recognized that hare populations are subject to periodic fluctuations of some magnitude. But the wholesale decline of the rabbit due to myxomatosis in 1954 and the years immediately following did not result in extensive increases in hares, as some people forecast it might. In fact since the late 1950s the

hare population in some parts of the country has not merely
dwindled but disappeared altogether. The reasons for this are
not known and are the subject of an investigation by the Game
Conservancy. However, it seems likely that changes in agricultural
practice, particularly the removal of hedgerow and other cover,
have been contributory causes.

But in some areas, such as parts of the North and South Downs,
hares remain plentiful, and when special shoots are organized to
deal with them the day's bag may amount to several hundred.
On some shoots in the south of England the hares are left alone
on partridge and pheasant days and dealt with on their own in
February. Where hares are genuinely numerous this seems a sound
policy. But in Scotland they are usually taken as they come on
shooting days throughout the season and can comprise a substantial part of the bag.

Hare Shoots

Hare shoots and their organization have already been briefly mentioned in Chapter 8. On large areas of open ground, such as
prevail on many downland farms, it is necessary to organize these
shoots on a big scale. One such place, where I have been a guest
gun, has three days of hare drives in February, at which a grand
total of over 800 hares is normally killed. It is always a pleasure
to shoot there because the organization is excellent. About 30
guns attend and a selected number of beaters also carry guns.
Both the host and his keeper maintain a very tight control over
the proceedings and I have never once seen anyone even attempt
a dangerous shot. No dogs are allowed, which some people may
question, but having so often seen a hare drive turned into something more resembling a coursing meeting, their exclusion is in
my opinion fully justified, provided, as in this case, there is a
pick-up afterwards. A mistake frequently made is to site the guns
too far apart, so that hares which make a dash through the gap
mid-way between two guns are not properly within range at a safe
angle of fire. 35 yards is quite far enough between guns
and 20 yards between beaters. Also if the guns standing in the line
want to enjoy good sport, they should remain concealed until the
moment arrives to take their shot.

When the beaters have reached a point 250 yards from the
guns, a signal should be given either by blowing a whistle or

sounding a horn, after which all hares must be allowed to pass through the line of guns or beaters and only be shot behind that line. On flinty or frozen ground, where the risk of ricochets is considerable, this is an important precaution.

A criticism often levelled at drives where a line of beaters advances towards a line of guns is that many hares escape to the flanks unshot at. By forming the line of beaters in the shape of a crescent, and having walking guns well forward on each flank, this can to some extent be overcome, though not entirely. At hare shoots in some continental countries, guns and beaters are lined out on the circumference of a huge circle, and then at a given signal start to walk inwards towards the centre. Shooting inwards is prohibited on the sounding of a further signal. Although in theory this should overcome the problem of hares being able to escape, it does not in practice, because in the early stages the distance between guns is such that some hares that run through the circle are out of range. Another disadvantage is that unless the ground being encircled is really open so that everyone can see each other, it is very easy for people to get out of position, and subsequently find themselves in somebody else's line of fire. I have never felt happy participating in this form of circular driving on the continent, and on two or three ocasions have seen accidents narrowly averted. In my view therefore the British method of marching a line of beaters towards a static line of guns is much the safer and is not so much less efficient as continental sportsmen would have us believe.

There is no sight more to be deplored in the shooting field than a botched shot at a hare. We have probably all been guilty of it at some time or other and this is, I believe, the reason why many of us find hare shooting the least attractive of a season's sport. If hares are to be shot at all, the deed must be done well. Hare shoots should not be occasions to which every Tom, Dick, or Harry who owns a gun is asked, as they are in some places. There are usually plenty of keepers, pickers-up and others who are competent shots, who will gladly fill the ranks if difficulty is experienced in finding enough guns.

Shooting the Hare

A hare is a large animal and, if it is to be killed cleanly, it must be hit well forward, with a shot charge centred on the head and forequarters. This is almost impossible to achieve in a direct going-away shot, as the hind-quarters obscure the true target to such a large extent. But whatever kind of shot is attempted, the shooter must begin by fastening his eye on the head of the hare. If a hare is properly within range, i.e. at not more than 35 yards, it should be possible actually to look it in the eye, which will help to rivet the shooter's attention and prevent it straying elsewhere. Then as soon as he decides the moment to fire has arrived he should mount his gun smoothly and briskly to the shoulder, and as always pull the trigger on first aim. Some people noticeably dither on their aim after the gun has been brought to the shoulder and this is disastrous to their shooting. It is probably because they don't shoot hares very often, and so are put off by the size of the target. This causes them at the critical moment not quite to trust their eye. The way to overcome this hesitancy is to really 'go' for the shot. Then as soon as a few hares have been success-fully bowled over, self-confidence will be restored, and the fault eliminated.

With winged game a shooter learns to hold well up on a crossing target. But with ground game this may lead to him shooting over the quarry. He should therefore always aim to shoot the ground from under crossing hares and rabbits, just as he should with a pigeon perched in a tree, or any stationary target; this is especially important when shooting downhill.

The size of a hare often leads to misjudgements in range, and shots being taken too far out. To avoid this, the gun as he waits at his stand should pick out two or three distinctive marks on the ground to his front at an estimated 40 yards. If he does not start to mount his gun until an approaching hare has crossed this imaginary line, it should be within 35 yards range at the moment he actually fires.

It has been estimated that at full speed a hare travels at about 40 mph, so that one moving fast, but not flat out, will probably be doing some 30 mph. But a hare often approaches the line of guns rather hesitantly, pausing every now and again to see what is happening. Then, having lulled the shooter into anticipating an easy shot for which he will have plenty of time, it makes a sudden dash for safety and is missed handsomely behind with both barrels. So one wants to be alert and watch the quarry closely.

A man who was probably one of the best shots of his day invariably used No. 3's at hare drives. A standard 12-bore load of these will just give an adequate pattern density (i.e. of 70— see Chapter 3) with an improved cylinder barrel at 40 yards. But my own preference is for No. 4's which give a denser pattern, and also have more than ample striking energy up to 40 yards. No. 5 shot likewise has sufficient striking energy up to this limit, but any smaller shot size is too light, and can only lead to unnecessary wounding if a hare is further out than a shooter has appreciated.

I have heard of hare drives being held in the second half of March. Although there is no close season laid down in law for hares, this is in my view too late in the season, and the end of February should see the finish of hare shooting. If hare drives are well organized, and the guns competent shots, then in my experience they can be enjoyable occasions. It is when these conditions are not fulfilled that they become instead a rather badly conducted exercise in pest control, from which a sportsman can derive little pleasure.

CHAPTER TWENTY-SEVEN

RABBITS AND RABBIT CONTROL

The Rabbit as a Pest

BECAUSE of the charming myths created by Beatrix Potter, and others, many townsmen do not understand that in real life the rabbit is not simply a lovable little furry creature but an unmitigated pest. Furthermore it has a long history as such. In Roman times the inhabitants of Majorca and Minorca sent a deputation to Rome asking if they could be given new land because they were being driven from their own by the vast hordes of rabbits in the islands. In more recent times, in the 1930s and 1940s, the counties of Carmarthen, Pembroke and Cardigan in Wales were so overrun with rabbits that a greater tonnage of rabbit meat was produced by those counties annually than of either beef or mutton. In fact so bad had the situation become prior to myxomatosis that hedges and banks were all undermined by rabbit burrows, and, as no worthwhile crops could be grown, so no farms could be let; trapping was blatantly carried on in the open, in defiance of the law, as a result of which gamebirds had become practically extinct, and there was hardly a dog or cat in any parish that went sound on all four legs. From my own experience I can recall fields in Sussex which were never cultivated because of the damage done by rabbits, and if a person stood in the gateway the whole of the far side of the field would appear to get up and run into the wood in a sea of brown bodies and bobbing white scuts.

It has been calculated that a pair of rabbits in Britain is capable of founding a family which could number four million within three years. This allows for natural predation, but not for the effects of epidemic disease, or those of control measures taken by man. It indicates the vast problem which rabbits can pose.

The actual amount of damage done by rabbits in terms of hard cash was sometimes argued to be offset by their value in meat and fur. But this is a fallacy. Prior to 1954 the annual damage to crops of all kinds in England and Wales caused by rabbits was officially estimated at £40–£50 million; the concurrent trade in rabbit meat and skins amounted to not more than £15 million, of which only £2 million was recouped by the farmer.

With cereal and brassica crops, rabbit damage can be reasonably accurately valued, but with grassland it is necessarily more a matter of intelligent guesswork. However, trials, which were carried out at Aberystwyth with rabbit-free grass plots and those to which rabbits were allowed access, showed conclusively that the former can carry approximately double the amount of farm stock.

Forestry as well as farming and gardening suffers severely from rabbit predation, particularly nursery trees of all kinds of which the bark and leading shoots are eaten.

On the credit side rabbits do exercise a useful controlling influence over the spread and density of undergrowth, such as briars, which as explained in Chapter 11 can have a beneficial effect on ant populations, and hence on those of partridges. If it was easier to keep rabbit populations within reasonable bounds this might weigh more in their favour.

The Romans were mainly responsible for the westward spread of the rabbit in Europe, but it was the Normans who introduced it to Britain. They established warrens for their rabbits in order to provide themselves with a self-perpetuating supply of meat with which to feed their retainers.

Natural History

The rabbit is covered in dense fur, generally brown in colour with white on the belly. A fully grown specimen is about 15 in long and 3 lb in weight. Bucks are slightly larger than does and have rather more massive heads. The species is polygamous, not promiscuous as popularly supposed. Breeding takes place mainly from January to June, during which time litters may be produced at monthly intervals, and sporadically in the remaining months of the year. Gestation lasts for 28 days. The young in a litter vary from 2 to 8 in number. They are born in a 'stop', or short tunnel, off the main burrow, scratched out by the doe, at the far end of which she makes a nest lined with grass. After their birth they are suckled by her once every twenty-four hours, and each time on her departure she seals up the entrance to the stop with earth.

This is necessary to thwart the cannibalistic tendencies of the buck. At 16 days old the young start eating herbage, and are weaned at 30 days. They become sexually mature at about 4 months.

Myxomatosis

In 1954 the disease myxomatosis spread to this country from the Continent and decimated the rabbit population here. However, pockets of survivors have continually emerged during the subsequent years, though further outbreaks of myxomatosis have checked any widespread resurgence in numbers. Nevertheless, nineteen years after the initial outbreak, a small but noticeable general increase in rabbits does seem to be occurring throughout the country.

The disease first attained prominence in Australia, where it killed off large numbers of rabbits. But it was considered by scientists there that in time rabbits might build up immunity to it, and that within twenty years it could be a spent force. There are some indications that this may be happening in Britain, but the issue is complicated by the fact that there have been changes in the strain of myxomatosis which may be prolonging its virulence. There is therefore no clear indication as to how rabbit populations may move in the future. My own guess, and it is no more, is that we are faced with the likelihood of a slow but sustained comeback by the rabbit, which could by the 1980s mean that we have a major problem on our hands again, unless we take effective action in the meantime to prevent it.

Rabbit Control

Effective rabbit control on a grouse moor is hardly less essential than it is in farming and forestry. In the management of pheasants and partridges it is less critical, but certainly desirable. With the aid of guns, nets and ferrets the shooter can make a valuable contribution.

Prior to 1939 the principal means of control were traps and snares. But these have now been superseded by lethal gas, such as the proprietary brand 'Cymag'. Where gassing is impracticable traps and snares can still play a useful part in places. But probably the most efficient method of clearing out small rabbit colonies which cannot be effectively gassed is to ferret them. Long nets, except for sealing off burrows being ferreted, have now little practical use.

Gassing

The first and most important thing to understand about Cymag, or any other brand of lethal gas, is that it is a deadly poison. The precautions laid down by the manufacturers regarding handling and usage should be strictly observed. Cymag is in fact a powder which, when exposed to the moisture in the air, gives off hydro-cyanic gas. It is sold in sealed tins which should be stored under lock and key. When setting out on gassing expeditions any dogs should be shut in their kennels or in the house and kept well out of harm's way.

A gassing party should always consist of at least two persons, so that if a mishap occurs and one is overcome by fumes the other can give first-aid and fetch help.

There are two basic methods of employing gas; spoonfuls of the powder can be placed inside each hole; or it can be blown down the hole with a pump, either hand or mechanically operated.

Whatever method is used the operators should work from the upwind side of the burrows with which they are dealing so that any fumes blow away from them. Placing spoonfuls of powder inside rabbit holes is not in my experience a very satisfactory method. But if it is employed, the powder must be placed sufficiently far down the hole, so that when this is blocked with turf the powder is not covered. Any other entrances to the same burrow should be similarly treated and blocked.

Except in very large rabbit burrow systems, the most economical and satisfactory method of gassing is with a hand pump. A hole on the upwind side of the burrows should be selected and the hose from the pump inserted well down it. The hose should then be firmly sealed in place with a turf placed grass-side downwards in the hole and any additional earth necessary tamped in place round it (see Figure 72). Adjacent holes should be similarly sealed. Having filled the container on the pump with powder, a start can be made to pump it down the hole. After a short while the gas will probably be seen to appear as a white smoke from the un-plugged hole. Pumping should immediately be stopped, and the holes concerned plugged with turves, which should be cut and

K

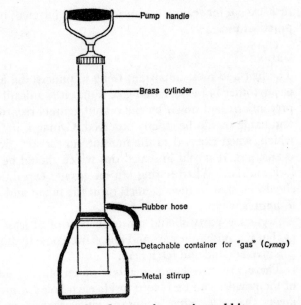

Fig. 72   A typical hand pump for gassing rabbits

waiting in readiness, and any extra earth required to make an airtight seal tamped in place. Pumping can then be continued, and the process repeated as necessary, until the gas has obviously penetrated the whole system. The hose should then be pulled out, and the sealing of the hole completed.

Gassing should only be done in fine weather when there is no more than a light breeze blowing. Operators handling the pump, etc., must not put their hands to their mouths, and should anyone suffer a cut or scratch, he should quit at once, so that there is no risk of any powder getting in the open wound. On completion of operations, empty Cymag tins should be flattened and then buried. On no account should they be disposed of in ponds or streams, or powder residues may prove lethal to fish and farm stock. Having done this and put away the rest of the equipment, the men concerned should wash their hands thoroughly, and be sure that they do not touch any food or animal feeding stuffs until they have done so.

Burrows which have been gassed should be inspected daily thereafter for several days to make sure there have been no break-outs or break-ins. If there have, it will be necessary to gas them again, and continue repeating the dose until they remain closed.

Gassing is simple and effective, but I would stress again that proper precautions must be observed if accidents are to be avoided, not only to humans, but animals as well; I know of a man who lost a valued and valuable Labrador through failure to take the necessary safety measures.

In some situations, such as where rabbit burrows are among tree roots, gas may escape through cracks in the ground, particularly when it is very dry, and therefore not be effective. In such circumstances trapping may be the best alternative.

Trapping

All rabbit traps now have to be of an approved pattern. There are three of these, but at the time of writing only two are apparently in production, namely the *Imbra* (see Figure 73) and the *Lloyd*. By law traps cannot be set in the open and so have to be placed in the mouth of a rabbit hole. Setting traps correctly calls for considerable skill; the level of the floor of the entrance must not be altered; so the trap has to be counter-sunk and the plate then lightly covered with fine soil so that all appears normal. The chain of the trap should be firmly secured with a peg pushed into the ground beside the hole. It is claimed on behalf of the Imbra that over 90% of the rabbits taken in these traps are killed outright. This is a very big improvement on the gin, formerly used for this purpose. No equivalent figures are available for the Lloyd trap, but I have heard it well spoken of by those who should know.

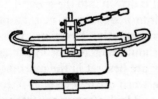

Fig. 73   The Imbra rabbit trap

This trap has proved very successful, and achieves a high percentage of kills. When set in a rabbit hole, it is essential that the pan, when set and covered, conforms to the original floor level.

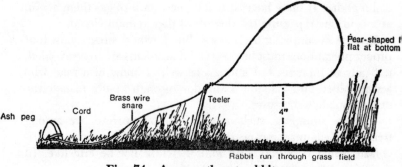

Fig. 74 A correctly set rabbit snare

Snaring

Snaring really is an art. Almost more depends on knowing precisely where in a rabbit run is the right place to set a snare, than how to set it. To discover a run from the edge of a wood out into a field is not difficult for any moderately observant person. But it requires sharp and knowing eyes to be able to pick out a rabbit's tracks in the run. A rabbit appears to move in a series of bounds, and the snare should be set just in between them. In deciding the right place, it has to be remembered that the marks of a rabbit's hind feet appear in front of its forefeet. A correctly set snare is shown in Figure 74. It will be noted that the loop is pear-shaped, but flat on the lower side, which should be about 4 in, i.e. a handspan, above ground level, though on hill sides it will need to be set rather higher. The loop is held in position by a slender stick stuck in the ground, known as a 'teeler'. The other end of the wire is attached to a length of cord, which is secured to a peg about 10 in long that is driven into the ground.

If a rabbit goes into a snare at a run, its neck is usually dislocated and it dies instantly. However, this does not always happen, and snares should therefore be inspected after an interval of a few hours. They are best set in the morning, so that any taint of humans will have worn off by evening. A competent operator should be able to set and look after up to 400 snares.

Ferreting

Long netting depends for its success on large numbers of rabbits being present, and in my view has no real part to play in controlling the small populations which have to be dealt with on shoots today. However, ferreting can make a very useful contribution, and one which possibly because of its sporting overtones is often underrated by officialdom.

The first requirement is to know how to handle and manage ferrets. This is a big subject, and space here will only allow a few salient points and guide lines to be set down. Those who wish to know more should go and learn at first hand from somebody who keeps and works ferrets.

The ferret is a member of the family *Mustelidae* in Britain, of which its largest relative is the otter, and its nearest the polecat. In fact brown or skewbald ferrets are usually known as 'polecats'. It has a characteristically fierce, alert and fearless nature, like others of the family.

Success with ferrets is just as dependent on obtaining stock sound in body and temperament, and bred from a good working strain as it is with gundogs. The prospective ferret owner should therefore make discreet inquiries with a view to finding a reputable breeder, whom he should then visit so that he can see the animals in question and how they are kept. If they appear well fed and in good health and are obviously well housed in clean, decent quarters, then it will probably be worth opening negotiations to purchase. It is usually wise to avoid ferrets offered for sale by casual acquaintances picked up in markets and pubs, however reluctantly obliging the vendor may appear.

A male ferret is called a hob and the female a jill. Ferrets like the company of their own kind, so it is usual to house two of the same sex together. Some people prefer hobs, others jills. Part of the code of good ferret management used to be that a jill had to be mated at her second heat or she died. This is not such an old wives' tale as some people now assert; jills can survive unmated at their second heat, but modern veterinary evidence shows that it is desirable that they should be mated at this time, and complications which may be fatal can occur if they are not.

Line ferrets, or 'liners' as they are known, are different characters with a different role in life from their companions who work free of any such restraint. If one or more of the latter kills a rabbit underground and lies up with the kill, it is the liner's job to go down and act as chucker-out. He may have to drag a considerable length of line behind him, so it is essential that a line ferret is big and strong. In view of the unsociable part he has to play a liner is always housed on his own.

Ferrets are quartered in a hutch, or cub. This should be solidly constructed of wood, and one to accommodate two animals should be at least 4 ft in length with other dimensions as shown in Figure 75. The roof should be hinged and there should be well-fitting doors to both the run and sleeping quarters; the roof should have a fastening to hold it open, so that it cannot be blown shut accidentally by a gust of wind, and possibly kill or injure one of the occupants. The flooring and inner walls should have flush, smooth surfaces to facilitate cleaning out, which should be done daily. The cub should be sited under cover against a wall with a southern aspect, so that its occupants can enjoy the sunshine on fine days; a dank, dark shed in which one sometimes sees a ferret hutch is not a suitable site.

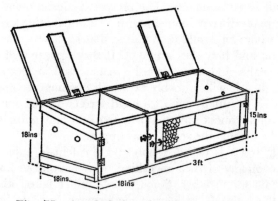

Fig. 75   A cub designed to house two ferrets

Well-managed ferrets are not treacherous. But they do need to be handled carefully and considerately. As mentioned above they are alert creatures with highly tuned reflexes; they react sharply if taken unawares by any sudden movement. So, provided they are treated as working companions rather than pets and sensibly handled, there is no reason to be fearful of being bitten.

Feeding utensils should be of heavy enamel ware so that they cannot be used as playthings. As ferrets are carnivorous they should be given raw meat from time to time, even if the basis of their diet is bread and milk. Whatever it is, some liquid, i.e. milk or water, should be supplied with every meal.

Rabbit burrows can be pretty dirty, flea-ridden places in which to work, and rat runs even more so. So, although ferrets are naturally hardy little creatures, they should be regularly inspected, so that any ailment they develop or parasites they pick up can be promptly dealt with. By far the most important factors in keeping ferrets in good health are general cleanliness and good feeding in the course of their everyday lives. But when prevention has to give way to cure, a qualified vet, with modern antibiotics, etc. at his command is the best person to effect this.

For transporting ferrets to and from their work a well-made box, with a web sling so that it can be carried over the shoulder, is best; one to carry two free ferrets and a liner in their respective separate compartments is shown in Figure 76. A sack or canvas bag is not suitable, as when placed on the ground it can easily be trodden on, or have something like a spade dropped on it.

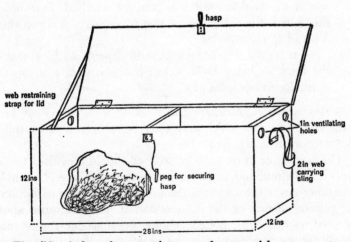

Fig. 76 A box for carrying two ferrets with a separate compartment for the liner

Some people might consider it preferable to have a separate lid for each compartment, but some well-made box of this style is a great asset. A sizeable wisp of hay should be put in each compartment every time it is used, and removed afterwards.

Some people muzzle their ferrets when they go rabbiting because they claim it makes the use of a liner unnecessary. In my experience this is not always so, and if the ferret by mischance meets one of its hereditary enemies such as a rat, it is completely defenceless. It is therefore preferable to work ferrets unmuzzled.

In addition to the box in which to carry the ferrets, other equipment needed for a day's rabbiting is :

a A leather collar and line for the liner. The line should be light, strong and durable; it should be attached to the collar by a swivel and clip; it should be twenty yards long, and each yard marked by a knot; it should be wound on a stick, and should be unwound and wound back again in use as occasion demands, and not left in coils on the ground. It should be hung out to dry like a fishing line after use.

b A light steel rod with a T-handle for use as a probe.

c A special long, narrow-bladed spade or graft with a long handle.

d A billhook, which should be both clean and sharp.

e A mattock, which also needs to be sharp, but which can be left in the vehicle until it is actually required. Fortunately this is not often, but where tree roots are a problem there is no adequate substitute.

f Purse nets; the number needed will depend on the extent of the burrows being tackled, but a dozen to a score should normally suffice, plus pegs.

A dog which is accustomed to working with ferrets can be a great help, but any which aren't are better left at home unless they are rock steady to fur.

The warren or burrows to be ferreted should be visited two or three days beforehand, so that any necessary clearance of brambles and other cover from around the holes can be made to facilitate the placing of nets or the introduction of ferrets. If guns are to be used to deal with bolted rabbits, positions for the shooters should be selected, and cover cut back as required to give them clear fields of fire.

A typical ferreting party may consist of three people, two guns, and one man to handle the ferrets. Silence is essential to success. The party should approach the site upwind as noiselessly as possible. A halt should be called at a point short of the destination where surplus kit can be left out of harm's way, and anyone's field of fire.

Sometimes, even if it is intended to bolt rabbits to the guns, some of the holes may be netted, and where this is the case the purse nets should be put in position. As soon as this has been done the guns should go to their places. If the burrows are reasonably extensive, it will probably be advisable to work two ferrets, which as soon as the handler sees the guns are ready can be introduced.

Rabbits can either bolt like cannon balls or slink away like shadows. But, however they elect to make their exit, they must be allowed to get well clear of the burrows before they are shot. Each gun must know exactly where the other members of the party are, even though he may not be able to see them; he must also know his arc of fire and not shoot outside it. If on a fine day rabbits are bolting well, grand sport can be had. But from the safety point of view it is essential that the participants stay where they are supposed to be, and in the excitement of the moment someone does not, for example, chase off after a wounded rabbit and get in somebody else's field of fire.

As soon as all the rabbits in a bury have been evicted, a ferret will normally surface of its own accord. It should be allowed to move well out from the mouth of the burrow and then be picked up round the shoulders, as shown in Figure 77. If it does not emerge when expected, it may be possible to tempt it out with a rabbit's paunch placed in the entrance to the burrow. If this does not succeed, recourse will have to be made to the liner, which may in turn have to be followed by digging. But a little hard grafting never did anyone any harm and, although it may interrupt the shooting, has to be accepted as just as much an integral part of the sport.

Shooting Rabbits

There are various other ways, apart from casual encounters on ordinary shooting days, in which rabbits can be tackled with a gun. Now that they appear to lie out much more instead of going to ground, hunting up areas of bracken and scrub with the aid of spaniels or German short-haired pointers can provide good sport in February and March, and again in October.

Shooting rabbits in the fields at harvest time as the corn was

K*

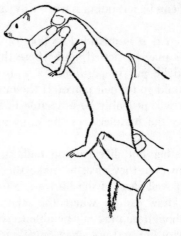

Fig. 77 The correct way to pick up and carry a ferret with the right hand

The use of the left hand as well is not essential.

cut used to be a popular sport, before the advent of myxomatosis in 1954. But the universal adoption of the combine harvester, with the swath of straw it leaves in its wake, and the greatly increased acreages of fields have changed conditions dramatically, and even should the size of rabbit populations again allow, I doubt whether circumstances will permit sport of that kind to be enjoyed again. However, dogging the stubbles before the straw is baled or burnt may be practicable for rabbits lying up under the swath, and two years ago I shot half a dozen in this way on one field.

Rabbits in cover can offer tricky shooting, as they bounce along, disappearing intermittently behind hazel stools, brambles and other low cover. But the shooter must not be put off by this. He must fix his eye on their head and 'go' for them with his gun. If he does so, and trusts his eye, he should soon be bowling them over without any trouble.

In the days when rabbits were legion in Britain they provided many people with a lot of sport. But in my opinion the shooting community as a whole is better off without so many rabbits in the countryside, and their place as the 'popular' quarry has been more than well filled by the ubiquitous woodpigeon.

Finally, I am sure all who have ever enjoyed rabbit shooting of one kind or another will heartily endorse the sentiments expressed by the anonymous author who wrote :

> If rabbits weren't so short behind,
> How many brilliant shots we'd find!

CHAPTER TWENTY-EIGHT

WOODPIGEON

T HE woodpigeon with its swift flight and smartly executed evasive tactics can provide splendid shooting and prove an elusive target to even the finest marksmen. It is a pity that its superb sporting attributes are not as handsomely matched by its subsequent attractions when it comes to the table. If they were, the problems which it now poses as a pest would long ago have solved themselves.

People often wonder why woodpigeon populations have grown to such huge proportions in recent years. The short answer is that modern farming, with its large acreages of arable land and fine young clovery leys, provides exactly the conditions the birds need in order to thrive and multiply. Unless there is a very harsh winter such as we had in 1962–3, at no month of the year are they short of food, though in some they may have to search a little harder than others.

Natural History

The generally grey plumage of the woodpigeon with its white collar and wing bars, and pink tinted underparts is so well known as to need no further elaboration. Male and female are generally the same size. Their average weight is $1\frac{1}{4}$ lb, length 16–17 in and wingspan 23 in. Their top flying speed is reckoned to be only 45 mph, which is a good deal slower than that of a pheasant or grouse, and somewhat slower than a partridge. But they have remarkable powers of acceleration, and it is these which enable them so often to wing their way to safety, and elude the shot intended for them.

The woodpigeon nests in almost any kind of tree but conifers in woodlands and quickthorns in overgrown hedges, especially if the latter are ivy-covered, are particularly popular sites. The breeding season lasts from April to September. The normal size of a clutch of eggs is only two, but three and often up to five

clutches are laid in the course of a season. However, the survival
rate from the earlier clutches is usually very low, and it is estimated
that two-thirds of the young which grow to maturity are from
those which hatch in August/September. Incubation is by both
the male and female, the former mainly by day and the latter by
night. The fledglings are fed by both parents and are able to fly
after about 28 days. Young birds of the year which are subsequently shot in the autumn can be distinguished by their lack of
a white collar, although they have white wing bars, and the
brownish grey tone of their body plumage. In October the birds
start to pack in flocks, which can sometimes number many
hundreds, and in which they feed and roost together. In autumn
and winter they like to roost in sheltered woodlands, and to those
specially favoured by them thousands of birds will flight of a
winter's evening.

Crops off which they feed vary with the time of year, and a
summary is given below :

Diet

a March-June	Clovers and other forage crop mixtures, spring sown cereals, sprouting peas, young kale and other brassicas; weed seeds of various kinds, especially chick-weed.
b July-August	Ripe peas : cereals from lodged patches of standing corn (N.B. wheat is generally, though not invariably pre-ferred to barley when it has ripened sufficiently); stubble gleanings.
c September-October	Wheat and barley stubble gleanings; autumn sown cereals; beech-mast, acorns, and other nuts; clovers.
d November-February	Late stubble gleanings, including those of oats; kale, rape, brussels sprouts and most other green crops; ivy and other woodland berries; spring sown cereals; clovers.

The above periods into which the pigeon's gastronomic year
has been divided have been chosen quite arbitrarily. Some experts
may think them in need of adjustment, but however much one
rings the changes there will always be a good deal of overlapping

in the menu of one period with that of another. But as a guide line, grain is generally preferred to greenstuffs, and clovers to brassicas. The only sure way to find out the popular dish of the day is to shoot three or four birds and examine their crop contents.

Shooting Pigeon

Some people argue about the time of day at which it is best to shoot woodpigeon. In my experience there are no hard and fast rules governing this. However, there are sometimes local trends; for example in one area where I have shot considerable numbers over decoys at varying times of year, the birds have frequently, though not always, lost interest after about 2.30 in the afternoon and the few that have pitched in after that time have really not been worth waiting for. In summer and early autumn the three or four hours after midday usually seem the least productive. But in the short winter days woodpigeon have so little time in which to feed that they cannot afford to play 'hard to get', and birds will normally pitch in continuously. On one farm where I have shot a great many on various occasions there is always increased activity over the decoys in the last two hours of daylight of a winter's afternoon as the birds start flighting back to the woods to roost. There is little to be gained in my experience by making an early start, in fact the advantage may lie in letting the birds settle to their feed before the shooting begins.

If one takes a walk with a gun, woodpigeon can sometimes be shot as they clatter out of a bush or tree. But owing to the disturbance caused by each shot, it will take an awful lot of walking to make a bag of any size in this way. The two principal ways of tackling woodpigeon are, therefore, to shoot them over decoys, or as they flight into roost in the woods of an evening. The latter is a winter sport, when the leaves are off the trees. The former can be undertaken whenever the pigeon have concentrated in sufficient numbers to make it worthwhile.

Gun and Cartridges

Before we take the field there is the question of the gun and cartridges we ought to take with us. A lot of idle chatter is bandied around about how difficult woodpigeons are to kill. As a result young shots gain an impression that the bird is like a sort of flying armoured vehicle that requires the nearest thing to an anti-tank weapon in shotguns in order to bring it down. This is quite wrong. A woodpigeon is as easily killed as any gamebird, but it can be rather more difficult to hit and that is the crux of the problem.

As explained in Chapter 3, the overall size of a pattern shot by a 28-bore is not significantly smaller than that of a 12-bore. Shot size for shot size the essential difference lies in the greater number of pellets contained in the pattern thrown by the larger gun. It is this factor which makes it so much more lethal. However, those who shoot with a small-bore can redress the balance in their favour by shooting with a smaller shot size. In practical terms, the idea which I have seen propounded in print that a larger bore gives a wider spread of shot in the sky is nonsense.

Again, as indicated in the tables in Chapter 3, a woodpigeon is reckoned to require a minimum pattern density of 130 pellets in the 30 in circle, and a pellet striking energy of at least ·85 ft/lb in order to make certain of a clean kill. These conditions are very adequately met by a 1oz load or No. 7 shot used in conjunction with an improved cylinder (12-bore) barrel up to a range of 45 yards, and a pigeon at that distance is a very high, or long bird indeed.

Shooting pigeon over decoys is mostly fairly close-quarter work at typical driven game ranges, though the shooter who likes to take some sporting chances at longer ranges will never lack the opportunity. It is where winter flighting of woodpigeon into tall beechwoods is concerned that people's thoughts turn to heavier shot. I have done quite a lot of experimenting with heavy loads of larger shot in these conditions, notably 'Maximum' 4's and 5's, but the results have been no better than those obtained with 1 oz of No. 7's, which seems to me the most lethal load for pigeon in all normal circumstances. It also has the advantage, where a considerable number of cartridges are fired, of having much the less noticeable recoil.

One other point can be conveniently disposed of at this juncture, namely the wearing of camouflage face veils. Most experts rather scorn these pieces of equipment, on the grounds that if a shooter knows his stuff they are an unnecessary and faintly irritating adornment. I am afraid I disagree; I have used one for many years, both for flighting and decoying, and am convinced that the advantage it allows the shooter in being able to move his head more freely to look around and see what is happening, more than compensates for any slight discomfort experienced; also on a summer's day they are invaluable for keeping the flies and midges off one's face.

Pigeon Flighting

Flighting pigeon as they swoop into their woodland roost on a windy winter's evening can be thrilling sport. But to obtain the best results in extensively wooded areas the birds should be kept moving over as wide a locality as possible, so the greater the number of guns who participate, the larger the area that can be covered and the better the sport likely to be enjoyed by all.

The guns should be ready in position at least an hour and a half before dusk. As they will all have different distances to go to their respective stands, shooting should begin at a stipulated time given out at the meet beforehand, or as otherwise appropriate. Each gun should be allotted a reasonably extensive beat within which he can place himself as he likes to best advantage in the prevailing conditions of wind and weather to deal with the incoming birds. Unless one has prior local knowledge, it may take a little time to discover by trial and error exactly where the best spot is. So it is advisable to keep the impedimenta down to the minimum necessary which I consider to be the gun, an ample supply of cartridges, i.e. a bag of at least 100, a gamebag containing a pair of secateurs, and a shooting stick.

It is a mistake to worry too much about concealment; if the shooter wears a face veil, finds a good background, such as a holly tree or laurel bush in front of which to stand or sit, so that his back is to the wind, and then *keeps still*, the birds will come to him just as well as they ever will to an elaborately and laboriously made hide, which may anyway be found to be in the wrong place and have to be abandoned. A pair of secateurs can be most useful for snipping off small branches to clear a field of fire, and is light and easily carried. A dog can prove a valuable aide on these occasions, but it does need to be sat where it has ample overhead cover from view.

If these winter flight shoots are well organized and attended by experienced guns, bags running into several hundred can be made of an evening. Where disturbance of game in the coverts is not a problem, they can be continued from the begininng of the year right through into March.

Decoying Pigeons

Unlike flighting, shooting woodpigeon over decoys is usually a solitary sport. If the birds come well and plentifully to the decoys, the shooter can virtually make his shots as easy or difficult for himself as he likes. So the man who claims to have shot x pigeon for the expenditure of a total number of cartridges only slightly in excess of x may not always be such a good shot as these figures imply. But for those who treat decoying as a sport as much as an exercise in pigeon control it can provide some of the most exciting and varied shooting a man is ever likely to enjoy.

Equipment

An important prelude to success is to have the proper equipment, and know how to use it. There are a lot of attractive gadgets with which a man can saddle himself which are of little real use. A Land Rover can often carry him and his kit right up to the site selected for a hide. But not all of us have Land Rovers and even those who do may sometimes have to carry their own equipment, so it is advisable to organize it on a man-pack basis, so that it can be carried reasonably conveniently in one lift for 500 yards or so. Having collected and discarded many items over the course of the years, my own kit has now become standardized with the following :

a 12-bore game gun carried in canvas cover with sling.
b Cartridge bag containing 100 cartridges.
c A dozen rubber decoys plus sticks, carried in a gamebag.
d Shooting stick with adjustable stick and leather sling seat.
e Face veil.
f Insect repellent.
g Ex-WD machete, and a pair of secateurs.
h Two small camouflage nets.
i An empty sack for carrying shot birds.
j *Binoculars.
k *Ropes of 'bangers' (i.e. agricultural bird-scarers).
l *Reserve of 500 cartridges.

The items marked * are left in the car until actually needed.
I have found I can carry items *a–i* above without feeling unduly overburdened for any reasonable distance across country.

Finding Pigeon

Having equipped oneself, the next thing is to find the pigeon. I do not propose to waste space giving people hints on how to obtain shooting. In my experience there are those who have the character, initiative and natural graces to obtain all the shooting they'll ever want, and those who are not so blessed, and no amount of advice, however well meant, will ever basically change this state of affairs.

There is an army slogan to the effect that time spent on reconnaissance is seldom wasted. It is just as applicable to the preliminaries for pigeon shooting as military operations. In the early months of the year, woodpigeon tend to be in penny packets all over the countryside, feeding on clovers in permanent pastures, or on whatever they can find. Occasionally one may discover an unploughed stubble in late December/January, particularly if the weather was bad at harvest time, which has become a centre of attraction. A strategically placed clover field in February/March can likewise draw in large numbers. Knowing the likely places in which to look can save a lot of time spent on reconnaissance. So also can good liaison with farmers and their staff, especially the herdsman if there is one, as he probably sees more of the farm as a whole every day than the other men. The number of birds on the ground will give a good indication of how well attended a field is, and if these are reinforced by a sizeable quantity of others waiting perched in nearby trees, then one has probably hit on the local jackpot. But it always pays to spend some time watching the birds' movements with field glasses to make sure it is the real thing, and that they have not temporarily vacated the field next door due to somebody exercising his dog, or some such interruption.

Having made certain of the field, the site for a hide has now to be chosen. Ideally one wants to sit with one's back to the wind, slightly to one side of a well-used flight line. Again it will pay to spend a short while watching how the birds are moving around, their lines of arrival and departure, the trees they favour for resting in, and so on. If one knows of a field with a similar crop fairly nearby, it will be advisable to go and inspect it in order to make sure, if it is being used, it is only a secondary attraction. Having confirmed this, two or three bangers can be tied to the branch of a tree, or the fence wire, and lit, so that birds which come to it when the shooting starts will be scared off.

Pigeon Hides

In my experience there are two kinds of pigeon shooters; those who want to shoot woodpigeon and those who want to build hides. The latter spend hours making elaborate erections, which are quite likely to be in the wrong place, and then there is another three-quarters of an hour's delay while a further rural development scheme is put in hand. I hear that one expert in this line has even managed to get a pigeon to come and perch on him, so well concealed has he been as a result of his endeavours, though why any honest-to-goodness shooter should want to try and emulate Long John Silver and his parrot I am at a loss to understand. I have always found that the simpler the construction of a hide can be kept the better it serves. There are four basic requirements for a satisfactory hide :

- *a* Good background; this will prevent the shooter's head and shoulders showing up in silhouette, particularly to low incoming birds.
- *b* Broken outline; this is a most important consideration when draping camouflage netting; straight lines stand out like the proverbial sore thumb.
- *c* Roominess; nothing is more irritating than not being able to reload without knocking one's gun barrels against the front or sides of a hide; one also wants to be able to reach one's cartridge bag easily.
- *d* Stillness; movement of some kind, either by the shooter himself, or of a part of the hide by him, is far more frequently the reason why birds are scared off than lack of concealment or camouflage.

Shadow intelligently used on a sunny day can greatly aid concealment. If natural cover is relied on for a hide, the less cutting of branches and other changes in the original scene that are made the better.

A hide always wants to be sited so that the shooter has his back to the wind if possible. If local conditions prohibit this, the next best thing is to try for a cross wind, or at least a partial cross wind.

With the wind from behind, the birds will flight in upwind from the front, so the shooter will have plenty of time to see them and prepare for his shot. The most lethal moment to take this is just as the bird spreads its wings prior to alighting. With a cross-wind he should also be able to see approaching pigeon in plenty of time. But with a head-on wind they will just appear suddenly from over his shoulder, and judging when and when not to shoot is something he will only learn from experience.

I always try and use a hide sited in a hedgerow or the edge of a wood. But in some situations this is impracticable, and a hide of some kind has to be set up in the middle of a field. For some years I had a length of hessian screening with five thin mild steel rods tied to it at intervals; the screening was green on one side and brown on the other. Although very basic, it served admirably, and was as successful as any hide of straw bales I have ever used. It is sometimes said that a hide in mid-field ought to be erected a day or two before it is used to enable the pigeon to get accustomed to it. On one occasion a baler, left in the field from the previous day, provided the basis of a hide, and a very satisfactory one it proved. So I am not convinced of the need to allow pigeon time to become used to a hide.

Decoys

When the hide is satisfactorily established, the moment has come to set out the decoys. Straightforward rubber decoys set up on sticks have always served me very well, but some people maintain that mummified real birds give better results. However, the former are more durable, less bulky, and simpler to store when not in use. I therefore prefer them.

Whatever decoys are used should be set out head to wind, or approximately so. If the wind is blowing either from straight behind or straight towards the hide, they should be placed directly in front of it. If it is a cross wind they should be slightly upwind of the hide. They should be set up at varying intervals from one another with the nearest about 20 yards from the hide, and the furthest 30 yards away. If the wind is head-on the whole lot should be ten yards further out.

As birds are shot they should be added to the picture. Some people prop up the heads of the dead birds with short forked sticks they carry specially for the purpose. This has always seemed to me rather a waste of time; provided the dead birds are placed to look as if they are feeding they will suffice. One or two can be set out with spread wings, which at times can prove an eye-catching attraction.

I usually start with 12 decoys, and then build up with shot birds as quickly as possible. The aim must be to create a lifelike and attractive picture to incoming woodpigeon, so avoid setting out decoys in straight lines or other regular patterns, and see that too many feathers don't litter the ground.

I have always found my dog a valuable asset when decoying. An intelligent animal soon learns that dead pigeon set out as decoys are nothing to do with him or her. Also if one is shooting from the edge of a wood, the dog can often get on with the retrieving of birds that have fallen well back in it, while his owner carries on shooting.

Once a shooter has mastered the knack of all these things, and it is not difficult, he should be able to look forward to making three-figure bags of woodpigeon in a day reasonably consistently, and enjoy a lot of good shooting in doing so.

CHAPTER TWENTY-NINE

HOW TO MAKE THE MOST OF A DAY'S ROUGH SHOOTING

T HERE is something about the friendly, informal atmosphere of a well-run rough shoot, with its undertones of quiet competence, which lends a good day's sport a magic peculiarly its own, and seems to me to capture the spirit of all those things of value in our field sports which one likes to believe command the approval of St Hubert, the patron saint of hunters.

An attempt has been made in Chapter 9 to show how good management can enable game populations on a rough shoot to be built up. The shooting programme should be complementary to, and reinforce these endeavours, so that although good sport is shown, it is not at the expense of good sport in the future. Because game populations are comparatively small, the balance between showing good sport and overshooting is often a fine one.

Overshooting

Overshooting can take various forms. A common one is to try and pack too many shooting days into January in order to end the season with a flourish. As a result the ground is disturbed too much; because of the shortage of game, shooting often goes on too late, and where pheasants are concerned too many hens are shot to make up for the lack of cocks. Rough shoots should be shot hard early in the season and lightly at the end. Thus on a typical shoot where pheasants in the hedgerows and spinneys are the mainstay of the sport, an outline programme for a season's shooting might be as follows:

a *October:* two days in the second half of the month, concentrating mainly on the outsides.
b *November:* four days.

c *December:* for the first fortnight of the month a mid-term break; then three days, including Boxing Day.

d *January:* three days, all cocks only.

An arrangement like this will provide 12 shooting days, which is a reasonable amount.

Elsewhere the possibility of shooting cocks only early in the season, rather than in January, has been mentioned. It seems to me sound policy to shoot cocks in preference to hens in October days, whenever a gun has the choice, as can quite often happen.

Planning a Day's Shooting

The plan for a day's shooting should be kept flexible. Early in the season wild pheasant populations on a rough shoot tend to congregate wherever there is a source of natural food, and move on from one to another as each is eaten out. However good the in-covert feeding arrangements may be, they do not materially affect this pattern until natural foods become hard to find from around the end of November onwards. As an example, there is a small beech wood I know which forms a peninsula jutting out into a field from the end of a much larger conifer plantation. On a day in the latter half of October in a good beechmast year up to 20 pheasants may be flushed from this rather bare little bit of woodland, though at other times one is lucky to find anything at all in it. On another shoot there was a stubble one year on which a number of birds from the ground next door always came to feed of a morning in October and early November, but were gone by midday. So for the first beat of the day the guns took post in a small glen just on our side of the march, and one man and his dog then walked these birds off the field. Plans should be adaptable so that situations like these can be exploited at once. To delay is to court disappointment. I remember an occasion when some wild duck were seen to flight into a stretch of river; it was suggested we ought to go after them immediately, but the person in charge would have none of it because it meant a change of plan. Thus when we came in due course an hour later to the river, there were no duck. If opportunities such as these are ignored on a rough shoot, it can mean a lot of walking and precious little shooting, which is both boring and exasperating for all concerned.

Dress

It must be appreciated that walking is basic to rough shooting, and those who turn out for such sport should be willing and dressed to do their share of it. Everyone is prepared to make allowances for the man who has accidentally left his gumboots behind—provided he does not make a habit of it. But to arrive obviously not dressed for the part at all is a very different matter; a certain gentleman appeared at a snipe shoot in Ireland in an immaculate plus-four suit and half-wellingtons. After an hour, having been heard to remark that it was not a bit like Sandringham, he retired wet, and nobody bothered to enquire if he was implying that he normally shot with royalty.

Manners

Although game may be much less abundant than at a covert shoot, the fellow who always tries to shoot your birds before you do is not less of a pest, whatever excuses he has to offer, and they are not usually in short supply. However poor a shot you consider your neighbour, and however much you want your grace birds at the day's end, do at least let him have one barrel at birds or ground game which rise in front of him before you demonstrate your own superior skill. It is simply good manners. But there is one exception allowed and that is when snipe are walked up; here it is only sensible that it should be understood and accepted that as soon as a snipe jumps any gun within range may shoot at it. There is, however, one proviso to this, in his enthusiasm to beat his companions to the shot, a novice is often inclined to fire at birds at extreme range, at which an experienced gun never even raises his weapon. This will put other birds to flight out of range, and spoil the sport for everyone; it should be tactfully discouraged.

Local Knowledge

Good local knowledge is probably the greatest asset a rough shooter can have. It will enable him to place guns in position without disturbing game feeding in the open. It will allow him to see and seize opportunities in the course of a day's shooting that would otherwise be missed. But those who manage rough shoots should remember that others may not possess their intimate knowledge of the ground, and when instructing guns where to go to head a beat, for example, must make sure that they give them clear directions. There may to them only be one holly tree 'over which all the birds will go' at the end of the path where the guest gun is told to take up his stand, but to that poor wretch when he gets there it could quite possibly be any one of twenty, and it is scarcely his fault if he picks the wrong one, and so never get a shot at the half-dozen birds which predictably all fly over 'that' tree. Precise instructions as to where guns, and particularly guest guns, are to go are sometimes sadly lacking at rough shoots.

Technique

At a covert shoot a gun goes to his peg, and is expected to stay there in default of any special instructions until the drive is over. At a rough shoot a gun sent forward to head a shelter belt or other covert, is often allowed more latitude in deciding for himself exactly where to stand. Because of rather inadequate instructions as to where he was to go, and his own selection of a rather improbable place in which to stand, I once saw an accident just prevented in the nick of time as a low-flying cock pheasant went forward at which one of the walking guns was about to fire. It is therefore most important that informality in the conduct of affairs does not lead to slackness in essential matters of safety, one of which is that everyone should know where everyone else is.

Dogs

At a guess, more sport is spoilt on rough shoots by unruly dogs than any other single cause. Having remarked on this with some force in earlier chapters it may be considered needlessly repetitive to do so again. But what is so incredible about this state of affairs is not how many such dogs appear in the shooting field, but how many shooters seem prepared to tolerate them, even allowing for the 'love me, love my dog' attitude which the British sportsman is apt to adopt at the drop of the slightest word of criticism. So strongly do I feel on this matter that I would even go so far as to suggest that a bad shot with a good dog is a more desirable combination and one which will serve the average rough shoot better than the converse. This is because game will at least be seen and shot at, whereas a good shot with a bad dog will probably mean that nothing is even seen. However, I realize my views may be considered extreme, and this is anyway a problem which rough shooting syndicates must solve for themselves.

Stock

There is another problem affecting rough shoots which is I believe of even more fundamental importance. The so-called 'wild' pheasant is now their staple gamebird, but these are becoming more and more reared birds which have strayed. As a result, even in a good breeding season, chick production and survival tends to be poor, with every likelihood of becoming poorer. It seems to me that rough shoots in this country urgently need stock birds from a really genuine wild pheasant strain. A possible answer to this may be the *Japanese Green Pheasant* mentioned in Chapter 14. This is a rather smaller bird than the English Blackneck, averaging about $2\frac{1}{2}$ lb in weight. In its native Japan it inhabits areas which experience high annual rainfall and intense cold. It is therefore a very hardy bird, which if it can survive in Japan, ought positively to flourish in the milder climate of Great Britain. There are such birds in aviaries over here, which have been imported. It would be interesting to obtain some, try to build up a breeding stock, and see if they might not be the answer to a rough shooter's prayer in forming the nucleus of a race of hardier, more truly wild pheasants, which would thrive better. They would doubtless interbreed with our existing native birds, which would benefit from the infusion of new blood.

Increase in Rough Shooting

In the last two decades many former rough shoots have either been incorporated in covert shoots or have otherwise disappeared. But with the current sharp rise in sporting rentals, and the increase in sporting rates consequent on the revaluation in 1973, one wonders if more sportsmen may not perforce in future turn from covert shooting to rough shooting, and the demand for good rough shoots grow substantially on account of the more modest demands they make on a shooter's purse. This in my view would be a welcome turn of events, and beneficial to the sport of shooting as a whole.

Most of my generation served a sort of apprenticeship at rough shooting before we were allowed to take our places in the line with the guns at covert shoots. In this way we learnt the fundamentals of safety and actual shooting, and also acquired a basic knowledge of game and their habits. But the growth of the syndicate system has made instant covert shooting available to virtually anyone who can afford the price of a 'gun' in both senses of the word. There are now people who sit on shooting sticks and fire guns who know almost nothing else about the sport. This can sometimes result in curious and unexpected situations. When picking up at a shoot one day I noticed one of the guests had no dog, and so went and stood with him at a beat where he was a flank gun. We greeted each other, and exchanged one or two pleasantries, as is usual on such occasions. A cock pheasant then came forward low along the covert side, and as it was obviously going to pitch in again, I expected him to let it go. However as soon as it came in range he raised his gun, missed with the first barrel, and had down a strong runner some 20 yards in front of us with the second. There being no point in delaying, I looked down at my dog and waved him forward with my hand. On looking up again I saw the guest gun running as fast as he could for the covert's edge where the pheasant was just disappearing with the dog already hard on its heels. Such was my surprise, that I called out rather tersely, 'That's the dog's job, not yours. Come back here.' He did; a moment later the pheasant was safely delivered to hand, and he was obviously overjoyed. It transpired in subsequent conversation that it was his first day's shooting, and the first pheasant he had ever shot, which he had been determined was not going to escape.

I believe, therefore, that rough shooting plays an essential part in a sportsman's education, and that those who have never enjoyed a day in the company of two or three friends and their dogs walking the fields, the hedgerows, marginal ground, or the moor have missed something of value, for which covert shooting even at its best is no substitute.

CHAPTER THIRTY

SHOOTING OVERSEAS AND FOR OVERSEAS VISITORS

THIS chapter is not intended as a complete guide to a painless passage through your shooting holiday, or how to fiddle a little bit extra on your duty-free allowance through Customs on your return journey. It is hoped, however, it may contain one or two hints to help you enjoy your sport on arrival.

Importation

Nowadays mention of the word 'guns' at an airport causes a far bigger stir than the cry of 'woodcock' at a covert shoot. However, it is perfectly legal in Britain to take your guns with you when you travel by air, and provided you declare them when you check in your baggage, and give the security men a chance to earn their pay by inspecting them and your shotgun certificate if they wish to, there is no reason why you cannot take them with you when you go to shoot abroad. However, on arrival at your destination things can be tricky unless you have checked prior to your departure with the appropriate embassy, and obtained any papers necessary to enable the Customs to clear them. In my somewhat limited experience of these matters, embassies conduct their business at a fairly leisurely pace, and it is advisable to apply in writing at least three weeks before you intend to travel. The only time I have applied at short notice, it appeared in the papers next day that the ambassador had had a heart attack. In view of the rather stuffy reply subsequently sent me, one hoped this might have been consequence, not merely coincidence.

In some countries the permit allowing a visitor to have a shotgun in his possession also allows him to shoot game, but in others a separate document is required for the latter. This point should be checked, so that one does not arrive with a gun which one then cannot use. The position regarding visitors to this country is ex-

316

plained in the next chapter, in the paragraph dealing with shotgun certificates.

Importation of Dead Game

The laws relating to the importing of dead game also vary from country to country. Once when going over to stay and shoot snipe in Southern Ireland, I took my hosts a couple of brace of grouse as a present. Knowing that some people are nowadays offended by the sight of dead game, I popped the birds in an army sandbag, tied a bit of string and a label round the neck of it and set off. All went well till Dublin Airport when I saw the Customs man looking quizzically at my sandbag, so I told him what it contained. His eyes lit up, he lent forward and whispered fiercely, 'Ye're not allowed to bring them in', at the same time marking the sandbag vigorously with his chalk, before moving on to the next customer.

Guns and Cartridges

Cartridges can pose one or two problems. In some places on the Continent cartridges suitable for use in $2\frac{1}{2}$ in chambered 12-bore British game guns are hard to obtain, and unless prior arrangements are made it may be found that only nominal $2\frac{3}{4}$ in cartridges are available, and these should not be used in $2\frac{1}{2}$ in chambered guns. Also the quality of cartridges varies quite a lot from country to country; however, excellent cartridges are obtainable in Austria, Belgium and West Germany if one knows the brands to ask for; but elsewhere, notably in some Iron Curtain countries, the cartridges are liable to give erratic ballistics.

In other countries generally there is a greater emphasis on walked-up game than in Britain, and because their game supposedly rises rather wilder, i.e. further out, these heavier $2\frac{3}{4}$ in loads and slightly larger shot are commonly preferred. Whether or not they are really advantageous, or merely encourage the taking of shots at excessive range, is another matter, and to try and argue it one way or the other is unlikely to change existing convictions on the subject, so I will only say that in the course of six years shooting in West Germany the results obtained with the British standard load seemed very adequate.

In the U.S.A., magnum loads for all bores have a big following. There are, for example, 20-bore loads available with $1\frac{1}{4}$ and $1\frac{1}{8}$ oz of shot, 28-bore ones with 1 oz and a $\frac{3}{4}$ oz of shot, and ·410 loads with a $\frac{3}{4}$ oz of shot. British cartridge makers do not market such loads. There is no real virtue in them. As has been explained in Chapters 2 and 3, their long shot columns merely produce higher pressures, more erratic patterns and greater noticeable recoil. These small-bore magnum loads are more efficiently handled by the appropriate larger gauges. They do not permit any saving in gun weight, in fact from a purely technical point of view, rather the contrary.

The 16-bore is a more popular gauge on the Continent than in this country. Those who come here and shoot with a 16-bore should not normally have any difficulty in buying cartridges in a shop. But because it is seldom seen in the field, they should take a good supply of cartridges with them when they go shooting, as in the event of a greater call on their resources than anticipated, they may not be able to find anyone from whom they can borrow some more to tide them over an emergency.

The numbered shot sizes in Belgium, Holland and Italy correspond with those in Britain. In Sweden the system of numbering is totally different. In many other countries, such as France, Spain, West Germany and the U.S.A., their No. 6 shot is the equivalent of our No. 5, and their 7 or $7\frac{1}{2}$ the same as our No. 7, there being no size comparable to our No. 6. When it comes to lettered shot sizes, e.g. our BB and SSG, every country seems to have a different system of designation.

Shooting Customs and Traditions

In Britain our shooting is conducted without any of the pageantry and ritual observed in a modest degree in the hunting field. But in some other countries, such as France and West Germany, custom decrees otherwise, and at big shoots certain traditional formalities are observed, particularly relating to the beginning and ending of the day's sport. As a visitor it is advisable to enquire beforehand about these things, so that one can conform, and avoid any awkwardness or possibility of giving offence. On another point of etiquette, it is wise to find out what game may and may not be shot. On the other side of the coin, when one is host to overseas visitors this point should be clarified. Thus repetition should be avoided of the apocryphal gaffe on the grouse moor, when the guest proudly announced to his host at the end of the first drive 'Les grouse trop difficile, mais les moutons sauvages, magnifique !'

Covert shooting abroad is sometimes conducted in a rather different way, in that the guns stand right up to the covert with their backs to it, and shoot outwards so that the birds are going away instead of coming to them. A few years ago a friend was peppered at a shoot on the Continent because he did not realize this. At a beat in thick woodland he stood well back as if for British covert shooting, and his neighbour who was out of sight round a corner of the ride in which the guns were standing shot at a low pheasant cutting across it, and some of the pellets hit him in the back and shoulders. Fortunately he was wearing thick clothing which saved him from serious injury.

Sportsmen of other nations I have noticed usually shoot low pheasants, irrespective of whether they are cocks or hens, without compunction. In Britain this practice, particularly where the hens are concerned, is frowned upon because it is liable to be dangerous, and does not call for much skill anyway. The incident related above seems to me to point the force of this argument; it is a matter which a host at a covert shoot might tactfully mention to a guest from overseas at the beginning of the day, and so forestall any possibly embarrassing contretemps *vis-à-vis* a beater who thinks he has come under fire.

Many Americans go game shooting with repeating or automatic shotguns. For the reasons already given I do not consider them suitable for such shooting in this country, although some shooters do in fact use them. It may be worth stressing that my objection to them is on grounds of safety, not snobbery.

Quality

It is always interesting to see how shooting is conducted in other countries, and the quality of the sport they have to offer. In the state forests of Czechoslovakia huge bags of pheasants can be made in a day, but with possibly rather too much emphasis on the quantity to suit really discriminating British tastes. Similarly vast numbers of grey partridges can be shot in Hungary. Excellent sport can be had with red-legged partridges in Spain, where quality and numbers go together. Capercaillie in Scandinavia also provide exciting shooting.

A lot of visiting sportsmen come to Britain to shoot grouse, and alas are sometimes disappointed in what they find. Unfortunately even good grouse moors have their bad years when bags are small, and unlike pheasants the matter cannot be put right by rearing more birds to compensate for the shortage of wild ones. This is a fact of life that is not always understood by the sporting visitor who comes here in a bad year, and in consequence leaves feeling he has not had a square deal. From the shoot owner's point of view however, his expenses in running the moor are much the same irrespective of whether it is a good or bad season, and he has to charge for his guns accordingly.

Although our covert shoots cannot match State-run continental shoots in sheer numbers, the quality of the pheasants shown to the guns is in many instances superb, and they provide uniquely demanding and exciting shooting. It is this which gives covert shooting in Britain a special appeal, of which a lot of sportsmen in other countries seem quite unaware, until they have sampled it.

Interchange of Information

But whether it is Britons going to shoot overseas or visitors coming to shoot in Britain, the interchange of information and ideas that result can but lead to improvements in conservation and management which are of benefit to game populations, and the betterment of sport in many countries. Also it must stimulate closer international co-operation in the wider aspects of conservation so necessary particularly in respect of migrant wildfowl populations at the present time, and in which the Wildfowlers' Association of Great Britain and Ireland is giving a valuable lead in this country. It is to be hoped therefore that in future visits by sportsmen of all nations to other countries will increase rather than diminish, as will the good that stems from them.

CHAPTER THIRTY-ONE

GAMEBIRD DISEASES

BY

T. H. BLANK, B.SC.

Assistant Director of The Game Conservancy

Introduction

BIRDS, like other animals, suffer from diseases, which may or may not cause death. Most of these are caused by organisms living as parasites on or within the bird's body, but some disease symptoms may be due to lack of certain essential chemicals and others to excessive amounts of poisonous chemicals in their diet.

In wild gamebirds, disease was at one time believed to be a major cause of mortality, particularly when they were living at relatively high density (e.g. grouse disease and partridge disease). Although the dead birds were shown to be carrying large numbers of disease organisms, which may have been the immediate factor, it is now considered that over-crowding, with all the attendant stresses, was the fundamental cause of death. In recent years disease in wild gamebirds does not appear to have caused any spectacular 'die-offs' such as those recorded among grouse and partridges in the early part of this century. Nevertheless in some years the incidence of 'gapes' (*Syngamus trachea*) and blackhead (*Histomonas meleagridis*) appears to have seriously affected grey partridges in certain areas, while outbreaks of fowl pest (Newcastle disease) in pheasants in 1970–1 decimated pheasant stocks locally, in many counties.

Unfortunately, even if we know that a certain disease is present and it is one for which we have an efficient cure, it is almost impossible to administer any medicines to wild birds. With reared birds however it is a different matter, and with relatively intensive rearing methods early recognition and prompt treatment of diseases are essential. Since effective remedies are not available for all diseases afflicting gamebirds, preventive methods are of prime importance. Such methods are most likely to be efficacious when based on an understanding of how diseases are spread.

Methods of Infection

Droplet infection, in which minute particles of saliva are coughed up, evaporate and float in the air, is responsible for the spread of some diseases of viral origin (e.g. fowl pest). Faecal contamination is the most common way in which bacterial and many animal parasites are transferred. Some of the most important avian parasites (e.g. round-worms) may have insects or other invertebrates as intermediate hosts which help to transfer the parasite from one bird to another.

Prevention

Preventive methods consist basically of providing the reared bird with adequate heat, ventilation and food since a well-grown bird is more likely to be resistant to disease. To offset the overcrowding intrinsic in modern rearing methods, movable pens may be used so that re-infection is less likely. And whenever possible new ground should be used each year for rearing, since there is no way of economically treating infected land so as to kill all eggs, cysts, etc., of the various disease organisms. While grazing by pigs and sheep that do not carry parasites of birds may help to destroy some of the infective stages, ground on which poultry or turkeys have been kept must be avoided. Disinfection of equipment should be routine; scrubbing with soap and a solution of soda or ammonia in hot water is most effective; an annual coating of creosote will not only preserve the wooden frames of pens and coops, etc., but also destroy disease organisms. Some special preventive methods, e.g. vaccination, and the use of drugs incorporated at a low level in foods will be discussed later.

Gapes—the Disease

Reared gamebirds are subject to many of the ailments which afflict poultry and one of the most commonly recognized diseases is 'gapes' caused by the parasitic round-worm (*S. trachea*). In pheasants the symptoms are quite characteristic, namely a sideways flick of the head accompanied by a juicy cough ('snicking') which signifies the bird's attempt to clear the obstruction caused by the parasite in the trachea. In partridges, symptoms are less reliable since the affected birds occasionally gasp with wide-open beaks, and this may be confused with other respiratory diseases. Both wild and reared birds may be affected. When the disease attacks young birds of from 2–6 weeks of age mortality can be heavy, but losses in older birds are usually relatively low. The adult worm lives in the birds' trachea, feeding on the hosts' blood. Heavy infestations result in loss of condition, while death from asphyxiation, due to the mass of worms preventing air reaching the lungs, is not uncommon. The mature female worm produces large numbers of eggs which are coughed up by the pheasant poult, subsequently swallowed and passed out in the droppings. Some of these eggs will hatch and the young gapeworm parasites may be accidentally picked up by other birds. Most commonly however the gapeworm eggs are swallowed by earthworms or some other invertebrate in whose intestine the eggs hatch and the larval gapeworms penetrate the hosts' muscles and encyst. In this highly resistant stage the parasite may remain as a potential source of infection as long as the intermediate host survives; and some earthworms may live for 3 or 4 years! An infected earthworm, if eaten by a pheasant poult, may release large numbers of gapeworm larvae into the bird's gut. These larvae rapidly make their way through the blood vessel to the lungs and in eight days from eating an infected earthworm a pheasant poult may have gapeworm in its trachea.

Gapes—Treatment

The small male gapeworm is permanently attached to the female which increases rapidly in size until at maturity it becomes an inch long and is readily visible through the wall of the trachea. At one time experienced keepers used to attempt to dislodge the worms from the epithelial lining of the trachea by manipulating a bent feather through the poult's epiglottis; this was a hazardous procedure, but sometimes effective when only small numbers were involved. Other methods involved blowing an irritant powder into a closed coop, the resulting coughing helping to remove some of the gapeworms. More recently a number of drugs have been found to be effective in either attacking the mature worm or in reducing its reproductive capabilities. Thibenzole, usually incorporated in the food for a 10–14-day period, has been found to be effective in controlling the disease, as has also ICI Game Bird Wormer which is administered as a one-day treatment in the drinking water. Treatment may however have to be repeated when the ground is heavily infected and it is usually uneconomic to medicate food or water until the poults are showing signs of the disease.

As we have seen, land which has become infected can remain so for several years. Although there is no practical economic way of removing all the potential invertebrate carriers (intermediate hosts) of the gapeworm, it has been claimed that a heavy dressing of iron sulphate, at 10 cwt/acre, gives a measure of control. The eggs and larvae of the gapeworm survive best in a neutral soil and so either heavy liming, to make it more alkaline, or sulphate of ammonia, to increase acidity, may have a beneficial effect. Even when ground is being used for the first time, losses from gapeworms can occur since several species of wild birds, notably rooks and starlings, may frequently suffer from this disease and should be discouraged from the rearing area.

Coccidiosis—the Disease

If 'gapes' is the most frequently recognized disease in young gamebirds, 'coccidiosis' is probably the most lethal. Indeed in cases where high mortality is associated with 'gapes' it is sometimes the more insidious 'coccidiosis' which is causing the deaths. But because the visible symptoms of coccidiosis are much less highly characteristic than the snicking which accompanies gapes, the disease itself is often unrecognized until severe losses have been experienced. The parasitic protozoan (a microscopic single celled animal) which causes coccidiosis is one of several different species of *Eimeria*. Although the pheasant claims the dubious distinction of having its own parasitic species (*E. phasianus*) it shares several other species of *Eimeria* with the domestic hen. These minute parasites live either in the blind guts (caeca) or the intestine of the poult. They can proliferate rapidly at certain stages, infesting the cells of the caecal or intestinal walls. As a result of the parasites' activity the affected birds soon lose condition. Food intake falls off rapidly and the birds have a 'humped up', dejected, ill-groomed appearance. Although a considerable amount of blood may be lost due to the break-down of the intestinal lining, this seldom shows in the birds' droppings and must not be relied on as a means of diagnosis. Although the disease may attack very young birds it is most frequently encountered in 3–5-week-old poults. When an inexplicable reduction in food intake occurs in birds of this age, and a few are showing a white 'scour' with typical signs of lethargy, it may be advisable to cull some of the ailing birds and send them away to be autopsied. If coccidiosis is present this will show itself in the inflamed blind-guts and in the cheesy consistency of their normally fluid contents. When portions of these contents are examined under the microscope large numbers of coccidia, the highly resistant resting spore stage of the parasite, may be observed. Early diagnosis is important since the disease can spread with rapidity and losses be heavy.

Coccidiosis—Treatment

There are several drugs which have been developed for the treatment of coccidiosis in poultry and since a number of the same species of *Eimeria* may be present in the pheasant, these drugs can successfully be used for gamebirds. Whitsyn S, Saquadil, Amprolium and several other compounds are widely used to control the disease. When the drug is given in the drinking water the usual procedure is to give medicated drinking water for three days, pure water for two days and then another three days of medicated water. Birds which have contracted the disease and survived have an immunity against further infection, and it is to develop this immunity that the 'three days on, two days off, three days on' treatment has been developed.

The resting pores (coccidia) of *Eimeria* are particularly resistant and can remain viable for a long time in the droppings on the surface of the ground. Equipment should be washed in an ammonia solution, but there is no satisfactory way of sterilizing infected ground.

Many proprietary chick foods contain a coccidiostat at a level which is capable of controlling a normal challenge from this parasite. However, if the ground has been used for rearing in previous years, and coccidiosis has occurred, the preventive level of the coccidiostat in the food may be too low to withstand a massive challenge. Curative treatment, as previously outlined, must then be adopted. Most cocciodiostats as well as being poisonous to the parasite are also more, initially, so to the 'patient', so do not exceed recommended dosage rates.

Although the spores of *Eimeria* are commonly found in wild gamebirds it is under semi-intensive rearing conditions that coccidiosis is most likely to spread quickly and losses can be heavy in pheasants, partridges, and grouse.

Blackhead—the Disease

Another protozoan parasite (*Histomonas meleagridis*) causes the inappropriately named disease, Blackhead. Even in turkeys, in which the disease was originally diagnosed, darkening of the skin at the back of the head is rarely characteristic, and is certainly not symptomatic in gamebirds. Although the disease occurs most commonly in partridges, its incidence in reared pheasants appears to be increasing. Red-legged partridges are particularly susceptible, and in some areas grey partridges are very difficult to rear unless preventive measures are taken.

In adult partridges Blackhead is usually a 'wasting' disease, the affected bird becoming extremely emaciated and unable to fly. Young partridges on the other hand may die from this disease while apparently still in good condition and losses can be severe. The blind guts may become very thick and enlarged, while in later stages of the disease, particularly in adults, lesions appear in the liver.

Blackhead—Treatment

Although it has long been suspected that round-worm *Heterakis gallinæ,* commonly found in gamebirds' intestines is involved in the spread of Blackhead, it is only relatively recently that the role of *Heterakis* has been diagnosed in detail. Good control of the disease can be achieved by the use of the drugs Entramin and Emtryl (in the food or in the drinking water), while treatment for the removal of the worm infestations with one of the anthelmintics used against gapes is also recommended. Unfortunately birds which have recovered from an attack of Blackhead do not acquire immunity and on infected ground continuous treatment through the drinking water may be necessary.

Although mainly a disease of gamebirds in captivity, the incidence of Blackhead is fairly high in wild partridges in certain areas.

Fowl Pest—the Disease

When Fowl Pest or Newcastle disease was recorded in wild pheasants in this country in 1963, the outbreak appeared to be an isolated one. But in 1970 when the disease, which is caused by a virus, spread rapidly amongst unvaccinated poultry, more widespread losses occurred among both wild and reared pheasants, being particularly heavy in East Anglia.

The symptoms of the disease in pheasants are similar to those of birds suffering from seed-dressing poisons, i.e. inco-ordination of the nervous system resulting in head twitching, staggering gait and eventually a paralysis accompanied by a dark green and white diarrhoea. Because of this it is extremely difficult to make an accurate diagnosis if these symptoms are observed in areas where autumn dressed corn has been recently sown and Fowl Pest is known to be present in poultry. Only by chemical analysis (for seed dressing poisoning) or by virus isolation (for Fowl Pest) can the cause of the trouble be diagnosed with certainty.

Since there is no curative treatment, preventive measures have to be adopted. Unfortunately there is nothing which can be done for wild birds except to ensure that all poultry units in the vicinity are properly vaccinated. But a measure of protection can be given to reared birds by adopting a vaccination programme.

Fowl Pest—Vaccination

Two types of vaccine are available—inactivated or dead vaccine which is given by injection, and live vaccines of two different strains (Hitchner B1 and La Sota). Adult pheasants caught up for laying pens should be injected (by means of a hypodermic syringe) in the thigh muscle with $\frac{1}{2}$ c.c. of dead vaccine. This should be followed with a second injection about six weeks later, and preferably at least a week before the birds begin to lay.

Live vaccine of the Hitchner B1 strain can be given to day-old pheasant chicks—by means of eye-dropping or beak dipping when the birds are transferred from chick boxes to the brooder house. With chicks from properly vaccinated parent stock this first vaccination may be omitted. When the chicks are three weeks old however they should be vaccinated with either dead vaccine (injection in the breast muscle) or live vaccine (Hitchner B1 or La Sota). Whilst it is possible to vaccinate the birds efficiently with live vaccine through the drinking water without handling the poults, beak dipping or eye dropping ensures that every bird is properly dosed. If vaccination is through the drinking water great care has to be taken to ensure that live vaccine is taken by all birds within two hours of reconstitution. When the birds are being caught up for moving to a release pen they should be given their final dose of vaccine—either dead vaccine (injected) or the La Sota strain of live vaccine (eye dropping). The use of either of these vaccines should give the poults an acceptable level of immunity to fowl pest until well into the shooting season.

Partridges, both red-legged and grey, can suffer from Fowl Pest and where stocks are penned for egg production vaccination with dead vaccine or the La Sota strain of live vaccine is recommended.

Other Diseases

In reared gamebirds, particularly during the first few weeks, various forms of the Common Cold (*Coryza*) are among the most frequently encountered ailments. This is also due to a virus but chicks may be more susceptible if they have been subjected to some form of stress such as chilling or overcrowding. Sometimes diseases due to certain bacteria, such as the pleuro-pneumonia-like organisms (P.P.L.O.), can occur at the same time and the causative agents may be difficult to determine. Bacteria, such as *Escherizia coli*, which may be present normally in small numbers, can proliferate rapidly and a broad-spectrum antibiotic is often used as a remedy.

Rarely encountered in young birds, but not uncommon in pheasants in captivity from their second year onwards, is Avian Tuberculosis caused by the bacteria *Mycobacterium avium*. At post mortem the heavily spotted liver and spleen is characteristic of the disease and the bird usually dies in an extremely emaciated condition. No cure is available and ground which has become infected should not be used for penning gamebirds for at least two years. Starling roosts are a potential source of infection and any recently occupied roosts should be avoided when pheasant release pens are sited.

Some diseases are caused by fungi. In pheasants (and also in wildfowl) a mould, *Aspergillus* spp. which is common on decaying vegetable matter can infect the respiratory system of pheasant poults and cause considerable losses. In the warm damp atmosphere of a brooder house, spores of the mould may be produced in vast quantities if infected straw or hay is accidentally introduced to block any gaps, etc., around the edge of the house. Again, if mouldy straw is used for 'strawing down' a feed ride, considerable mortality may result in 8–10 week-old poults. Affected birds may gasp for air (they do not 'snick') and birds usually die in good condition. White or grey nodules of varying sizes may be seen in different parts of the respiratory system. Prevention, by using only clean straw for this purpose, is the only course, since there is no cure for the disease generally known as Aspergillosis.

Another fungus, the yeast-like *Candida albicans*, makes successful partridge rearing almost impossible in certain areas unless special precautions are taken. The fungus is probably widespread in nature, living on dead and decaying vegetation. It can however live successfully on the crop lining of the partridge chick and utilize the vitamin B in the partridge chicks' food. If two- to four-week-old partridges become infected growth is arrested, feathers distorted and after partial paralysis the death rate may be high. The disease is most common in grey partridges but red-legs may also be affected. Although there is no effective cure for this disease (known as Moniliasis or Candidiasis) in partridges preventive measures can be effective. If the disease has been encountered previously and partridge rearing occurs on the same ground in subsequent years, spraying the food with a dilute solution of formic acid prevents outbreaks.

In addition to the gapeworm, *S. trachea*, and the threadworm, *Heterakis*, already mentioned in connection with Blackhead, a variety of parasitic worms may occur in gamebirds. At one time 'grouse disease' and 'partridge disease' were associated with the occurrence of strongyle worms. *Trichostrongylus* spp. Strongylosis can under certain conditions be troublesome in penned partridges. Crop worms, *Capillaria sp.*, can also occur, and if infestation is heavy Tetramisole (I.C.I. Game Bird Wormer) should be administered.

Parasites

Although many birds carry external parasites such as lice, preening and dust-bathing usually keep any infestation under control. Broody hens however may need treatment and dusting with a

L*

suitable insecticide; e.g. *Lorexane* is recommended. Mites, particularly the scaly-leg mite (*Cnemidocoptes mutans*) which causes eruptions under the leg scales, is best dealt with by shaking up equal volumes of *Lorexane* and paraffin oil and brushing the mixture on to the affected areas.

Poisoning

Poisoning of captive birds is relatively rare although this can happen if recommended doses of medicaments are exceeded. In wild birds certain agricultural chemicals, e.g. some seed dressings and other insecticides, can cause severe mortality, but occasional deaths from yew poisoning (from both leaves and berries), lead poisoning (by swallowing lead pellets) and even 'toadstools' (*Amanita* spp.) have been recorded.

Always examine birds carefully when completing the pick up on the day after a shoot to be sure that death was due to shooting!

CHAPTER THIRTY-TWO

LAWFUL AND UNLAWFUL OCCASIONS

T HE title of this chapter should probably have been 'With Apologies to the Legal Profession'. However it is not intended as an authoritative work on sporting law, but a guide to the answers to some of the quasi-legal problems with which a shoot owner and his keeper have to contend.

Laws relating to the pursuit of game go back to pre-Norman times. But it was the Normans who first really put teeth into them, when the prerogative of taking game was arrogated to the Crown, which then permitted the landed gentry to share the privilege. The earliest Act of importance in current law is the Game Act of 1831. Various other pieces of legislation have since supplemented, or modified it, the most significant in recent times being the Criminal Justice Act of 1967. As a result there is now a considerable and complex body of law governing the taking of game and related matters. A further complication is that Scottish Law is in some respects different from that in England and Wales.

The police to whom one often instinctively turns for advice on simple problems are not always well versed in this aspect of the law, though where one is lucky enough to find an officer who is, they can be of great help, and in such circumstances it pays to encourage one's keeper to strike up a good working relationship. However on matters of any complexity the wisest course is to consult a qualified member of the legal profession.

SHOTGUN CERTIFICATES

In order to possess, purchase, or acquire a shotgun it is necessary to have a Shotgun Certificate. These certificates are issued by the chief police officer for the area in which a person lives, and application forms may be obtained from any police station. The form, when completed, should be sent together with the requisite fee stated thereon to the local police station. The certificate is then issuable at the discretion of the Chief Police Officer of the area. If he declines to issue a certificate, the applicant may appeal to the Court of Quarter Sessions having jurisdiction in the area.

It is illegal to sell, lend, or give a shotgun to anyone who has not got a shotgun certificate; on no account may a shotgun be given to anybody under 15 years of age.

A shotgun certificate is *not* needed if :

> *a* A shotgun is borrowed from the occupier of private premises, including land, and used thereon in his presence.
>
> *b* Someone else's shotgun is used on artificial targets at a place and time approved by the local chief police officer, e.g. at an established shooting ground.
>
> *c* Someone is visiting Great Britain and not staying for more than 30 days in any period of 12 months.
>
> *d* You are carrying a gun for somebody else (who has a certificate) for sporting purposes only, e.g. you are a loader.
>
> *e* A person possesses a Northern Ireland firearm certificate for a shotgun.

GAME LICENCES

(The Game Licence Act 1860)

Game licences can be obtained from Post Offices and County Council offices. The rates of duty payable (1973) are :

One year, expiring 31st July	£6
Three months, expiring 31st October	£4
Nine months, expiring 31st July	£4
Any continuous period of 14 days	£2
Gamekeeper's licence for the whole or part of a year, expiring 31st July	£4

A game licence holder may sell game to a licensed game dealer. It is an offence to sell hares between March and July inclusive. A game licence is *not* required for :

> *a* Taking woodcock or snipe in nets in the United Kingdom; however, it is for shooting them.
>
> *b* Killing rabbits in enclosed ground or a warren with the permission of the landowner or tenant farmer. (See also *Ground Game Act 1880* below.)

c Killing hares by hunting or coursing.

d Killing deer by hunting or other means on enclosed land with the landowner's consent, but subject to the Deer Acts mentioned below.

e The killing of hares and rabbits by a tenant farmer or a person authorized by him in accordance with the Ground Game Acts.

f Beaters or loaders, provided the owner of the shooting holds a game licence.

But a game licence is necessary to kill rabbits on unenclosed land, and anyone doing so without a licence is guilty of trespass and taking game without a licence. (See also Poaching Prevention Act 1862 below.)

The Game Licence Act permits the use of a gun, snare, traps, or other devices for killing game. If the act is contravened, it is the intention to kill game which constitutes the offence, and it is not a defence to claim, for example, that game was shot at and missed.

THE GAME ACT 1831

In this Act the following are named as game :

Grouse	Partridge	Pheasant
Blackgame	Moorgame	Hares

Precisely what constitutes moorgame has never been defined. Ptarmigan are designated as game in Scotland.

The shooting seasons are :

Grouse	12 August–10 December
Ptarmigan (Scotland only)	12 August–10 December
Blackgame	20 August–10 December
Partridges	1 September–1 February
Pheasants	1 October–1 February

There is no close season for hares, but on moorlands and un-enclosed non-arable lands they may be shot by the occupier and persons authorized by him between 11 December (1 July in Scotland) and 31 March only. It is illegal in England and Wales to shoot game on Sundays and Christmas Day, and in Scotland illegal to shoot any wild bird or creature on these days.

Amendment to Section 4 of this Act by the Game Act 1970 terminated the offence of having game in one's possession more than 40 days after the beginning of the close season, as from 1 February 1971 (i.e. it became legal to keep game in a deep freeze for as long as required). However it remains an offence to buy or sell any gamebird (except live birds for rearing or exhibition purposes or for sale alive) after the expiration of 10 days from the date on which the relevant close season begins.

Under the Night Poaching Act of 1828 the taking of rabbits in addition to game as already specified above is an offence.

Under the Poaching Prevention Act 1862, woodcock, snipe, and rabbits are added to the list of game for the purpose of the Act.

THE GROUND GAME ACT 1880

This Act vested every occupier of land with an inalienable right to kill ground game on the land in his occupation. This right can only be exercised by himself or one other person authorized by him in writing, who must be either a member of his household resident on the land he occupies, or someone in his regular employ on the land, or expressly employed by him for the purpose of killing ground game.

Where a person does not have to rely on this Act for his right to kill rabbits, e.g. he is the owner of the land, he requires no authorization, and can ask as many people as he likes to kill rabbits.

However the Prevention of Damage by Rabbits Act 1939, and the Pests Act 1954 have now placed an obligation on the occupier of land to control the rabbits on it. If he does not do so, action may be taken through the County Agricultural Committee to obtain an order requiring him to control them, and if he still refuses to take necessary action, measures can be enforced despite him, for which he will be required to pay. The second of these two Acts makes it illegal for a person wilfully to spread myxomatosis.

All this impinges closely on the wider question of the exercise of sporting rights; if a landlord in England and Wales has not reserved the shooting rights for himself, they belong to the agricultural tenant, who can grant them to other persons, or merely allow people to shoot over the ground he holds. In Scotland this is not so, and an agricultural tenant has no right to take game unless this is specifically granted to him by lease. Irrespective of whether it is the landlord or agricultural tenant who disposes of the rights to a shooting tenant, this must be in writing; in Scotland an agricultural tenant can only do this with the prior written authority of his landlord. Although 'ready-made' printed leases are obtainable, it is advisable that they be properly drawn up by a qualified solicitor.

THE PROTECTION OF BADGERS ACT 1973

This admirable piece of legislation prohibits the taking or killing of badgers absolutely, save by an authorized person, who is defined as the owner or occupier of land, his authorized servant, or a person authorized in writing by him. It also empowers authorized persons to order people in pursuit of badgers off the land, and demand their name and address.

However, the Secretary of State may at discretion designate special Badger Protection Areas, in which otherwise authorized persons are required to show special cause to justify the taking or killing of badgers, such as, for example, extensive damage to crops.

Special acts of cruelty are also designated and prohibited :

a Cruelly ill-treating a badger.
b The use of badger tongs.
c Digging for a badger. Except for authorized persons to prevent damage, etc.

There are restrictions on the use of firearms; a smooth-bore gun must be of not less than 20-bore; rifles must fire a bullet of not less than 38 grains in weight, and must have a muzzle energy of not less than 160 ft/lb.

There are in addition certain general exceptions :

d A person may take an injured or disabled badger in order to tend it.
e A person finding a seriously injured badger may destroy it in order to spare it unnecessary suffering.
f If a badger is unavoidably killed or injured as an incidental

result of an otherwise lawful action, an offence shall not have been committed.

The Act does not specifically prohibit the setting of snares by authorized persons for the taking of badgers. However if a badger is taken in a snare, whether by design or accident, it might constitute an offence of 'Cruelly ill-treating', though such an action might be successfully defended on the grounds that the snares were regularly inspected at least once a day between sunrise and sunset. The implications in this respect deserve careful consideration by those who employ snares in predator control, if a badger it liable to fall victim.

THE PROTECTION OF BIRDS ACT 1954

This Act provides for open and close seasons for the other birds generally classed as game, and also wildfowl. The permitted shooting seasons are :

Snipe	12 August–31 January
Capercaillie	1 October–31 January
Woodcock (Scotland)	1 September–31 January
Woodcock (England/Wales)	1 October–31 January
Duck and Geese (Inland)	1 September–31 January
Duck and Geese (Foreshore)	1 September–20 February
Golden and Grey Plover	1 September–31 January

Coot, moorhen, bar-tailed godwits, curlew, redshank and whimbrel may also be shot between 1 September and 31 January.

The species of wild duck which may be shot in these seasons are :

*Common Scoter	*Garganey Teal	*Golden eye
*Long-tailed Duck	*Velvet Scoter	*Scaup
Gadwall	Common Pochard	Mallard
Pintail	Shoveler	Teal
Tufted Duck	Wigeon	

The species of wild geese which may be shot in these seasons are :

*Grey Lag	Bean	Pink-footed
White-fronted	Canada	

37 A keeper with ferrets and terrier.

38 Decoying pigeon from a hide on an open field.

39 A good type of springer spaniel retrieving a woodcock.

40 A pigeon killed coming into the decoys.

41 Scottish keepers and pickers-up discuss the next drive.

42   A low flying capercaillie flushed from a woodland.

43   Shooting woodpigeon from a high-seat in the treetops as they come into roost, a method which can give excellent results provided one has a good, experienced retriever!

44   The kind of bird we would all like to kill as a finale to a day's shooting!

All species of duck/geese marked with an asterisk appear in Part II of the First Schedule to the Act, and the others in the Third Schedule.

All raptors, that is owls, eagles, buzzards, kites, falcons and hawks, etc., are fully protected by this Act. However the following wild birds may be killed or taken by authorized persons at any time:*

Cormorant	Magpie	Carrion and Hooded
Herring Gull	Jay	Crows
Jackdaw	Starling	Domestic pigeon gone
Rook	Stock-dove	feral
Woodpigeon	Greater and Lesser	House Sparrow
Shag	Black-backed Gulls	

THE DEER (SCOTLAND) ACT 1959†

Scottish landowners were largely instrumental in having this admirable piece of legislation enacted in order to curtail the activities of poachers who were inflicting abominable cruelties on Red Deer in Scotland. Its passage through Parliament was hotly opposed by anti-field sport factions on the grounds that it was 'class' legislation!

The Act established the Red Deer Commission to conserve and control red deer in Scotland. It also stipulates close seasons for deer, as hereunder, and a nightly close time, in which deer may not be taken or killed.

The close seasons for deer in Scotland are:

Red Deer:	Stags	21 October–30 June
	Hinds	16 February–20 October
Fallow Deer:	Buck	1 May–31 July
	Does	16 February–20 October
Roe Deer:	Buck	21 October–30 April
	Does	1 March–20 October
Sika Deer:	Stags	1 May–31 July
	Hinds	16 February–20 October

* As already mentioned shooting on Sundays and Christmas Day is forbidden in Scotland, and by local statute in certain parts of England and Wales, information about which is obtainable from the local police.

† This, and the concomitant Deer Act 1963 (see below), are properly out of context in this book. But so many farmers, land-owners and shootingmen are unaware of their content and implication that it seems relevant to include details here.

The taking of deer during the nightly close time is prohibited during the open, as well as the close seasons. Poaching is prohibited at all times, and penalties for this, and contravention of the close seasons and nightly close time are included in the Act.

But it also provides that it is not an offence to kill a deer when a person:

a Acts to prevent suffering by an injured or diseased animal.
b Acts on instructions of the Red Deer Commission, provided he duly observes the nightly close time.
c Is authorized in writing by the occupier of agricultural land or enclosed moorland, he may kill deer found on arable land, grassland (excepting moorland or unenclosed land), garden grounds, or woodlands. In this instance killing is permitted during the nightly close time.

It is an offence under the Act to take or kill deer wilfully by any means except shooting with a lethal barrelled weapon, but the use of repeating firearms, e.g. any type of machine gun or submachine gun, is expressly forbidden, and so also are weapons which discharge a noxious substance, except that a deer may be taken alive with the permission of the occupier of the land in any manner which does not cause unnecessary suffering.

The nightly close time is defined as a period from one hour after sunset to one hour before sunrise.

THE DEER ACT 1963

This is the equivalent Act to provide protection for deer in England and Wales. A nightly close time is specified which is the same as in the Scottish Act, and also close seasons, which are:

Red Deer:	Stags	1 May–31 July
	Hinds	1 March–31 October
Fallow Deer:	Buck	1 May–31 July
	Does	1 March–31 October
Roe Deer	Buck	No close season
	Does	1 March–31 October
Sika Deer:	Stags	1 May–31 July
	Hinds	1 March–31 October

The taking of deer during the nightly close time is prohibited during both open and close seasons.

The use of certain firearms and ammunition for the killing of deer is forbidden; these are :

Firearms

 a Any smooth bore gun of a smaller gauge than 12-bore.

 b Any rifle of a calibre less than ·240 in, or having a muzzle energy of less than 1700 ft/lb.

 c Any air rifle, gun or pistol.

Ammunition

 d Any cartridge for use in a smooth-bore gun which is loaded with shot smaller than ·269 in in diameter; i.e. it must be SSG or larger.

 e Any rifle bullet which is not soft-nosed or hollow-nosed.

At the discretion of the Secretary of State other species of deer may be added to the list for which close seasons are prescribed, and the list of prohibited arms and ammunition may also be amended.

The Act concedes that if a person shoots a deer on pasture, cultivated land, or enclosed woodland in the close season, or nightly close time, in order to prevent serious damage to crops, vegetables, growing timber, or other property on the said land, he will not be guilty of an offence, provided he uses an authorized weapon and ammunition, and is the occupier of the land, or acting with the written authority of the occupier.

OWNERSHIP OF SHOT GAME

Sometimes one may shoot a pheasant or other bird which falls dead over the boundary on a neighbour's land. It is then the shooter's property, but if it is collected without permission, he is guilty of trespass. If by chance it is not a dead bird, but a runner which he goes to retrieve, then in law he becomes a poacher as well as a trespasser. However, if he sends his dog for it, he at least escapes the stigma of poaching.

If you shoot a bird over your neighbour's land which falls on your own it constitutes a trespass, but if it lands on his side it becomes poaching as well.

In Scotland the law is slightly more sensible, in that if you retrieve a dead bird which was shot over your own land, but has fallen on your neighbour's, you do not commit trespass. However, if it is a runner of which you go in pursuit, you again become both a trespasser and poacher in the eyes of the law.

If any action against a person for trespass is brought under Common Law, an injunction may also be sought to prevent repetition of the offence. If a trespasser does not obey a request to leave enclosed land he may be removed by force, provided only the minimum necessary is used. If a trespasser compounds his offence by inflicting malicious damage, or acting violently, he can be prosecuted under Criminal Law. However this is unlikely to arise unless one has to deal with real poachers to whom we will now turn.

POACHING AND POWERS OF ARREST

Basically anyone who takes 'game' from land without due authority is guilty of poaching, and in such circumstances, as explained earlier in this chapter, woodcock, snipe, and rabbits may count as game, and in Scotland wild duck are included as well. An interesting point in respect of rabbits is that although a tenant farmer cannot be guilty of day poaching, he can of night poaching.

The law regards poaching by night as a more serious offence than by day, and where at night it is committed by a gang of three or more in number and possessing offensive weapons, the penalties attaching to it are much heavier.

Under the Game Act 1831 the shooting tenant, or the occupier of the land, or any gamekeeper employed by either of them, or any other person authorized by either of them can require a person found on the land to leave and give his name and address. If that person gives a false name and address, or wilfully refuses to give this information, or to leave the land, or having done so returns upon it, he may be apprehended. The owner or occupier, or any gamekeeper employed by either of them can order a person seen in possession of game to hand it over, and if this is not promptly complied with they may seize it. However only a policeman has power to search a poacher.

By virtue of the Poaching Prevention Act 1862 a police officer may stop a vehicle in any street or highway on suspicion of it having come from land where it has been used in furtherance of poaching, and search it for game unlawfully obtained, and any gun, ammunition or other equipment used for so obtaining it. If any of these things are found, the officer may impound them, and apply to a magistrate for a summons.

At night the owner or occupier of the land, or their game-keepers or servants (N.B. But NOT the shooting tenant or his gamekeeper) can arrest any person found poaching, but may not search him or seize his gun. The culprit must then be handed into police custody. If a police officer is present when the arrest is made, he can both search the culprit and seize any game, gun, or equipment used for poaching in his possession.

Under the Firearms Act 1965 a policeman can arrest without warrant anyone whom he has just cause to suspect has entered any land or buildings in possession of a firearm, and is a trespasser with no right to be there.

USE OF POISONS

The use of poisons is very strictly controlled by law. An Agricultural Executive Commitee can grant a licence to poison harmful birds, as specified in the Protection of Birds Act 1954, and already listed above. It is otherwise illegal to use poisons except for the purpose of killing insects, rats, mice, and certain small ground vermin, such as moles, and in the manufacture of grain or seed dressings used for agricultural purposes. When poisons are used, precautions must be taken to prevent harm to dogs, cats, farm and other domestic animals, game, and wild birds. A Ministry of Agriculture permit is necessary to obtain and use strychnine to control moles.

As described in Chapters 7 and 27 lethal gas, such as Cymag, may be used in the control of rabbits. It may also be used to control foxes, but it is illegal to kill badgers with it.

Since 1961 a voluntary ban has been observed on the use of the persistent poisons of the organo-chlorine group, such as aldrin, dieldrin, and heptachlor in seed dressings used for spring sown corn. However the right has been reserved to use these dressings in special circumstances if required.

TRAPS AND TRAPPING

All traps used for both pests and predators must now be of a pattern approved by the Ministry. No licence is required to use traps, but by virtue of Section 10 of the Protection of Animals Act 1911, traps may not be set in the open, and all traps which are set must be inspected at least once a day between sunrise and sunset.

The use of pole traps has been illegal since 1904. However in 1972 the R.S.P.B. reported that over 90 instances of keepers using traps of this kind had been discovered, and the Society obtained court convictions in a number of the cases concerned.

Since the use of gin traps in Scotland was made illegal by the Agriculture (Spring Traps) (Scotland) Act 1969, their use has been prohibited throughout Great Britain.

DECOYS

No live bird which is blind, maimed, injured, tethered, or has had its wings clipped may be used as a decoy for catching, or killing any wild bird. Where live birds are used as decoys, for example in crow traps, they must be provided with shelter, food and water.

MUIRBURN

The times of the year when this is permitted are as follows :

    a Scotland   * 1 October—15 April
    b England and Wales   * 1 November—31 March

In Scotland an extension may be obtained up to 30 April, and on deer forests over 1500 ft above sea level a further extension is permissible up to 15 May.
(*See also page 230 *et seq*).

YOUNG PEOPLE, FIREARMS, AND THE LAW

The relevant legislation is contained in the Firearms Acts 1937 and 1965, and the Air Guns and Shotguns Act 1962.

No one under fourteen years of age may possess, purchase, or acquire any firearm or ammunition, nor may he be lent any such weapon or ammunition. But he may :

a Possess and use firearms and ammunition as a member of an approved club, or when shooting in a shooting gallery where only air weapons, or miniature rifles are available.

b Possess and use any air weapon if he is not in a public place, and is under the supervision of a person over 21. But it may not be used for firing a missile beyond the bounds of the premises or land where he is being supervised.

c Carry a firearm or ammunition under the instruction of another person over 21, who holds a valid shotgun, or firearms certificate relating to the weapon or ammunition in question.

When a youngster is fourteen or over, he may be lent or given an air weapon or ammunition for it.

If a young person is under fifteen years of age, and has a shotgun certificate, he may have an assembled shotgun with him provided he is supervised by a person over 21, or the shotgun is carried in a gun cover securely fastened. But when he is fifteen, or over, and has a shotgun certificate, he may be given a shotgun as a gift.

Until a young person is seventeen years of age he may not purchase or hire any firearm or its ammunition. But on reaching that age, provided he has a shotgun certificate, he may possess, purchase, acquire, and use a shotgun and ammunition subject only to the normal legal restrictions applicable in these respects to grown-ups. Also at this age there are no restrictions on his acquisition of all weapons.

ANIMALS DESIGNATED AS PESTS

The under-mentioned animals are all designated as 'pests' at the time of writing :

Rats	Rabbits	Grey Squirrels
Mink	Coypu	

SUMMARY

I have tried not to bombard the reader with vast verbatim quotations from the law, but to write in plain words the sense of what the law intends. As I said at the beginning of this chapter, the proper person to resolve any doubts as to what the law means in any particular case is a qualified lawyer. But I hope the above may prove a reasonably reliable guide to some of the small change of shooting law about which people quite frequently want to know, but don't want to have to pay a half-guinea fee in order to find out.

CHAPTER THIRTY-THREE

GAME COOKERY
(or the Gourmet's Concise Guide to Game)

BY CAROLINE VERNEY AND RODERICK WILLETT

T HE object of shooting game is to be able to enjoy eating it afterwards. Having spent thirty-two chapters describing how to accomplish the former it seems fitting in this, the last, to move from gunroom to kitchen, and discuss a few ways of transforming the fruits of the chase into mouth-watering dishes to grace the sportsman's table.

Few cookbooks really do justice to game. The redoubtable Mrs. Beeton's *Household Management* is unquestionably among the most comprehensive, and the *Robert Carrier Cookbook* one of the most exciting. But the treatment accorded game in the majority of popular cookbooks is positively pedestrian, and having cursorily described how to roast a grouse, a partridge, and a pheasant, stew a rabbit, and jug a hare, their authors return with almost audible sigh of relief to variations on a steak and chips theme.

The English—the Scots are an exception to this—are generally singularly unimaginative in their cooking of game, and seem to regard any departure from straightforward roasting as a sort of heresy in which foreigners may indulge, but Englishmen don't. As a youngster I can remember invoking a scene reminiscent of a Bateman cartoon in the famous series, 'The man who . . .', by suggesting there might be other ways of cooking a pheasant just as good as roasting. One old gentleman choked on his port, and spent the rest of the evening muttering about people who liked their birds 'drenched in Kirsch', a gastronomic excess he had apparently once experienced when dining at a foreign embassy.

But this is in no way intended to denigrate roasted gamebirds; they are excellent when properly cooked and served. However, if one is lucky enough to have a well stocked larder in due season,

HINTS ON HANGING AND PREPARATION

GAME	AVERAGE DRESSED WEIGHT	RECOMMENDED TIME FOR HANGING*	CHARACTERISTICS	BASIC GUIDE LINES FOR COOKING	COOKING TIMES
Wild Rabbit	2–2½ lb	4–5 days	If buying, look for bright, unglazed eyes.	Roast if young; otherwise marinade and/or stew.	Roast 45 mins Stew 1–2 hrs
Hare	4–8 lb	7–10 days	Unlike rabbits, normally hung undrawn.	Saddle excellent roasted; the rest makes delicious pâtés, pies, and braises.	Roast 35–45 mins Braise 1–2 hrs
Pheasant	2–3 lb	1–2 weeks	Cocks inclined to be dry, but improve if hung a little longer.	Roast, casserole, pâtés, or pies.	Roast 45–60 mins
Partridge	About 12 oz	7 days, but beware warm weather	Needs to be well barded to keep moist.	Roast young birds; braise old ones.	Roast 25–30 mins Braise 2 hrs
Grouse	16–20 oz	7–10 days, but beware warm weather	To prevent dryness must be well barded, and basted.	Roast, or casserole.	Roast 25–30 mins Casserole 1½–2 hrs
Ptarmigan	About 16 oz	4–7 days	Otherwise treat as for grouse.		
Blackcock	3–3½ lb	7–10 days	Inclined to be dry unless well barded.	Roast if young; otherwise braise or casserole.	Roast 45–60 mins Braise 2–2½ hrs

	Weight	Hanging	Treatment	Cooking time
Capercaillie	4–10 lb	7–14 days	Inclined to taste of turpentine; to discount this soak overnight in milk, and then for 8 hours in vinegar before cooking.	Old birds are not worth cooking. If young, roast, braise, or casserole.	Roast 1–1½ hrs Braise 2–3 hrs
Woodcock	8–12 oz	7 days	Often cooked undrawn.	Roast (and baste lavishly), or casserole.	Roast 20 mins Casserole 45–60 mins
Snipe	About 4 oz	3–7 days	Pluck but do not draw; skin head and neck; skewer body with beak.	Roast; baste with butter.	Roast 15 mins
Golden Plover	About 6 oz	3–7 days	Cook undrawn, unless otherwise specified.	Roast well barded.	Roast 20 mins
Wild Duck	2–2¼ lb But Teal only approx 10 oz	4–7 days	Some species have a fishy or muddy taste and should be basted in salt water and onion for 15 mins. But Mallard, Teal, Pintail, and Gadwall do not normally suffer this handicap.	Roast, braise, pâté, or salmis.	Roast 30–35 mins
Wild Geese	4–7 lb	7–14 days	Grey geese and Canada geese do not normally have fishy flavour.	Roast well barded, and baste frequently.	Roast in slow oven, 300°F.; allow 20 mins per lb

* N.B. Irrespective of whether you like your game only mildly 'gamey', or distinctly 'high', it is the weather which dictates precisely how long it ought to be hung; thus in warm weather these times may need to be considerably shortened.

a little variety is often appreciated. For those prepared to be adventurous, there are ample appetizing alternatives to roasting well within the scope of any reasonably proficient cook, and there is no need to go berserk with a bottle of Kirsch, or any other expensive liqueur. However, the judicious use of the occasional soupçon of wine, or spirit, can add immeasurably to the enjoyment of many a dish.

Under the able guidance of Caroline Verney, I have tried to put together in this chapter a number of fairly simple, but delicious recipes for cooking game. In addition there are some notes on deep-freezing procedure, also a table of hints on hanging and preparation, and a section devoted to gamebird sauces. Finally, to round off the meal, so to speak, there are a few ideas on suitable wines.

DEEP FREEZING

All game should be hung for the full, recommended time before it is deep frozen, as otherwise, when it is thawed out, it is liable to deteriorate too quickly. It is easier to pluck, or skin and draw game before freezing, than postpone this task until it is required for eating; however, if desired, it can just as well be frozen with feather or fur left intact.

When freezing game which has already been plucked and drawn, the giblets can be put in a polythene bag which is placed inside the body; but remember to remove it before cooking.

When the bird or beast is withdrawn from the freezer prior to cooking, allow plenty of time for it to thaw out. It should be removed from the plastic freezer bag, and placed somewhere at room temperature—out of reach of that member of the household who may have retrieved it last season—a half-hour per pound weight should be allowed for defreezing. Whatever happens do NOT re-freeze game, unless it has first been cooked.

The normal 'frozen' life of game is about nine months.

RABBIT

LAPIN À LA BRABANÇONNE (RABBIT IN BEER)

N.B. The rabbit should be jointed and soaked overnight in water and vinegar, prior to cooking.

Ingredients

1 young rabbit	1 tablespoon flour
4 oz streaky bacon	Bouquet garni
4 onions	1 tablespoon butter
½ pint ale	2 lumps sugar
1 tablespoon vinegar	Salt and pepper
1 teaspoon French mustard	

Slice the onions and chop the bacon; fry until gold. Take the jointed rabbit from the liquor in which it has been soaked, and fry until brown. Empty rabbit, etc., into casserole. Add sugar lumps, bouquet garni, mustard, and a pinch of pepper and salt. Sprinkle with flour; cover with beer. Bring to the boil. Cover the dish and cook in a slow oven for 2 hours.

Encyclopaedia of European Cooking

RABBIT STEW

Ingredients

2 rabbits	2 large onions
4 oz breadcrumbs	2 oz margarine
Flour	1 pint milk
Salt and pepper	

Wash rabbits in salted water and dry well. Dip into seasoned flour. Chop onions and put in bottom of casserole. Cover with 1 oz of margarine and sauté in oven. Put rabbit joints on top of onions. Place the other ounce of margarine over them and put in oven for 15 minutes. Bring the milk to the boil and pour over the rabbit. Cook for two hours in slow oven. After 1½ hours sprinkle on breadcrumbs.

HARE

HARE BAKED WITH BEER

Ingredients

1 hare	Dripping
Fine oatmeal	1 pint light ale
Butter	Salt and pepper

Joint the hare, and roll the joints in seasoned fine oatmeal. Lightly fry in dripping. Place in a baking dish covered with a few shavings of butter, and pour over the beer. Roast in a very moderate oven, basting frequently with the beer, until the meat is tender, i.e. in about 1½ hours. Serve with gravy made from the basting beer, and red-currant jelly.

Encyclopaedia of European Cooking

LIÈVRE À LA TRENTINA

Ingredients

1 young hare	Pinch of nutmeg
½ pint of red wine	4 oz butter
½ pint meat stock	1 teaspoon sugar
Salt and pepper	Bouquet garni
3 tablespoons raisins	Boiled rice
2 strips lemon peel	

Joint the dressed hare. Take the heart, liver and kidneys and chop finely; marinate them in a deep dish by covering them with raisins, chopped lemon peel, sugar, nutmeg, bouquet garni, and red wine. Allow to stand for at least 2 hours. Brown the pieces of hare in the butter; add the stock and the marinade. Season with salt and pepper. Simmer gently for 2 hours. Serve accompanied by boiled rice.

Encyclopaedia of European Cooking

PHEASANT

A LINCOLNSHIRE RECIPE FOR PHEASANT

Ingredients

1 young cock or hen pheasant	1½ pints of stock (approx.)
1 onion	1 carrot
Salt and pepper	Dripping
4 tomatoes (or 1 small tin)	½ lb mushrooms
1 tablespoon chopped parsley	2 tablespoons flour

Chop the onion and carrot, and fry in the dripping. Cut up the pheasant, and add the pieces of meat, well seasoned, to the onion and carrot; fry for a further five minutes, stirring all the time. Add the flour, and cook until brown. Gradually stir in the stock and boil. Add the tomatoes, mushrooms, and parsley, and allow to simmer for ½ hour. Serve in a casserole.

The Sporting Wife

PHEASANT WITH GREEN APPLES

Ingredients

1 pheasant
1 Spanish onion, finely
  chopped
2 tablespoons butter
4 small cooking apples
½ pint cream

¾ lb green bacon, diced
1 clove of garlic
2 tablespoons olive oil
4 tablespoons Cointreau
Salt and pepper

Sauté the bacon, onion, and garlic in the oil and butter in a casserole until golden; remove and keep warm. Brown the pheasant in the same fats, and likewise remove. Peel, core and slice thickly the four apples; sauté them until they start to turn. Pour over the Cointreau. Remove the apples. Skim the fat from the pan, leaving the juices. Return the pheasant to the casserole. Surround with apple slices, bacon, onion and garlic; allow to simmer for 10 minutes. Stir in the cream; add salt and pepper to taste. Cover the casserole, and cook in a slow oven (275°) until the pheasant is tender. When ready to serve remove the pheasant and bacon to a clean casserole, and keep warm. Purée the sauce and the apples. Correct seasoning and re-heat the sauce; pour it over the bird.

Robert Carrier

PHEASANT WITH COTTAGE CHEESE

Ingredients

1 pheasant
Cottage cheese
Fat bacon or pork

⅓ cup of brandy
3½ tablespoons butter

Stuff the pheasant with cottage cheese; secure the opening, and tie the bird with fat bacon or pork. Paint generously with melted butter. Melt 3 tablespoons of butter in a casserole; insert the pheasant; season, cover and cook gently, basting frequently, for 1 hour. About 15 minutes before the bird is ready, remove the bacon and allow the bird to brown. Place the pheasant on a serving dish and keep warm. Add ⅓ cup of brandy to the casserole, scraping the bottom of the pan to ensure mixing in all the juices. When just simmering pour over the pheasant, and serve.

The Alice Toklas Cookbook

PANCAKES BONNIE CHARLIE

Ingredients (For 6 people)

12 pancakes	4 oz butter
1 medium size roast pheasant	½ glass of dry white wine
	1 small glass of brandy
1 lb braised lambs' sweetbreads	¼ pint of single cream
	salt and pepper to taste
4 oz chopped shallots	2 medium size cooking apples
4 oz sliced mushrooms	

Melt the butter in a sauté pan and lightly fry the chopped shallots and mushrooms; add the wine and brandy, and reduce by half; then pour in the cream. Heat in this mixture the pre-cooked and sliced pheasant and sweetbreads. Season to taste, and simmer for a few minutes until the sauce thickens. Divide this mixture equally on the pancakes, and roll them, folding in the edges to prevent the sauce from coming out.

Arrange the rolled pancakes on a silver entrée dish, and place on each a few slices of stewed apple. Pour a little brandy over the pancakes and serve flambé'd.

From a Recipe found amongst Family Papers, and updated for the Author by Peter Strong

PARTRIDGE

PARTRIDGE WITH LENTIL PURÉE

Ingredients

6 partridges	1 glass white wine
6 carrots	1 cup chicken stock
3 onions	1 lb brown lentils (soaked overnight)
4 oz butter	
	Seasoning

Place the partridges in a casserole just large enough to hold them, pack tightly round with sliced onions and carrots. Add 4 oz butter. Place in moderate oven; when the birds have taken colour, pour the glass of white wine over them, and season. When the liquor has reduced by half, add the cup of stock. Cover and finish cooking slowly.

Simmer together for two hours the 1 lb of lentils, 1 onion stuck with a couple of cloves, 2 cloves of garlic, and 2 carrots. When quite soft purée. Mix the purée with half the sauce from the partridges over a low heat until it is quite smooth. Serve with the purée all round the birds, and the remainder of the sauce poured over them.

The Sporting Wife

PERDREAUX À LA BARETTA

Ingredients

6 partridges	3 glacé cherries
1 pint double cream	1 medium sized apple
6 green grapes	1 small glass of whisky

Place the partridges in a casserole; add the cream, season, cover and cook in a slow oven for approximately 2 hours. After one hour add the grapes, cherries, and apple cut in quarters. Half-an-hour before the birds are ready add the whisky.

Lady Maclean's Cookbook

PERNICIOTTE ALLA MILANESE

Cut the partridges in two lengthways, and flatten with a meat flattener. Allow to marinate for 1 hour before cooking in oil seasoned with salt, pepper, a little parsley, and a crushed bay leaf. Then dip each half of the partridge in crisp breadcrumbs, and fry on both sides in olive oil. Arrange on a heated dish, and serve with anchovy sauce.   *Encyclopaedia of European Cooking*

GROUSE

GROUSE PIE

Ingredients

2 grouse	Salt, pepper and herbs
½ lb short crust	3 hard-boiled eggs
Game forcemeat, or bacon	A few slices of raw ham or bacon

Cut up each grouse into five parts and season. Cover the bottom of a pie dish with game forcemeat (for recipe see under sauces at end of recipes), or with a layer of streaky bacon. Place the pieces of grouse on this and sprinkle with herbs. Fill the gaps between the portions of grouse with sliced hard-boiled eggs, and place a few slices of raw ham or bacon on top of the grouse. Make a good gravy or stock, and pour in enough to come halfway up the side of the pie dish. Cover with pastry; paint with egg; put in a moderate oven (375°) for 1½ hours.

This is an excellent way of cooking old, or rather heavily-shot birds.   *The Sporting Wife*

M

SPORTSMAN'S GROUSE

For this recipe the grouse must be well hung*. After plucking and trussing, stuff with butter and rowan berries, or alternatively raspberries, preferably wild ones. Roast for 25 minutes in a hot oven; the fruit almost disappears in the cooking, but the resultant juices are all that is required in the way of gravy.

(* *Author's note.* The original recipe recommends hanging for 'at least a fortnight', but by present day standards I think this will be regarded as excessive, and certainly so in warm autumn weather.)

The Sporting Wife

DEVILLED GROUSE

Ingredients

2 grouse	3 oz long grain rice
½ pint cream	2 oz sultanas
1 bay leaf	1 tin consommé soup
Worcester sauce	Curry powder
Sauce diable	Bovril, or equivalent

Prepare the grouse as for roasting, with bacon and dripping, and cover in foil; roast for 30 minutes in a hot oven. Remove and place in a saucepan; add the rice and consommé, the bay leaf, one teaspoonful of curry powder, and the sultanas. Allow to cook very slowly until the rice is almost dry; do NOT stir. When the birds are cooked, remove, cut in half, and place on a serving dish. When cool, cover with whipped cream to which has been added 2 teaspoonfuls of Worcester sauce, 1 teaspoonful of Bovril, and 2 tablespoonfuls of sauce diable. Place cooked rice around the birds, and place in a hot oven for 10 minutes to heat thoroughly. Serve with game crisps.

Lady Maclean's Cookbook

PTARMIGAN

ROAST

Place 2–3 slices of bacon over the breast and roast in a moderate oven for 30–35 minutes basting frequently with butter. When nearly cooked, remove bacon, sprinkle with flour, and baste well. Serve on toast, with bread sauce, breadcrumbs, and gravy.

The Sporting Wife

BLACKGAME

GENERAL

Can be treated in the same way as grouse. When roasted, use a hottish oven, cover the bird with rashers of bacon, and wrap in vine or cabbage leaves; baste frequently, and allow 45–60 minutes. Serve on thick slices of buttered toast, with a clear gravy and bread sauce.   *The Sporting Wife*

CAPERCAILLIE

GENERAL

An important preliminary with these birds is to try and discount the strong flavour of turpentine to which they are prone, as they feed largely on pine needles. This can best be done by first soaking the bird overnight in milk, and then for a further 8–10 hours in vinegar. It is only worth going to all this trouble with young birds, old ones are not worth eating anyway. Thereafter a young caper should be roasted in the normal way, allowing from 1–1½ hours according to weight. A useful recipe is as under.

Ingredients

1 young capercaillie	Butter
Flour	Chestnut or sausage stuffing
1 cup chicken stock	Salt and pepper

Rub the bird all over with salt and pepper and softened butter. Dredge with flour. Insert stuffing. Cover with fat bacon, and roast covered in fat in a hot oven (425°) for 10 minutes, then lower the heat to 300°. Baste well with stock and dripping. When almost cooked remove foil and bacon, and allow to brown. Reckon cooking time as 20–25 minutes per lb weight.

Serve with gravy to which has been added some red currant or crab apple jelly, and bread sauce.   *The Sporting Wife*

WOODCOCK

BÉCASSE RÔTI

Ingredients

2 woodcock	2 slices of bread
2 slices salt pork, or fat bacon	Salt and pepper

Draw the birds, and replace their livers inside with a pinch of salt. Place them in a roasting pan on a grill, with the slices of pork over their breasts, and the slices of bread under them. Roast in a hot oven for 25 minutes. Sprinkle with salt and pepper, and serve.

Encyclopaedia of European Cooking

SNIPE

GEBRATENE SCHNEPFE (FROM AUSTRIA)

Ingredients

4 snipe	1 egg yolk
Fat bacon for covering	Bread slices
1 tablespoon chopped lemon peel	Pineapple
	Sour cream
Browned breadcrumbs	Watercress
2–3 shallots	Butter
Stock	Parsley
1 gill red wine	

Draw the birds, but do not remove the head and neck. Cover each bird with a slice of fat bacon, and tie with string. Tuck the long beak underneath. Roast in a quick oven in butter and stock for about 20 minutes. Chop the livers and hearts and mix with the chopped shallots, parsley, breadcrumbs, and lemon peel. Stir in the egg yolk and a little wine. Cook this mixture till the hearts and livers are well done. Fry the bread. Just before the birds are ready, add the rest of the wine and the sour cream to the roasting pan; stir in the juices. Remove the birds, etc., to serving dish; surround with fried bread on which is piled the liver mixture. Decorate as desired with watercress and pineapple.

Encyclopaedia of European Cooking

GOLDEN PLOVER

PLOVER STUFFED WITH OLIVES

Ingredients

4 golden plover	2 egg yolks
2 oz bacon	6 oz sliced belly of pork
Plovers' livers	6 oz sausage meat
1 tablespoon chopped herbs	3 tablespoons butter
Salt and Pepper	¾ glass white wine
½ glass madeira	2 handfuls green olives

Mix the minced bacon with finely chopped livers and sausage meat. Simmer in the butter for a few minutes and add the herbs, and Madeira. Mix well and cool.

Put the stuffing through a sieve, or in the liquidizer, add the egg yolks; stuff the birds with the mixture, and brown them in the butter. Add the wine and simmer for 10 minutes. Then add the olives and cook for another 10 minutes. Serve on croûtons of fried bread, basted in their own juice. *Chicken and Game*

CAILLES AU RIZ

Ingredients

4 golden plover	2 small onions
6 oz rice	1 pint stock
3 oz bacon	Black pepper
1 bouquet garni	1 oz lard

Melt the lard in a heavy saucepan. Add the cleaned birds, with the bacon cut in strips, and the onions. Cook for about 7 minutes. Remove the birds. Add 1 pint of stock, and bring to the boil again; then add the bouquet garni, and some black pepper. Cover and simmer for 10 minutes. Place the birds on top of the rice, cover and place in oven, and simmer for a further 12 minutes, or until the rice has absorbed all the stock. Serve.

Encyclopaedia of European Cooking

WILD DUCK

TERRINE OF WILD DUCK*

Ingredients

1 wild duck	$\frac{3}{4}$ lb duck's liver or pig's liver
$\frac{1}{2}$ glass whisky	$\frac{1}{2}$ glass sherry
Bouquet garni	3 cloves garlic
Ham or fat pork to same weight as duck	2 shallots
	Streaky bacon

Cut the breasts off the bird in neat slices and marinade for 2 hours in the $\frac{1}{2}$ glass of whisky, and same of sherry, plus the bouquet garni and 1 clove of garlic. While this is marinating cut the remainder of the meat from the bird, and make stock with the pork together with the shallots and remaining 2 cloves of garlic. Season with salt, pepper, and mixed spice.

Line a fireproof dish with streaky bacon. Then put in alternate layers of the duck, the liver, and minced meat, ending with the mince and a layer of bacon. Stand in a bain marie, and cook in a hot oven for 1 hour. When the terrine leaves the side of the dish top up with the remains of the marinade and a little stock. Cook for another ½ hour in a slower oven.

*N.B. This recipe can be equally well used for other game, or any collection of left-overs.   *Margaret Harford*

CANARD SAUVAGE À L'ANCIENNE

Ingredients

1 wild duck	2 teaspoons flour
1 tablespoon butter	¾ cup white wine
1 shallot	Juice of 1 lemon
1 teaspoon chopped parsley	4 tablespoons stock
Salt, pepper, nutmeg	

With a sharp, small-bladed knife, cut the breasts and legs from the raw duck. Sauté the pieces in a tablespoon of butter, together with a chopped shallot, a teaspoonful of chopped parsley, salt, pepper, and some grated nutmeg. When the meat is browned on all sides sprinkle 2 teaspoonfuls of flour into the pan; scrape up all the juices and add the ¾ cup of white wine. When it begins to boil add the juice of the lemon and 4 tablespoonfuls of stock. Stir until the sauce thickens and reduces a little.   *Bouquet de France*

WILD GOOSE

SCANDINAVIAN ROAST GOOSE

Ingredients

1 grey, or Canada goose	6 cooking apples
½ lemon	½ teaspoon pepper
1 tablespoon salt	20 prunes

Wash and dry the goose well. Rub the outside with lemon. Rinse the prunes well in tepid water, and boil them until soft; then stone them. Wash, peel, core, and slice the apples; then mix them and the prunes together, and place inside the goose. Sew up both ends. Rub bird with salt and pepper; place in a roasting tin covered tightly with foil, and roast in a moderate oven for about 2 hours. Remove foil, replace bird in oven to become brown.

Serve with a gravy made from pan juices; red cabbage, and roast potatoes.   *Encyclopaedia of European Cooking*

WOODPIGEON

PIGEONS À LA CRAPAUDINE

Cut down the breastbone of the bird. Flatten out the two halves as evenly as possible. Dip each in melted butter seasoned with salt and pepper, and cover with breadcrumbs. Place under a moderate grill for approximately 25 minutes, basting from time to time. Serve with sauce diable, remoulade, or any piquant sauce.

Encyclopaedia of European Cooking

MISCELLANEOUS

(With an Eye to Shooting Lunches)

KINGDOM OF FIFE PIE

Ingredients

1 young rabbit	3 tablespoons white wine
½ lb pickled pork	Stock
Forcemeat	1 hard-boiled egg
Salt, pepper and nutmeg	

Skin the rabbit and cut into joints. Soak for 1 hour in cold water. Make a good stock with the carcass and liver, or use a stock cube. Slice the pork and season. Make forcemeat balls and pack the rabbit, pork, and forcemeat balls into a pie dish with sliced hard-boiled egg, a cup full of stock and the white wine. Cover with a puff pastry, in which several holes are made for ventilation. Bake for an hour in a moderate oven. *The Scots Kitchen*

POACHER'S BROTH (OR SOUP À LA MEG MERRILEES)

Ingredients

Venison, beef or mutton trimmings, game	Carrots
	Onions
Celery	Parsley
Turnips	Seasoning and spices
Potatoes	Essence of mushroom or water
Cabbage	
Red wine	

Take from 2–4 lb of the trimmings of any cheap cuts of meat, or venison, or if game is in season, and you have plenty, then use only game, e.g. grouse, partridge, pheasant, blackcock, woodcock, etc.

Make a stock from bones, celery, carrots, turnips, onions, a bunch of parsley, and some peppercorns. When it has boiled for 3 hours, strain it. If you are using game only, flour and brown in dripping the pieces of meat, and place in the stock with some small onions, a head of celery sliced, and six peeled potatoes. When it boils add a small white cabbage quartered, black pepper, mixed spice and salt. Let the soup simmer until the meat is tender, but not overdone.

The Scots Kitchen

SAUCES, ETC., FOR GAME

MARINADE FOR REMOVING THE FISHY OR MUDDY FLAVOUR FROM DUCK

Place an onion in the duck, and put the carcass in a roasting dish of boiling salty water, with a bay leaf. Baste frequently for 15 minutes. Then cook normally.

GAME FORCEMEAT

This can be used for forcemeat balls, stuffing game, or game pies.

Ingredients
2 oz suet	$\frac{1}{2}$ teaspoon mixed herbs
1-2 oz ham	Grated rind of $\frac{1}{2}$ lemon
4 oz breadcrumbs	Salt and Pepper
2 teaspoons chopped parsley	Beaten egg

Chop the suet and ham. Mix with the breadcrumbs. Add the parsley, herbs and lemon rind. Season well, and add enough beaten egg to bind.

MARINADE FOR GENERAL PURPOSES

Ingredients
$\frac{1}{2}$ cup vinegar	1 cup red wine
Nutmeg	Bay leaf
Salt and peppercorns	Thyme
Finely chopped onion	Juniper berries (optional)

The meat should be placed in a shallow dish, and the marinade poured over it, and used to baste it frequently.

This is excellent for breaking down the tissues of tough meat, and adding a flavour to pâtés, terrines, etc.

ESPAGNOLE SAUCE

Ingredients

1 onion	1 pint stock
1 carrot	Bouquet garni
2 oz mushrooms	Peppercorns
2 oz lean bacon	1 bay leaf
2 oz flour	¼ pint tomato pulp
2 oz butter	½ glass sherry

Chop the vegetables and the bacon; fry them for a few moments until golden. Sprinkle on the flour. Add stock, herbs, and spices, and simmer for ½ hour. Add tomato pulp, and continue simmering for another ½ hour. Season and add the sherry. Put through a sieve, or in a liquidizer.   *The Sporting Wife*

GAME SAUCE

This is especially recommended with hare, rabbit, duck or goose which is marinading, as the marinade can be incorporated.

1½ tablespoons butter	1 tablespoon grated orange peel
1 tablespoon flour	¾ cup red currant jelly
1 cup of marinade	Pinch of cayenne pepper
Juice of 1 lemon and grated peel	

Melt the butter and add the flour. Cook for a minute until brown. Add slowly the cup of marinade, the lemon juice, and the grated rind, cayenne, and red currant jelly. Bring slowly to the boil, and simmer for 20 minutes.   *The Alice Toklas Cookbook*

SAUCE BIGARADE (For wild duck or any rich game)

Ingredients

½ pint demi-glace	1 bay leaf
2 shallots	Rind and juice of 1 orange
A nut of butter	1 teaspoonful red currant jelly
1 glass red wine	

Chop the shallots and soften the butter. Add the wine and bay leaf. Reduce by a third. Add the juice and half the pared rind of the orange to the demi-glace. Simmer from 5–7 minutes, and strain. Shred the remaining orange rind, and blanch for 5 minutes; add the red currant jelly to the sauce. Bring slowly to the boil, stirring

N

a full-bodied Burgundy, such as a Pommard or Chambertin is needed to set it off to advantage. Likewise I find venison, whether of red, fallow or roe deer, needs a good Burgundy or Rhône wine to keep it company, and for those who wish a modestly priced wine I would strongly recommend a Jules Regnier, Nuits St. George, or Echezeaux. This house produces some really splendid Burgundies, and for those who do not have to count their pennies too closely, I can thoroughly recommend their domaigne bottled wines.

The best wild goose I have ever eaten, a young greylag, was made doubly memorable by the excellence of the bottle of Château Neuf du Pape which accompanied it, as well as the company of those who enjoyed both with me.

To round off a meal at which game and wine have fulfilled their expectations, a glass of port should set the seal of satisfaction. For those who have them, can afford them, and know how to look after and serve them, good vintage ports are pearls beyond price. But for those who find a tawny, however excellent, a little thin by comparison, there are nowadays some extremely good 'vintage type' ports available, which are both drinkable and first class value for money. One that I particularly appreciate in each of these respects is Graham's 'Six Grapes', which will ensure a good dinner ends on a happy note, as I hope this book has; so let us take our brandy or liqueur with us, and join the ladies.

APPENDIX 'A'

INDIVIDUAL PELLET STRIKING ENERGIES IN FOOT-POUNDS FOR DIFFERENT SHOT SIZES AT RANGES AND OBSERVED VELOCITIES SHOWN

OBSERVED VELOCITY 1070 f.p.s.

SIZE OF SHOT	RANGE IN YARDS							
	10	20	30	35	40	45	50	60
BB	15·78	12·32	9·98	8·97	8·11	7·34	6·57	5·25
1	10·61	8·46	6·62	5·88	5·25	4·65	4·11	3·18
3	7·83	5·79	4·47	3·94	3·43	2·99	2·61	1·93
4	6·43	4·66	3·52	3·04	2·65	2·28	1·96	1·42
5	4·98	3·51	2·59	2·22	1·89	1·61	1·35	0·94
6	4·94	2·79	2·01	1·71	1·43	1·21	0·99	0·66
7	3·20	2·17	1·51	1·26	1·05	0·86	0·69	0·45
8	2·40	1·57	1·06	0·86	0·70	0·56	0·45	0·27
9	1·88	1·19	0·77	0·62	0·49	0·39	0·29	0·17

OBSERVED VELOCITY 1120 f.p.s. (H.V.)

SIZE OF SHOT	RANGE IN YARDS							
	10	20	30	35	40	45	50	60
BB	17·23	13·32	10·68	9·62	8·71	7·94	7·04	5·70
1	11·36	9·18	7·12	6·33	5·66	5·01	4·46	3·47
3	8·53	6·23	4·81	4·26	3·71	3·25	2·84	2·11
4	7·04	5·01	3·77	3·30	2·85	2·46	2·13	1·54
5	5·43	3·77	2·77	2·38	2·04	1·73	1·47	1·02
6	4·40	2·99	2·16	1·83	1·54	1·32	1·07	0·72
7	3·48	2·31	1·62	1·36	1·13	0·93	0·75	0·49

OBSERVED VELOCITY 1030 f.p.s.

SIZE OF SHOT	RANGE IN YARDS							
	10	20	30	35	40	45	50	60
5	4·61	3·31	2·45	2·09	1·78	1·51	1·27	0·88
6	3·71	2·63	1·91	1·61	1·35	1·12	0·93	0·62
7	2·98	2·08	1·43	1·19	0·98	0·80	0·65	0·42
8	2·24	1·49	1·00	0·82	0·66	0·52	0·41	0·25
9	1·74	1·11	0·73	0·58	0·45	0·35	0·27	0·15

INDEX

Actions; Anson & Deeley Boxlock, 37, 40; Anson & Deeley Hand-detachable boxlock, 40; Boxlocks generally, 37; Generally, 35, et seq; The Dickson Trigger Plate, or 'Round Action', 38, 39; The Holland & Holland Self-opening, 43; Over and Under Actions, 41–2; Purdey Action—*See* Purdeys; Sidelocks generally, 36, 38; Webley & Scott boxlock action, 35; Westley Richards Hand-detachable boxlock, 40
Alder; 194
Aldrin; 341
Amprolium; 325
Anson & Deeley; see Actions
Ants; 152
Anvil; 47
Aquatic Plants; 252
Artichokes; 110, 113
Aspergillosis; 328
Austria; 93, 317
Automatic Shotguns; 33, 100
Avian Tuberculosis; 328
A.Y.A. Shotguns; Chopper Lumps, 28; 28-bores, 70

Badger; Generally, 124, 128; Illegal to gas, 127, 341; Protection of Act, 325
Bag; Disposal of, 147
Balance; 81
Ballistics; Effect of Cork Wadding on, 48; Generally, 51, et seq.; Importance of consistent, 46
Bantams; 160, 167, 168
Barley; For Wild Duck, 255; For Winter Feeding, 114
Barrel Length; Effect on Ballistic Performance, 70, 71; Effect on Gun Fitting, 70
Barrels; Alignment of, 28; Blueing of, 27; Browning of Damascus, 27; Chrome-lining of, 93; Damascus, 27; Generally, 27, et seq; Inertia of, 81; Length—*See* Barrel Length; Methods of Joining, 29; Sleeving, 93
Beaters; 134, 219, 220–1
Beech; 186, 187

Belgium, 93, 171, 317, 318
Bend; 76, 77
Bits (For Pheasants), 207
Blackcock; Generally, 59, 64, 247, 271–4; Record Bag of, 273; Shooting of, 272–4
Blackgame; See Ch. 23; Cooking of, 355
Blackhead; 321, 326
Bols Woodcock Club; 260
Bore(s) Generally, 24–26; Other than 12-bore
Borings; (See also Choke) 30, 66
Boss, Messrs Ltd; Single Trigger Mechanism, 45
Box; 130
Boxlock; See Actions
Bracken; As cover for Woodcock, 261; on Grouse Moors, 236
Brailing; 195
Bramble (Blackberry); 187, 188, 261
Breech; 24, 33
Brewers' Grains; 255
Broodamatic; 202, 203
Brooders; For Partridges, 163; For Pheasants, 202
Broodies; For Partridges, 160; For Pheasants, 197, 201, 209
Buckwheat; 110
Burrard, Major Sir Gerald, Bt. DSO.; 54, 93
Bursa Test; 181
Butts; 239, et seq

Caecum; 228, 229, 324
Canada Geese; 256
Canary Seed; 110
Candidiasis; 329
Cap, (of Cartridge); 47
Capercaillie; See Ch. 24; Cooking, 355; Generally, 59, 64; Natural History, 275; Shooting, 276
Caraway, 110
Cartridge(s); See Ch. 2; Bags for, 103; Belts for, 104; Cases, 49; Choice of, 55; Closure of, 51, 53; Extractors for, 104; Generally, 106; Results Achieved by—*See* Ch. 3; Storage of, 55
Cast Off; 76, 77
Catching up; 196